The Consensus of the Church and Papal Infallibility

The Consensus of the Church and Papal Infallibility

A Study in the Background of Vatican I

Richard F. Costigan, S.J.

The Catholic University of America Press
Washington, D.C.

Copyright © 2005
The Catholic University of America Press
All rights reserved

The paper used in this publication meets the minimum requirements of American National Standards for Information Science—Permanence of Paper for Printed Library materials, ANSI Z39.48-1984.
∞

Library of Congress Cataloging-in-Publication Data
Costigan, Richard F.
 The consensus of the church and papal infallibility : a study in the background of Vatican I / Richard F. Costigan.
   p. cm.
 Includes bibliographical references and index.
 ISBN 13: 978-0-8132-3238-6 (pbk : alk. paper)

 1. Popes—Infallibility—History of doctrines. 2. Catholic Church—Doctrines. 3. Vatican Council (1st : 1869–1870) I. Title.
 BX1806.C57 2005
 262′.131—dc22
 2004015232

*To my brother, Joe, and my sisters,
Ann, Dorothy, and Pat*

Contents

Acknowledgments ix
Abbreviations xi

1. Introduction   1
2. Jacques-Bénigne Bossuet   35
3. Honoré Tournely   63
4. Giuseppe-Agostino Orsi, O.P   78
5. Pietro Ballerini   94
6. Louis Bailly and Nicolas-Sylvestre Bergier   109
7. César-Guillaume La Luzerne   129
8. Alfonso Muzzarelli   145
9. Giovanni Perrone, S.J.   165
10. Conclusion   186

Bibliography   205
Index   215

Acknowledgments

I wish to thank the editors of *Theological Studies* for permission to use here two articles that appeared in their pages, "The Consensus of the Church: Differing Classic Views," 51 (March 1990), which became the chapters on Honoré Tournely and Pietro Ballerini, and "Bossuet and the Consensus of the Church," 65 (December 1995), which is the chapter on Jacques-Bénigne Bossuet. Research for this book stretched over many years, and I regret not writing down the names of people in various libraries who helped me unearth the venerable treatises that are the prime matter of the work. This would include persons at the Centre Sèvres Jesuit theological library in Paris, Gregorian University Library in Rome, and the Biblioteca Apostolica Vaticana. The staff members at my own Loyola University Library, especially those in the Rare Book Room, have always been helpful. I am grateful also to the Loyola University administration and the Department of Theology for the year of research leave, 1999–2000. That, combined with the enforced leisure that came along a year later when a broken leg knocked out a semester of teaching, enabled me to do the bulk of the writing. I also really appreciate the help of the staff of the Catholic University of America Press: its director, David McGonagle; acquisitions editor, Gregory LaNave; former managing editor, Susan Needham; and copyeditor, Robin DuBlanc, whose help on the text has been very valuable. Of my many Jesuit brethren who have been supportive I especially want to thank Fr. Frans Josef van Beeck and Fr. Pierre Blet for their stimulating comments. I hope I have not forgotten too many other people to whom I owe thanks.

Abbreviations

DHGE   *Dictionnaire d'histoire et de géographie ecclésiastiques.*

DS   Denziger, Henry, and Adolf Schönmetzer, eds. *Enchiridium symbolorum definitionum et declarationum.* 34th ed.

DTC   *Dictionnaire de théologie catholique.*

The Consensus of the Church and Papal Infallibility

CHAPTER I

Introduction

On Friday, July 15, 1870, in the tension-filled final days of the First Vatican Council, the council minority sent a delegation to Pope Pius IX to plead for the insertion into the draft of the *Pastor Aeternus* of even one phrase mentioning the role of the episcopate in formulating an important statement of the faith.[1] If this were done, they said, then nearly all those who had voted *non placet* in the preliminary vote on July 13 (who numbered 88 of the total of 601 voting) could vote *placet,* and there could be a near-unanimous final vote.[2] But all such phrases were rejected, and the phrase "ex sese, non autem ex consensu Ecclesiae" was *added* to the text, which was then voted through solemnly on Monday, July 18. "So little, it may seem now, ninety years after the event," says Philip Hughes, writing in 1960, "separated the Minority, at the crucial hour, from their brethren—the question which is the better form of words."[3]

    1. Cuthbert Butler, O.S.B., *The Vatican Council, 1869–1870* (London: Longmans Green, 1930), 2:157; in one-volume ed. (London: Collins and Harvill, 1962), 407.
    2. On this meeting of the minority with Pius IX, see Pierre Vallin, S.J., "Pour l'histoire du Vatican I: La démarche de la minorité auprès de Pie IX, le 15 juillet 1870," *Revue d'histoire ecclésiastique* 60 (1965): 844–848.
    3. Philip Hughes, *The Church in Crisis: A History of the Twenty Great Councils* (London: Burns and Oates, 1960), 322.

But in reality both sides were right in regarding the "form of words" as being far more than a "little" matter. The minority, with deep conviction, considered that the omission of any mention of the involvement of the episcopate in the preservation and teaching of the faith was an omission of something essential to the historic understanding of the Church. The majority, for their part, were determined to assert a strictly monarchical version of papal supremacy and to exclude any phrase that might suggest any kind of qualification or limitation of that sovereign ruling and teaching power. Specifically, as the precise wording of the *ex sese* clause indicates, they were determined to close and bolt the door forever on the dreaded spectre of "Gallicanism." The dogmatic constitution *Pastor Aeternus*, in its finished form, states that the definitions of the Roman Pontiff are irreformable "ex sese, non autem ex consensu Ecclesiae" (of themselves, and not from the consensus of the Church).[4]

This phraseology is clearly calculated to counter Article 4 of the Declaration of the Gallican Clergy of 1682. That article asserts that the pope does indeed have the leading role ("praecipuas partes") in teaching the faith to the whole Church but stipulates that his judgment is not irreformable "unless the consensus of the Church is present with it" (nisi Ecclesiae consensus accesserit).[5] The determination to prevent any possible revival of this idea associated with Gallicanism, with its evident nonacceptance of a totally monarchical papacy, was the reason why the majority refused to allow any mention of the episcopate in the text of the definition. It might somehow provide a possible opening to future "Gallicans."[6]

---

4. DS 3074.

5. The text of the Gallican Declaration is given in Latin in DS 2281–2284. An English translation is available in Sidney Z. Ehler and John B. Morrall, eds., *Church and State through the Centuries: A Collection of Historic Documents with Commentaries* (Westminster, Md.: Newman, 1954), 207–208. The translation given here is my own. The decision to render *consensus* throughout as "consensus" rather than "consent" is based on consultation with classical scholars. The word *accesserit* does not have to mean a *consensus subsequens*, that is, a consensus of the episcopate expressed *after* the Roman Pontiff has spoken. It certainly need not be subsequent in the Gallican authors studied here, as will be noted in a number of places.

6. Several scholars have written useful studies of the council debate on the word-

The definition of Vatican I, reaffirmed by Vatican II in *Lumen Gentium* 25, is clearly a product of a complex of historical factors, as the human persons on both sides strive according to their lights to assert what they consider right for the Church. Each side has an idea of the Church shaped by centuries of varied influences and aspirations. It is one same Church cherished by both sides, and one chair of Peter accepted and revered by both sides, despite very different ideas of the nature and function of the primatial office. Since these views developed in history, historical study can shed considerable light on them.

At least two questions deserve to be studied here. Looking at the council of 1870, a first question could ask to what extent, if any, the specific label *Gallican* is correctly applied to the minority at the council—especially, looking at the eighty-eight who voted *non placet*, the sixty-two (70 percent) who were not French. Despite the rather free use of the term by some then and since in describing the whole minority,[7] this question can really only be answered by careful study of what these many prelates actually said in their writings, in the council debates, and elsewhere.[8] The present study, however, will not deal with this specific question or with other questions about Vatican I itself.

---

ing of the *Pastor Aeternus*. One of the most illuminating remains that of Georges Dejaifve, S.J., "Ex sese, non autem ex consensu ecclesiae," *Eastern Churches Quarterly* 14 (Summer–Autumn 1962): 360–378. This article has been reprinted in several places.

7. For an outstanding example of this, see M. R. Gagnebet, O.P., "L'infaillibilité du pape et le consentement de l'Eglise au Vatican I," *Angelicum* 47 (1970): 267–307, 428–455. He bluntly labels the whole minority "Gallican" (271, 273–277). Throughout this long two-part article he gives abundant, precise references to the conciliar sources but makes no references to Gallican sources.

8. For a comprehensive study of the ideas of the French minority bishops at the council, see Margaret O'Gara, *Triumph in Defeat: Infallibility, Vatican I, and the French Minority Bishops* (Washington, D.C.: Catholic University of America Press, 1988). Austin Gough provides much information on this in the last chapter of his *Paris and Rome: The Gallican Church and the Ultramontane Campaign, 1848–1853* (New York: Oxford University Press, 1986). See also the excellent study by Jean-Rémy Palanque, *Catholiques libéraux et gallicans en France face au Concile du Vatican, 1867–1870* (Aix-en-Provence: Publications des Annales de la Faculté des Lettres d'Aix-en-Provence, 1962), and the informative article by Jacques Gadille, "L'épiscopat français au Premier Concile du Vatican," *Revue d'histoire de l'Eglise de France* 56 (July–December 1970): 327–346.

4 Introduction

Given that abhorrence for Gallicanism produced the *ex sese* clause, a second question must inquire into the actual thought on the Church and the papacy of the historic Gallicanism of the seventeenth and eighteenth centuries in France. One must ask whether the basic convictions of that ecclesiological tradition need to be described only in abhorrent terms and branded as simply incompatible with a genuine acceptance of papal primacy. This is particularly so in view of the rediscovery in recent decades of the more collegial and consensual ecclesiology of the early and medieval centuries, which Gallicanism knew well and on which it consistently drew.[9] The present work studies what Gallican theologians actually said about Church authority, and especially what they said in defense of Article 4 of the Declaration of 1682, dealing with the concurrence of the Church with papal statements. It is disconcerting to find how little attention has been devoted even by scholarly historians to the actual Gallican sources on this subject. Authors such as Thils, Fries, Nau and Aubert, to name only four, speak of "the Gallican doctrine" without citing even a *single* Gallican treatise or any study about Gallicanism.[10] The present work studies those treatises very closely.

9. Concerning Gallican authors' knowledge of Church history, see Yves Congar, O.P., "L'ecclésiologie de la Révolution française au Concile du Vatican, sous la signe de l'affirmation de l'autorité," in Maurice Nédoncelle et al., *L'ecclésiologie au XIXe siècle* (Paris: Cerf, 1960), 105. Aimé-Georges Martimort discusses the Gallican study of history in *Le gallicanisme de Bossuet* (Paris: Cerf, 1953), 90–91 and at greater length on 154–174. See also on this matter his *Le gallicanisme* (Paris: Presses Universitaires de France, 1973), 83–84, 86.

10. Gustave Thils, in *L'infaillibilité pontificale: Source, conditions, limites* (Gembloux: Duculot, 1969), speaks of "la théorie gallicane" (173, 174), giving no reference except to cite Article 4 as quoted in *DTC*. Heinrich Fries, in "Ex sese, non autem ex consensu ecclesiae," in Remigius Bäumer and Heimo Dolch, eds., *Volk Gottes: Zum Kirchenverzeichnis der katholischen, evangelischen und anglikanischen Theologie* (Freiburg: Herder, 1967), talks about the Gallican view (490–491) without giving *any* references. Paul Nau, O.S.B., in "Le magistère pontifical ordinaire au premier Concile du Vatican," in Roger Aubert et al., eds. *De doctrina Concilii Vaticani Primi* (Vatican City: Libreria Editrice Vaticana, 1969) says that the Gallican position demands a *consensus subsequens* (207, 208) but cites no sources at all. (The essay was originally published in *Revue Thomiste* 62 (1962): 341–397.) Roger Aubert, in "L'ecclésiologie au Concile du Vatican," in Bernard Botte et al., *Le concile et les conciles: Contribution à l'histoire de la vie conciliaire de l'Eglise* (Paris: Cerf, 1960), speaks of the Gallican view (281) without citing any sources.

A natural correlate to a study of the classic Gallican tradition is an examination of the opposing papalist, or Roman or Ultramontane, ecclesiology, which eventually triumphed at Vatican I. Papalist authors writing treatises *de Ecclesia* after 1682 explicitly reacted to the Gallican Declaration, and this enters into their rearticulation of monarchical papal authority. Studying the specific terms in which they criticize the Gallican view on the consensus of the Church helps to understand how two conceptions of the same Church can differ so markedly that what is properly integral to one is totally foreign to the other. Attending closely to the one specific question of the consensus of the Church, we shall study several important representatives of each school.

Gallicanism

Actually, by 1870 Gallicanism was already effectively extinct, and there was really no serious likelihood of its being revived. Thus it is surprising that the papalist majority at the council thought that so much effort to counteract it was needed in the drafting of *Pastor Aeternus*. Gallicanism was really a phenomenon of historical conditions that had all but ceased to exist in France itself, and whose equivalents were rapidly passing away in other countries also. In addition, the extraordinary success of the Ultramontane Movement by the middle of the nineteenth century had already brought about a general recognition of papal supremacy so strong that a new definition could hardly add anything to it. Ultramontanism's extolling of papal sovereignty featured a very explicit and forceful rejection of Gallicanism as a discredited system whose time had passed, and whose appeal could not compare in any case with that of the Holy Father in Rome.[11]

---

11. Several works of Roger Aubert and Yves Congar, O.P., remain the best scholarly, and most interesting, sources on the Ultramontane Movement. See Aubert, "Les progrès de l'Ultramontanisme," in his *Le pontificat de Pie IX*, vol. 21 of Augustin Fliche and Victor Martin, eds., *Histoire de l'Eglise* (Paris: Bloud et Gay, 1963), 262–310; and his "La géographie ecclésiologique au XIXe siècle," in Maurice Nédoncelle et al., *L'ecclésiologie au XIXe siècle* (Paris: Cerf, 1960), 11–55. In the same volume is Congar's excellent article "L'ecclésiologie de la Révolution française au Concile du Vatican, sous le

Authors have identified several kinds of Gallicanism, but it would not be useful to undertake a lengthy discussion of them here. Yves Congar's names of two general kinds are probably the most apt for our purposes: "Gallicanisme des ecclésiastiques," and "Gallicanisme des politiques."[12] The Gallicanism "of men of the Church" is the kind that we mainly deal with in this book. We will encounter only a few times in passing the other kind, that of "men of politics," which is essentially what is often called "parliamentary," and which will be briefly described shortly. As a matter of history the Gallicanism of churchmen included two principal elements, one ecclesiopolitical and the other ecclesiological. The two are closely related and may at times seem almost inseparable, but it really is necessary to note the distinctive character of each. The ecclesiopolitical, entailing a close and generally friendly association of the Church and the monarchy in France, emerged in the course of some particular French experiences in late-medieval controversy. The ecclesiological was rooted in much earlier periods of Christian history, when the Catholic Church was less centralized and the faith was preserved and extended through more collegial and consensual means. This element is obviously not specifically French but is part of the general tradition of the whole Church. Both elements entail the belief that papal primacy should not mean that the Roman Pontiff can either determine the faith or govern the universal Church in an absolutely monarchical way. In this book the authors we study, both the Gallican and the papalist, focus their attention mainly on ecclesiological questions, that is, on papal authority in teaching and governing the Church.

Gallicanism, says Congar, "before being a system was a current of history transmitting a certain temperament and a practical attitude

---

signe de l'affirmation de l'autorité," 77–114. Hermann Josef Pottmeyer has written a major study on Ultramontane theorists in several countries: *Unfehlbarkeit und Souveränität: Die päpstliche Unfehlbarkeit im System der ultramontanen Ekklesiologie des 19. Jahrhunderts* (Mainz: Matthias Grünewald, 1975). See also Richard F. Costigan, S.J., *Rohrbacher and the Ecclesiology of Ultramontanism* (Rome: Università Gregoriana Editrice, 1980).

12. Yves Congar, O.P., "Gallicanisme," in G. Jacquemet, ed., *Catholicisme* (Paris: Letouzey, 1956), 4:1736.

linked to the situation of France under the authority of the kings."[13] This concurs with Victor Martin's classic definition of Gallicanism: "If there is need to define it, you could say that it consists in the accord of the king and the clergy to govern the Church of France by controlling and restraining the interference of the Holy See, and claiming to rely on rights anciently acquired."[14] French churchmen believed that they were right in resisting papal demands that they saw as going beyond the legitimate traditional role of the Roman Pontiff. Like churchmen in every country of Christendom, they also thought that the king, their fellow member of the Church, was a natural and proper ally in these endeavors.

Problems and frictions involving a number of western European countries in the fourteenth and early fifteenth centuries led to acts by the French that are significant in the early history of Gallicanism. The frictions centered around major efforts by the papacy to make the whole Church a more centralized and pope-controlled system. Prominent among papal claims resented by churchmen in France and other countries was the papal assertion of an increasingly greater role in the apportionment of ecclesiastical benefices, overruling previously established customs and rights of conferral, and demanding numerous financial payments to the papal treasury in connection with the benefices. Victor Martin lists and describes these ever-multiplying demands, arguing that in the effort to shake off this financial yoke, Gallicanism was born.[15] French popes during the Avignon period (1305–1377) greatly increased these demands, and then during the schism (1378–1417) the Avignon pope continued this tendency. (The French had no dealings with the pope of Rome during the schism.)[16]

Historians of the Avignon papacy offer particularly valuable information and insightful comment on the great ecclesiastical centraliza-

13. Ibid., 4:1731.
14. Victor Martin, *Les origines du gallicanisme* (Paris: Bloud et Gay, 1939), 1:31. This work remains unsurpassed for its clear, detailed information on the views and goals of the participants at each phase of development.
15. Ibid., 1:269. Martin gives an extended account of the many fees entailed, 1:247–269.
16. For this whole development see also Karl August Fink, "The Curia at

tion undertaken by popes during that period and specifically on the great increase in financial demands entailed in it. Guillaume Mollat states, "The progressive centralization of the Church [during this period] is nowhere more clearly shown than in the manner in which the Avignon popes laid claim to an ever-increasing share in the collation [conferral] of benefices."[17] He describes numerous kinds of papal taxes and ways in which they were collected.[18] One example of a tax was the "annate," which consisted of the revenue from a benefice in the first year of a new incumbent.[19] That the papacy had legitimate needs for funds was recognized, but it was also known that popes were spending enormous amounts on their Italian wars, that is, campaigns to retain or recover papal territories in Italy, and this aroused great resentment not only in France but in other countries, including England and Germany.[20] The French were taxed especially heavily. Yves Renouard, after another useful and clear listing of the numerous kinds of revenue that the papal curia undertook to collect, states, "Examination of papal finance in this period leads to two conclusions: that the greater portion of revenue came from the French kingdom (where there were fifteen out of thirty collectories) and that the vast majority of expenditure was on the armies which for more than forty years struggled to recover the Papal States."[21] He adds that John XXII and his chief financial officer, Gasbert of Laval, had as their general principle "that funds collected in France would be spent in Italy."[22]

Avignon," in *From the High Middle Ages to the Eve of the Reformation*, vol. 4 of Hubert Jedin and John Dolan, eds., *History of the Church* (New York: Crossroad, 1970), 333–344. See also E. Delaruelle et al., *L'Eglise au temps du Grand Schisme et de la crise conciliaire (1378–1449)*, vol. 14 of Augustin Fliche and Victor Martin, eds., *Histoire de l'Eglise* (Paris: Bloud et Gay, 1962), 315–368, esp. 329–344.

17. Guillaume Mollat, *The Popes at Avignon, 1305–1378* (London: Thomas Nelson, 1963), 335.

18. Ibid., 319–329.

19. Ibid., 322; and see also Yves Renouard, *The Avignon Papacy: The Popes in Exile, 1305–1403* (New York: Barnes and Noble, 1994), 103.

20. Mollat, *Popes at Avignon*, 330–341.

21. Renouard, *Avignon Papacy*, 104. A collectory was a specific collection area.

22. Ibid. He devotes two chapters to this development, 96–115.

Louis Caillet, in a valuable major study, offers a more nuanced analysis that ultimately concurs with the perception of Mollat and Renouard. Studying in great and painstaking detail the pontificate of John XXII (1316–1334), a pope of considerable intelligence and competence, Caillet tries to show that John XXII generally applied responsible norms in appointments to benefices, and that this resulted in some salutary effects in many parishes and dioceses.[23] But the sheer volume of his interventions in French Church life was eventually counterproductive. His pontificate, great though it was in some ways, also prepared the way for the doctrinal developments of conciliarism and some other doctrines "of the 15th and 16th centuries favorable to the limitation of the authority of the Holy See."[24] John XXII, "without really willing it, but by reason of his 16,773 interventions in French benefices, sowed the seed of Gallicanism in its two forms of ecclesiastical Gallicanism and political Gallicanism of which the results were the Concordat of Bologna of 1516 and the Declaration of the four articles of 1682."[25]

It was not only, the French thought, that the financial demands were excessive and bothersome. Martimort stresses that they were convinced that there were also basic ecclesial traditions and theological principles at issue. He says that the phrase "liberties of the Gallican Church" expresses "in an original and specifically French fashion the need for a general reform of the Church," a need felt across Christendom more and more pressingly throughout the fourteenth century.[26] Reform meant that there needed to be a restoration of traditional institutions threatened by the new papal demands. This was the theme of a series of meetings in France in the 1390s. Pierre Le Roy, highly respected abbot of Mont-Saint-Michel and a man ad-

23. Louis Caillet, *La papauté d'Avignon et l'Eglise de France: La politique bénéficiale du Pape Jean XXII en France (1316–1334)* (Paris: Presses Universitaires de France, 1975), passim, with an important summary, 429–460.
24. Ibid., 428.
25. Ibid. Geoffrey Barraclough's *Papal Provisions* (London: Basil Blackwell, 1935) deserves to be reread for his considered judgment that popes of the fourteenth century were relatively intelligent and responsible.
26. Martimort, *Le gallicanisme*, 34.

mired as the most learned canonist in France, gave eloquent expression to the complaints and the reform ideals at one of these councils in Paris in 1398. He said that the primatial authority conferred on St. Peter by Jesus Christ is conditioned by the nature of his mission. Christ "gave Peter the authority necessary to pasture his flock, the lambs and the sheep, that is to guide the faithful and the pastors in the way of salvation. To have the right to obedience the successor of Peter must devote himself to things that have salvation as their end; his power is circumscribed in these limits. One is bound to accomplish the will of the pope only when it reflects that of God, [that is] if his orders tend to the good of the Church."[27] Thus, to refuse to the pope the power to confer benefices, and to resist the financial exactions of the curia, is simply to restore the authentic rights of the Church, which have been transgressed by the pontiffs of the present time. "The principle of [episcopal] elections goes back to the apostles themselves, the councils have sanctioned it, and it has been held in honor for twelve hundred years and more."[28] Now the Church "must free itself from recent servitudes and reestablish the common law, that is, 'the decrees of the ancient holy fathers.'"[29] Since it appears that we cannot rely on either popes or councils to achieve this, it is necessary that the king take the lead. He is the patron of the Church of France, and it is the duty of a good prince to come to the aid of oppressed subjects.

After lengthy debate, the French clergy at this council decided on July 27, 1398, to withdraw their obedience from Pope Benedict XIII (pope of the Avignon line since 1394). They declared: "[T]he king and the Church of France will not endure any longer that the pope usurp, confound, and enervate . . . , as he has done for some time, the power and the authority of the prelates of the Church of France in the conferral and disposition of benefices, which is something being

---

27. Martin, *Origines*, 1:281. Martin gives interesting information on Pierre Le Roy, 1:271 and 357.
28. Martin's wording, attributed to Le Roy, ibid., 1:284.
29. Martimort, *Le gallicanisme*, 39; wording attributed to, not quoted from, Le Roy.

done against all reason, the authority of the holy councils and canons and the good of ecclesiastical discipline; and [we declare] that the Church of France is returned to its liberties and ancient usages."[30] With this act, says Martin, "the idea triumphed that the pope is not an absolute monarch in the Church and that his power is not arbitrary." This is an idea heavy with consequences, he adds, for it will always be easy to claim that the papal will is not oriented toward salutary ends.[31]

Several years of more vicissitudes followed, during which the French at least once (1403) decided to resume their allegiance to Benedict XIII. Finally, assembled in a council in 1406, French churchmen asked King Charles VI to establish vis-à-vis Benedict XIII their ancient freedoms, assure their maintenance, and decree an end to the payments to the papacy. Charles VI complied with these requests in the Ordinances of 1407, which among other things rejected all financial exactions by the Holy See and asserted that bishops should be elected by cathedral chapters. Martin says that this can be considered the "official birth of Gallicanism," for though the concurrence of interests and concerns between the king and the clergy was of long standing, this unified action based on the appeal to "Gallican liberties" was new.[32] Pierre Le Roy, he thinks, provided the ecclesiological basis for the doctrine asserted here, and his learning and eloquence gave it the appearance of a legitimate reform. "To define the Gallican liberties as the right, for the Church of France, to administer itself conformably to ancient discipline and to deny the obligatory character of papal decisions that contravene it, was to formulate a whole program for the future: it was to create Gallicanism."[33] This French event was not, of course, taking place in isolation from similar developments in other countries that were reacting to the same increases in papal demands. Martin adds some perceptive

---

30. This wording is that of Martimort, ibid.; Martin gives a fuller version, *Origines*, 1:287–288.
31. Martin, *Origines*, 1:289–290.   32. Ibid., 1:333.
33. Ibid., 1:356. This is the end of volume 1 of *Origines*.

comments on the influence of the English on the French during these years. He cites some specific terms borrowed by the French from the English Statutes of Provisors, which were calculated to prevent papal appointments to benefices in England and the payment of money from England to the papacy.[34]

During the same years that saw this development of the Gallicanism of churchmen, the other principal kind of Gallicanism also emerged and became a major perennial factor in French church history. Brief mention of this "Gallicanisme des politiques" should suffice, for it will not figure prominently in the course of this book. The expression "parliamentary Gallicanism" is a fairly well-accepted name for this viewpoint, for its articulation is associated firstly with theorists and spokesmen of the *parlements* (essentially judicial bodies in France). It includes some ideas and attitudes markedly different from ecclesiastical Gallicanism, for it tends to be unfriendly not only to undue papal influence in France but also to the clergy and the Church itself. It stresses the independence of the temporal power from papal or any ecclesiastical authority, relentlessly opposes any Church authority in any way independent of the state, and asserts the power of the state over the functioning of the Church.[35] M. Dubruel, in a particularly useful description of parliamentary Gallicanism, says that its exponents "extended the right of the secular power to the point of overrunning almost the whole spiritual domain."[36] The name "political Gallicanism" is sometimes applied, appropriately, to this viewpoint. Victor Martin, in his *Le gallicanisme politique et le clergé de France* (1929), uses this term for the doctrine contained in Article 1

---

34. Ibid., 1:348–357. William E. Lunt, *Financial Relations of the Papacy with England, 1327–1534* (Cambridge, Mass.: Medieval Academy of America, 1962), gives abundant information on controversies relating to financial payments from England to the papacy during these years, esp. 307–446.

35. Congar, "Gallicanisme," 1734; Martimort, *Le gallicanisme,* 42–43, 62–65.

36. M. Dubruel, "Gallicanisme," *DTC,* 6.1:1125. A lengthy section of this article deals with "Le gallicanisme des politiques," 1124–1137. Regarding parliamentary Gallicanism, see also Adrien Dansette, *Religious History of Modern France* (New York: Herder, 1961), 1:31–37, esp. 34–35; and Léopold Willaert, S.J., *Après le concile de Trente: La restauration catholique, 1563–1648,* vol. 18 of Augustin Fliche and Victor Martin, eds., *Histoire de l'Eglise* (Paris: Bloud et Gay, 1960), 367–407, esp. 376–377.

of the Declaration of 1682, which strongly rejects any papal authority over kings in temporal matters.[37]

The Gallican authors whom we study in this work do not concur at all with the anti-Church attitudes of parliamentary Gallicans or with their real hostility toward the papacy. However, papalist authors frequently blur the important differences between the two kinds of Gallicanism, either from lack of studying them very carefully or in order to add a little more odium to their adversaries with the suggestion of disloyalty to the Holy See. Going even a little farther, papalist authors sometimes imply that the Gallicans, to whom they attribute a separatist tendency, might someday decide to break away from the Roman Catholic Church. We simply do not find this sentiment in our Gallican authors. Victor Martin states emphatically that the French always had "the deliberate will not to break from the Roman Church." The French were Catholic and always intended to remain so. If they seemed at times to approach the brink of schism, they never went that far "because they did not want to."[38] This comment is borne out in the authors studied here.

The Declaration of 1682

The event that led to the Declaration of the Gallican Clergy, or Gallican Articles, issued on March 19, 1682, was a decree by King Louis XIV on February 10, 1673 extending the right of *la régale* to all the dioceses of France.[39] The *régale* was of two kinds: the *régale temporelle* and the *régale spirituelle*. The temporal meant that the king, as general guardian of the Church, could, after the death of a bishop, administer the revenues of the diocese until a new bishop was installed. The spiritual meant that he could also appoint new clerics to benefices not having the care of souls that were at the disposition of

---

37. Victor Martin, *Le gallicanisme politique et le clergé de France* (Paris: Picard, 1929). This book deals largely with the content of Article 1 of the Declaration of 1682.

38. Martin, *Origines,* 1:31.

39. For brief treatments of this controversy, see André Latreille et al., *Histoire du catholicisme en France,* 2nd ed. (Paris: Spes, 1962), 2:420–431; and E. Préclin and E. Jarry, *Les luttes politiques et doctrinales aux XVIIe et XVIIIe siècles,* vol. 19 of Augustin Fliche and Victor Martin, eds., *Histoire de l'Eglise* (Paris: Bloud et Gay 1955), 149–164.

the bishop. These had been long-established prerogatives of the king of France for most of the dioceses of the country, but not for some in the south of France. The decree of 1673 extended the *régale* to those southern dioceses also. For some time no one objected to this decree, either in France or in the Rome of Pope Clement X (Emilio Altieri; pope 1670–1676). The archbishops and bishops of the southern dioceses affected calmly acquiesced as the decree was implemented.

However, there was one, Nicholas Pavillon, bishop of Alet, who felt that the king's move was wrong because the Council of Lyon in 1274 had forbidden such an extension of royal power. After lengthy study and discernment, by March 1676 he decided that he simply would not comply with the decree. By July 1677, after resisting the efforts and blandishments of many other French churchmen, he appealed to the pope, by that time Innocent XI. Within a few months, a second bishop, Etienne Caulet of Pamiers, decided to follow his example, and he also appealed to the pope in September 1677 for advice and support. He persevered in this after the death of Pavillon in December 1677.

Innocent XI (Benedetto Odescalchi; pope 1676–1689) was a man of austere personal habits, great religious and moral integrity, and earnest dedication to the highest spiritual standards of the Church. In fact, before he accepted his election as pope he demanded that the cardinals sign a fourteen-point program of reform in the Church.[40] On studying the appeals of Pavillon and Caulet, he decided that Louis XIV's extension of the *régale* was an unjustified encroachment on the spiritual terrain of the Church. Between March 1678 and January 1680 he sent the king three briefs condemning the extension and calling on him to retract it; the third brief spoke of the possibili-

---

40. Ludwig von Pastor, *History of the Popes* (St. Louis: B. Herder, 1902–1953), 32:10. See also Bruno Neveu, "Culture religieuse et aspirations réformistes à la cour d'Innocent XI," in his *Erudition et religion aux XVIIe et XVIIIe siècles* (Paris: Albin Michel, 1994), 235–276. Also see his more recent "L'esprit de réforme à Rome sous Innocent XI (1676–1689)," *XVIIe siècle* 50 (1998): 203–218. On this question of the very strict piety of Innocent XI, see the interesting article by André Latreille, "Innocent XI, pape 'janséniste,' directeur de conscience de Louis XIV," *Cahiers d'histoire* 1 (1956): 9–39.

ty of ecclesiastical sanctions. Louis was not willing to comply, and tensions between France and Rome mounted over the next year and a half, culminating in the meeting in Paris that produced the Gallican Declaration.

A long-accepted view of this meeting was that King Louis XIV initiated and dominated it, and really dictated the declaration to a compliant French clergy assumed to be rather weak in the area of religious convictions. Roman Catholic bishops, according to this view, should definitely have disagreed with a king who defied the papacy and should have refused to support him. Instead, the French bishops were so weak that they simply signed a statement placed before them by the king. Nineteenth-century Ultramontane writers especially pushed this interpretation, and did so in very polemical terms. Some prominent examples of this include Joseph de Maistre,[41] Félicité Lamennais,[42] and René-François Rohrbacher.[43] This reading of the event of 1682 was presented again by Charles Gérin in 1869 in *Recherches historiques sur l'Assemblée du Clergé de France de 1682*, a book considered at the time a substantial work of history.[44] Historians generally accepted this view, though not necessarily echoing the disparaging comments on the French bishops. For example, Victor Martin, in 1929, considered it correct to say that Louis XIV ordered the declaration and that the bishops yielded to the royal pressure.[45]

---

41. Joseph de Maistre, *De l'Eglise gallicane dans son rapport avec le Saint-Siège*, vol. 3 of *Oeuvres complètes de J. de Maistre* (Paris: Emanuele Vitte, 1931). The Declaration of 1682 is targeted scornfully throughout this book.

42. Félicité Lamennais, *De la religion considérée dans ses rapports avec l'ordre politique et civile*, vol. 7 of *Oeuvres complètes de F. de Lamennais* (Paris: Daubrée et Cailleux, 1836–1837; Frankfurt: Minerva, 1967). It is in chapter 7, 148–239, in particular that Lamennais polemicizes against the Gallican Declaration.

43. For Rohrbacher's polemic against the Gallican Declaration, see Costigan, *Rohrbacher*, 219–234. Rohrbacher (1789–1856), a close associate of Lamennais for a number of years, wrote a huge history of the Church extolling the papacy: *Histoire universelle de l'Eglise catholique*, 3rd ed., 29 vols. (Paris: Gaume Frères, 1857–1859).

44. Charles Gérin, *Recherches historiques sur l'Assemblée du Clergé de France de 1682* (Paris: Lecoffre, 1869). He published a second edition of this work with some modifications in 1870.

45. Martin, *Le gallicanisme politique*, 303–316. Paul Sonnino, in his *Louis XIV's View of the Papacy (1661–1667)* (Berkeley: University of California Press, 1966), offers much

But two major works have necessitated the abandonment of this view. Aimé-Georges Martimort in his *Le gallicanisme de Bossuet* offers a superbly informed study of the ecclesial views of Bossuet himself, the growth and articulation of French ecclesiology in the seventeenth century, a valuable account of the controversy that produced the declaration, and the response of Rome to the declaration.[46] More recently, Pierre Blet, S.J., has produced the really definitive work on this subject, *Les Assemblées du Clergé et Louis XIV de 1670 à 1693*.[47] Embodying exhaustive archival research, this work presents in meticulous day-to-day, at times even hour-to-hour, detail the statements of all the participants relating to the *régale*, the ensuing controversy, the assembly of the clergy, the writing and content of the declaration, and the terms of the eventual settlement between the French Crown and the Holy See. Both Martimort and Blet show that the articles of 1682 express the genuine long-held views of the French clergy and were not simply dictated by Louis XIV and his minister Jean Colbert.[48]

After hoping for over a year to work out a settlement with Innocent XI by diplomatic means, Louis XIV reluctantly yielded in June 1681 to the urgings of several men who pressed for a strong public act of the combined Church and Crown of France: an Extraordinary General Assembly of the Clergy of France that would be convoked

---

information on the thinking of Louis, though without dwelling very much on ecclesiological issues.

46. Martimort, *Gallicanisme de Bossuet*.

47. Pierre Blet, S.J., *Les Assemblées du Clergé et Louis XIV de 1670 à 1693* (Rome: Università Gregoriana Editrice, 1972).

48. Martimort, *Gallicanisme de Bossuet*, 441–460, 549–563; Blet, *Assemblées du Clergé et Louis XIV,* 348–362, esp. 350–351, and 560–561. R. Darricau has written an extended appreciation of this work of Blet, pointing out in detail its significance for the event of 1682: "Lumières nouvelles sur l'histoire du clergé de France sous Louis XIV," *Revue d'histoire ecclésiastique* 69 (1974): 93–102. Blet has also written a most interesting article on Jean Colbert, showing that this famous minister of Louis XIV did not initiate or encourage the declaration, and moreover that he was not as anti-Roman as writers like de Maistre and Rohrbacher thought: "Une légende ténace: Colbert et la Déclaration du Clergé en 1682," Académie des Sciences Morales et Politiques, Communications de la séance du 4 octobre, 1971, 25–45.

by the king and that would produce a statement that would then be confirmed by the king. Three men in particular urged this: Michel Le Tellier, chancellor of the realm; his son Charles-Maurice Le Tellier,[49] archbishop of Reims; and François de Harlay de Champvallon, archbishop of Paris. The event showed that the ecclesial views of these three were shared by a very large number of French clergy. When the king convoked the Extraordinary Assembly, elections following traditional forms were held in all eighteen ecclesiastical provinces of France, each province electing two bishops and two other priests.[50] The resulting assembly of thirty-six bishops and thirty-six other clergy began with a formal opening on October 27, 1681, in the historic convent of the Grands Augustins in Paris. On November 9 Bossuet gave his famous "Sermon on Unity" in which he extolled the papacy as the historic and essential center of unity in the Church but recalled also the Church's conciliar and collegial traditions. He also dwelt at length on the historic and rightful role of the kings of France as pillars of the Church and included reasons why it was appropriate for the king to exercise rights like the *régale*.[51]

Weeks of discussion were concluded on March 19, 1682, when the assembly voted unanimously in favor of the text of a declaration prepared mainly by Charles-Maurice Le Tellier, Gilbert de Choiseul du Plessis-Praslin, bishop of Tournai, and Bossuet, with the latter being the redactor of the final draft.[52] The assembly then appealed to King Louis XIV to promulgate as a royal edict this "Declaration of the

49. Pierre Blet, S.J., in "Fidèle au pape, fidèle au roi," in Yves Durand, ed., *Hommages à Roland Mousnier: Clientèles et fidélités en Europe à l'époque moderne* (Paris: Presses Universitaires de France, 1981), 315–332, describes the leading role taken by Charles-Maurice Le Tellier in the meeting of 1682 and shows that he considered his views on the relation of the episcopate and the papacy to be in line with longterm Catholic tradition.

50. A full list of the electees, province by province, is given by Blet, *Assemblées du Clergé et Louis XIV,* 603–610.

51. Both ibid., 273–276, and at great length, Martimort, *Gallicanisme de Bossuet,* 392–427, discuss the content of this sermon, the full text of which is available in Bossuet, *Oeuvres complètes,* ed. F. Lachat (Paris: Louis Vives, 1862–1866), 11:588–632.

52. Blet, *Assemblées du Clergé et Louis XIV,* 339, 344; Martimort, *Gallicanisme de Bossuet,* 443–460.

Gallican Clergy on Ecclesiastical Power" (*Cleri gallicani de ecclesiastica potestate declaratio*). At the urging of Choiseul, the bishops asked that the king should decree that the declaration be registered with the parlements, that all in France should be forbidden to teach a contrary doctrine, and that all professors of theology should subscribe to and teach the four articles of the declaration.[53] The king immediately complied with all these requests.

The assertions in the four articles are as follows.[54] Article 1 states that God has bestowed on Peter and his successors power over spiritual things but not over civil and temporal matters. Thus kings are not subjected by the ordinance of God to any ecclesiastical authority in temporal affairs, nor can they be deposed directly or indirectly, nor can their subjects be dispensed from obedience and the oaths of loyalty to the king that they have taken. This first article is the longest of the four; the other three are all very brief. Article 2 asserts that full authority in spiritual matters is inherent in the Apostolic See, while at the same time the decrees of the Council of Constance concerning the authority of general councils are to remain valid and unchanged. This is of course the doctrine of conciliarism, which asserts the supremacy of the council over the pope. Article 3 says that the exercise of the apostolic authority should be moderated by the canons established by the Holy Spirit and consecrated by the respect of the whole world. Also the rules, customs, and institutions accepted in the French kingdom and Church are to keep their force, and the bounds fixed by our fathers are to remain undisturbed.

The fourth and final article, the only one studied in the present work, must be quoted verbatim and in at least three languages. "In questions of faith the leading role is to be that of the Supreme Pontiff; and his decrees apply to all churches in general and to each of them in particular. But his judgment is not unchangeable, unless it receives the consent of the Church." This English translation, in the

---

53. Blet, *Assemblées du Clergé et Louis XIV,* 342–343.
54. The text of the Declaration in English is given in Ehler and Morrall, *Church and State through the Centuries,* 205–208.

Ehler and Morrall collection, is a pretty good rendering of the Latin original, which says: "In fidei quoque quaestionibus praecipuas Summi Pontificis esse partes, eiusque decreta ad omnes et singulas ecclesias pertinere, nec tamen irreformabile esse judicium nisi Ecclesiae consensus accesserit."[55] A standard French translation reads, "Que, quoique le pape ait la principale part dans les questions de foi et que ses décrets regardent toutes les Eglises, et chaque Eglise en particulier, son jugement n'est pourtant irréformable, à moins que le consentement de l'Eglise n'intervienne."[56] Rendering *accesserit* by *intervienne* can be considered useful in view of one of the points of discussion about the Gallican doctrine of the consensus of the Church. As will be seen in a number of the chapters in this book, it has been commonly said both by Ultramontane writers and by modern historians that the Gallican doctrine expressed in Article 4 demands a "consensus subsequens" by the Church to a papal definition of faith. That is, the pope issues a definition of a doctrine, and then after the pope has issued it the bishops of the Church indicate their agreement with it or reception of it. *Intervienne* can be translated as "be involved [with it]," and this is very similar to the "is present with it" that will be used in this book to render the *accesserit* of the Latin original. Both these renderings of the Latin word are non-chronological, that is, they do not mean *subsequent* consensus.

It was not until April 11 that news of the declaration, and a copy of the text, was brought to Rome by the courier of the nuncio. The reaction of Innocent XI and the curia was of course quite negative. Cardinal César d'Estrées, French ambassador to the Holy See, reported that the pope showed "extreme displeasure" when he heard what the French had done.[57] Even several Roman cardinals who had disapproved of the pope's intransigence in regard to the *régale* felt that the four articles could not be ignored and agreed with the pope that

---

55. DS 2284. The Latin is given also in many of the works on Gallicanism.
56. This French version is given in Blet, *Assemblées du Clergé et Louis XIV,* 341; and Martimort, *Gallicanisme de Bossuet,* 471; and is the same as given in C. Constantin, "Déclaration ou les Quatre Articles de 1682," *DTC,* 4.1:197.
57. Blet, *Assemblées du Clergé et Louis XIV,* 371.

some response must be made. But Innocent was not minded to act precipitately, and after some consideration he appointed a special commission to study the French declaration.[58] The commission studied and debated the matter for years, and indeed were still debating it when Innocent died on August 12, 1689. Several thought that outright condemnation should be meted out to these "propositions so impious, so detestable, so temerarious and schismatic that no ecclesiastic could sustain them without infamy in this world and reprobation in the next."[59] These sentiments of Cardinal Decio Azzolini were shared by only a minority of the commission. The majority, throughout their several years of study and discussion, thought that the articles could not be declared heretical. They were well aware that theses on papal supremacy, and papal infallibility in particular, had been the subject of debate for centuries. Innocent XI himself noted in a letter to Cardinal d'Estrées as early as May 3, 1682, "These matters have been disputed and can still be [disputed]."[60] Another reason for great care in drafting a response, thinks Martimort, was the general opinion that the French clergy were the most learned in Europe, and they could be expected to pinpoint any defects in a Roman statement.[61]

Eventually, the commission decided that they had to content themselves with declaring null and void the act of the French assembly, reserving judgment on the doctrine to later decisions of the Holy See. This decision, proposed by the majority of the commission in meetings as early as the summer of 1682, was eventually adopted by Alexander VIII (Pietro Ottoboni; pope October 1, 1689–February 1, 1691) and promulgated in his *Inter multiplices* on January 30, 1691. The term "null and void" is of course juridical rather than doctrinal. The strongly worded judgment stated in *Inter multiplices* also stays carefully on that juridical level. It declares that the propositions of the Gallican

---

58. Ibid.
59. Quoted by Martimort, *Gallicanisme de Bossuet*, 506, in his ten-page section on this papal study commission, 505–515.
60. Quoted in ibid., 511n.   61. Ibid.

clergy are "null, void, invalid, empty, and altogether and completely devoid of power and effect from their very beginning and will be in perpetuity."[62] This judgment, stated after giving the whole text of the four articles, applies to all four of them. *Inter multiplices* does not make any particular comments about the conciliarism in Article 2 or the consensus of the Church in Article 4.

This unwillingness to assert that the doctrines of the Declaration were heretical, of obvious importance for our present study, comes through in a most interesting way in subsequent negotiations over episcopal appointments for men who had signed the Declaration of 1682. This took place under the next pope, Innocent XII, (Antonio Pignatelli; pope July 12, 1691–September 27, 1700) who was not inclined to make a major issue of the *régale,* and who was more interested in reaching a settlement with the French. His nuncio to France, Giovanni Cavallerini, said on December 22, 1692, to Charles Colbert de Croissy, the royal secretary of state: "His Holiness does not demand a retraction of the doctrine. He leaves to each one to believe what his own conscience dictates. But that some bishops [and priests] had the audacity to assemble to publish a declaration against the authority of the pope is a thing that cannot be excused from being a manifest affront and a lack of respect. It is well known that these opinions have been at various times sustained and also attacked as problematic."[63] But that some priests who declare them sound and constant doctrine should still be promoted by the pope to the episcopate without their retracting the "injurious act" is really too much.[64]

Rome was willing to confirm as bishops men who committed the injurious act, if they were nominated by the king, but not before they made some kind of retraction. The wording of the retraction was debated for months, as each side studied texts suggested by the other.

---

62. DS 2285. The Latin reads, "nulla, irrita, invalida, inania, viribusque et effectu penitus et omnino vacua ab ipso initio et fuisse et esse ac perpetuo fore."
63. Quoted by Blet, *Assemblées du Clergé et Louis XIV,* 559.
64. Ibid. "Really too much" renders *vraiment exorbitante.*

That Rome did not demand a retraction of the doctrine of the articles was noted at several points. For example, Cardinal Fabrizio Spada, papal secretary of state, said in a dispatch to Cavallerini on May 26, 1693, that the pope was not demanding even "the appearance of a retraction of the doctrine" but only of the "offense done to the pontifical authority."[65] Finally, in August of 1693, agreement on a formula was reached. In it the priest signatories of the declaration stated: "[W]e declare that everything that could be considered as decreed on ecclesiastical power and pontifical authority at the assembly [of 1682] should be held as not decreed and that we hold it as such."[66] They add that they certainly never had any thought of decreeing anything prejudicial to the laws of the Church. This studiously noncommittal statement, which does not mention any doctrines, provided the gentlemanly accord that both sides, tired of the long stalemate, wanted. The controversy over the *régale* soon became a nonissue also, as both Innocent XII and his successor, Clement XI (Francesco Albani; pope November 23, 1700–March 19, 1721), tacitly accepted Louis's extension of that royal prerogative.[67]

This settlement of the controversy did not mean that the Gallican Articles were not taught in French schools of theology from that time and throughout the eighteenth century and into the nineteenth. They did continue to be a standard part of Gallican theology. Indeed, Martimort comments that they actually gained in clarity and solidity by virtue of the conflict.[68]

Bellarmine on Papal Authority

The papalist doctrine against which the Gallicans were reacting is well known, but since the authors studied in this book all wrote after 1682, it will be useful to review the ecclesiology of one whose work was already current in the seventeenth century. Jesuit Robert Bellarmine (1542–1621), one of the most widely read authors of the pa-

---

65. Reported, not quoted, in ibid., 567.
66. Quoted in ibid., 570. 67. Ibid., 576–580.
68. Martimort, *Le gallicanisme,* 102. See also Antoine Degert, *Histoire des séminaires français jusqu'à la Révolution* (Paris: Beauchesne, 1912), 2: chap. 2.

palist school, was well known in France and was considered by Gallican writers a major adversary.[69] For him, papal monarchy in ruling and teaching is really a divine given that is perfectly well known as integral to Catholic faith and piety, so well known that there should be no need to try to "prove" it. Papal supremacy and infallibility, he believes, are plainly taught in the New Testament in Christ's words to Peter in the Gospels. But he does not begin his treatise on papal authority with any matter from Scripture or tradition, but by asking what is the best form of government. Surely no one would doubt that Jesus Christ, supremely and divinely wise and benevolent, would choose for his Church the form of government that was "the best and most useful."[70] Of the three forms of government—monarchy, aristocracy, and democracy—he briefly shows that the best is monarchy. For temporal kingdoms, some mixture of the three forms seems best, but "monarchia simplex" is really the best system intrinsically, for it is one most conducive to maintaining order in a society. For this reason, Jesus Christ, supremely and divinely wise and benevolent, chose this system for his Church.[71]

For Bellarmine, "simple monarchy" means that the pope-monarch governs the Church and teaches the faith untrammeled by constitutional structures. But it is not a "monarchia absoluta et libera" (monarchy absolute and arbitrary); it is one that is appropriate to "ministers and dispensers" of the faith and grace of God, for all Catholic doctors agree that this monarchy is "tempered . . . by aristocracy and democracy."[72] Unfortunately, he does not explain here or elsewhere what he means by "tempered," nor do any elements resembling aristocracy or democracy appear in his ecclesiology in any

---

69. The edition of Bellarmine's work used here is his *Opera omnia*, ed. Justin Fèvre (Paris: Louis Vives, 1870; Frankfurt: Minerva, 1965). In this edition *Tertia controversia generalis: De summo pontifice* begins in volume 1 and continues into volume 2. *Quarta controversia generalis: De conciliis* is contained in volume 2. They will be cited here as *III controv.* and *IV controv.*, giving Bellarmine's book and chapter numbers with volume and page numbers of the Fèvre edition. The *Controversiae* were first published at Ingolstadt beginning in 1586.

70. *III Controv.*, I, 1 (1:461).   71. Ibid., I, 5 (1:469) and I, 9 (1:479).
72. Ibid., I, 5 (1:469), citing I Cor 4.

recognizable way. But it should be noted that, unlike some later papalist authors, he does not mind calling the papal authority "ministerial."[73] Though he takes papal supremacy as a divine given, he adds lengthy and detailed arguments from the New Testament, offering some thirteen chapters and forty-seven pages of exegesis on the Petrine texts.[74]

For Bellarmine, the Roman Pontiff is the supreme judge in controversies of faith and morals, and his judgment is certain and infallible. The Protestants totally reject any such teaching authority, even exercised by the pope together with a council. Sadly, some Catholics also dissent, maintaining that infallibility belongs only to the whole Church and is exercised by a general council. Bellarmine does not call these Catholics Gallicans; the name *Gallican* seems to be unknown to him. He calls them "Parisians," naming Jean Gerson as a leading exponent of this view.[75] This position, unlike that of the Protestants, "we do not dare to call properly heretical, for thus far we see those who adhere to this view tolerated by the Church." However, it seems to be "altogether erroneous and proximate to heresy," so that it could be deservedly declared heretical by the judgment of the Church.[76] The pope must be accepted by Catholics as the infallible teacher of the faith. "The Supreme Pontiff," asserts Bellarmine, "when he teaches the whole Church on a matter of faith, cannot in any case make a mistake."[77] Christ teaches this plainly when he says to Peter in Luke 22, "strengthen your brothers." The Parisians are wrong when they say that Christ addressed those words to the whole

---

73. Two other places in *III Controv.* where he says that popes and bishops are ministers or have a ministerial role are I, 7 (1:474) and I, 9 (1:479).

74. Ibid., I, 10–22 (1:488–535). These are double-column pages with rather small type.

75. Ibid., IV, 2 (2:79). Jean Gerson (1363–1429), chancellor of the University of Paris for many years, author of many valuable theological and other works, believed in conciliar supremacy and was a leader at the Council of Constance (1414–1418). On the Church thought of Gerson see Olivier de La Brosse, *Le pape et le concile: La comparaison de leurs pouvoirs à la Veille de la Réforme* (Paris: Cerf, 1965), esp. 81–145; see also Louis B. Pascoe, S.J., *Jean Gerson: Principles of Church Reform* (Leiden: Brill, 1973).

76. *III Controv.*, IV, 3 (2:80).   77. Ibid.

Church, for he addressed them to Peter alone. In like manner, Christ's words to Peter in John 21, "Feed my sheep," mean that there is no appeal from a papal pronouncement on the faith. Who could judge whether the pontiff has taught rightly or not? "It is not for the sheep to judge whether the shepherd has made a mistake."[78]

There is no appeal from Peter's successor to a general council. Christ spoke the words "Feed my sheep" to Peter alone, not to a council. "He called Peter alone the rock and the foundation, not Peter and a council. From this it is apparent that all the firmness of legitimate councils comes from the pontiff, not partly from the pontiff and partly from the council." Sometimes a general council cannot be convoked, as was the case during the first three centuries of persecution. "There must be in the Church even without a council some judge who cannot err" in teaching the faith. Moreover, at a council there may be dissension, and dissension means the council cannot be a certain judge. But there must at all times be a sovereign certain judge that the faithful can believe. "Therefore it remains that the pope is the judge, and for that reason he cannot err."[79]

This does not mean that councils are useless, for the pope should not neglect the use of ordinary and human means for arriving at truth, and a council is an ordinary means for that. His discussion of this point is the one place where Bellarmine mentions the consensus of the Church, or Churches. He says, "Definitions of the faith depend mainly on apostolic tradition and on the consensus of the Churches. To ascertain what is the opinion of the whole Church [*totius Ecclesiae sententia*] and what tradition the Churches of Christ have preserved on a question that has arisen, there is no better way than that the bishops of all the provinces gather together, and that each one reports the custom of his Church."[80] He adds that councils are very useful, and sometimes necessary, to end a controversy. The fact that all the bishops have gathered together to testify to a doctrine, and also show

---

78. Ibid., IV, 3 (2:84).   79. Ibid.
80. Ibid., IV, 7 (1:89). "Custom" renders *consuetudo*, which is an unusual word for faith or doctrine.

their readiness to teach the doctrine, is very conducive to the unity and harmony of the Church.[81] This is the whole extent of Bellarmine's comment on the consensus of the Church on a matter of faith.

Quarta controversia generalis: De conciliis spells out further this basic view that a general council is at times necessary for practical reasons, but it is *not* simply or absolutely necessary.[82] Indeed, most of the *Quarta controversia* is devoted to strong assertions of papal supremacy over any council. Contrary to the view of the Parisians (none are named) and other conciliarists, a general council is not superior to the pope. Rather, "I think" (ego tamen existimo) that a council not confirmed by the pope can err. That is because (1) a statement of a council is "not the ultimate judgment of the Church"; and (2) the firmness of a council comes from the "concurrence and conjunction of the body *with the head,*" and not from a consensus of the body of believers.[83]

A council does not have supreme power because the Church is not like a temporal kingdom. "For in the kingdom of Christ supreme power is in Christ and is not in any way derived from the people."[84] In a human kingdom the power of the king is from the people because the people make the king. They concede the power to the king, and they can in the extreme case withdraw it, if he becomes a tyrant. However, "the Church [community] does not have any authority by itself, for all [authority] is in Christ and in those to whom Christ concedes it." Christ gave to Peter the keys of the kingdom of heaven and to the other apostles only what was needed for their episcopal functions. No power was given to the congregation of the faithful. "Thus if no authority was given to the whole Church [*Ecclesiae universitati*], then none was given to a general council as representing the universal Church."[85] Finally, "The Supreme Pontiff is simply and absolutely over the universal Church, and over a general

---

81. Ibid.
82. *IV Controv.,* I, 10 (1:207–210).
83. Ibid., II, 11 (2:260); emphasis added.
84. Ibid., II, 16 (2:268).
85. Ibid., II, 16 (2:268–269).

council, and he does not acknowledge any judgment on earth over himself." This, he adds, is "almost of faith" (fere de fide).[86] If the pope does wrong, judgment is reserved to God, for there is no Church authority that can judge him.[87]

Bellarmine respects Gerson enough to devote several pages to his objections to such enormous power vested in one man. Remonstrating against such absolute papal claims, Gerson says, "So only the Church remains with no remedy if it has a bad pontiff, and that pontiff can with impunity harass and destroy everybody, and no one can resist[!]"[88] Bellarmine responds with some striking comments that are not mentioned by any Gallican or papalist writers studied in the present work. He says that it is not surprising that the Church has no effective *human* remedy for papal wrongdoing, since its salvation depends not on human effort but on divine protection. Still, though the Church cannot depose a pope, it does have some recourse. The Church can and should ask God to provide some remedy, and it is certain that God will help, perhaps by converting the pope or removing him from the scene before he destroys the Church. "But it does not follow that it is illicit to resist a pope who is destroying the Church" (Non tamen hinc sequitur, non licere resistere Pontifici Ecclesiam destruenti). In the extreme case of a pope who seems incorrigibly bent on a course very harmful to the Church, there is an extreme remedy. "It is licit to admonish him respectfully, and to try moderately to stop him, and even to resist him by force of arms if he is willing to destroy the Church. For to resist and repel force with force does not require any authority" (Licet enim cum servata reverentia admonere, et modeste corripere, repugnare etiam vi et armis, si Ecclesiam destruere velit. Ad resistendum enim, et vim vi repellendam, non requiritur ulla auctoritas).[89] There could be interesting dis-

---

86. Ibid., II, 16 (2:269).
87. Ibid., II, 19 (2:274).
88. Ibid., II, 19 (2:275). This is Bellarmine's wording of a complaint of Gerson in a text that he does not identify; "bad," renders *malum*.
89. Ibid.

cussion of the anomalous position that there is no peaceful, or constitutional, solution to the problem of the extreme misuse of power by a pope, but that there is a violent solution if the community has enough armed men to overcome him.[90] In the papalist perspective propounded by Bellarmine, the members of the community may take this drastic step provided they do not claim any higher *authority* in doing it. Surely Gerson would have some intelligent and probably pointed comments. But this is not the place to launch a discussion on that point.

It is clear from this brief summary of one famous and representative exponent of the papalist doctrine that it does not recognize any constitutional limits on papal power, nor any constitutional means whereby the Catholic faith community can influence the Supreme Pontiff, who exercises essentially absolute divine power. It is this exaltation of monarchical papal power that the French clergy gathered in Paris in 1682 did not consider really sound and traditional Catholic doctrine. On March 17 they listened to a lengthy position paper delivered by Gilbert de Choiseul du Plessis-Praslin, bishop of Tournai, who served as the rapporteur for the group that drafted the declaration. Choiseul, himself a doctor of theology, concludes his long and erudite report by reproaching the papalism that insists on "this infallibility, this independence of the canons, this absolute monarchy, and this enormous power, that some theologians of these latter times have attributed to the pope, against what Scripture and the whole of tradition teach us."[91] He frequently names Bellarmine as a leading teacher

90. Bellarmine cites Joannes de Turrecremata (Juan de Torquemada, O.P., 1388–1468) as making a similar comment, and the Spaniard does say that if an incorrigible pope will not mend his ways a council can invoke the secular arm, that is, the emperor or another king, to resist the evils being committed by that pope. Such a pope is, in his vivid terms, a "delapidator" of the Church (breaks it down by throwing big stones at it). He does not explicitly mention military force as does Bellarmine. See Turrecremata's *Summa de ecclesia* (1453), II, 106, as in Juan Tomàs de Rocaberti, O.P., ed., *Biblioteca maxima pontificia* (Rome: Joannes Buagni, 1697–1699; Graz: Akademisch Druck, 1969), 13:440; see also Thomas M. Izbicki, *Protector of the Faith: Cardinal Ioannes de Turrecremata and the Defense of the Institutional Church* (Washington, D.C.: Catholic University of America Press, 1981), 87–91.

91. Text of the Rapport by Bishop Choiseul as given in Pierre-Toussaint Durand

of this doctrine. "Is it not a duty of our pastoral charity finally to draw aside the curtain and declare our true sentiments to the whole world?"[92] On March 19 all the assembled clergy voted for the declaration, and the ecclesiological views contained in it were, according to all the indications we have, those of a very large number of French clergy, probably a majority, until the Ultramontane Movement got under way in the years after Napoleon.

But there were always some in France during these centuries who adhered to the Ultramontane, or papalist or Roman, standpoint, including some highly respected theologians. This was true even of the Faculty of Theology of the Sorbonne, frequently considered a Gallican stronghold.[93] Bellarmine thought of these "Parisians" as adversaries of papal supremacy but was not well informed as to their diversity. He would have been surprised to learn that a majority of the Sorbonne theologians were actually unwilling at first to register the declaration of March 19 and did so only under pressure from royal officials.[94] André Duval (1564–1639), a leading doctor of the Sorbonne, was a defender of papal infallibility so able that even some of the men who signed the declaration hesitated because of their admiration of Duval.[95] In 1684 Bossuet felt compelled to do more work on his defense of the Gallican Declaration when he read Antoine Charlas's *Tractatus de libertatibus ecclesiae gallicanae*, a book published in

---

de Maillane, ed., *Les libertés de l'Eglise gallicane prouvées et commentées*, 5 vols. (Lyon: Pierre Bruyset Ponthus, 1771), 4:343–454, at 451. This is a major collection of documents illustrating France's defense of its Gallican liberties.

92. Ibid.

93. See Martimort's opening chapter in *Gallicanisme de Bossuet*, "L'antique sentiment de la Faculté de Théologie ou les 'Maximes de l'Ecole de Paris,'" 17–56.

94. Martimort, *Gallicanisme de Bossuet*, 498–505. See also Jacques Gres-Gayer, "The Magisterium of the Faculty of Theology of Paris in the Seventeenth Century," *Theological Studies* 53 (September 1992): 440. Gres-Gayer also gives a wealth of specific information on this in his valuable article on the papal nuncio's personal "scorecard" of theologians faithful or unfaithful to the Holy See: "Gallicans et Romains en Sorbonne d'après le nonce Bargellini (1670)," *Revue d'histoire ecclésiastique* 87 (July–December 1992): 682–744. He offers a wealth of specific information on this in his major new book, *Le gallicanisme de Sorbonne: Chroniques de la Faculté de Théologie de Paris (1657–1688)* (Paris: Honoré Champion, 2002).

95. Martimort, *Gallicanisme de Bossuet*, 472–474.

Belgium that offered a detailed and impressive critique of Gallican positions and defended papal supremacy.[96]

But books defending papal supremacy and infallibility were not generally welcome in France even before 1682. The Faculty of Theology itself severely censured a book written by Jacques de Vernant promoting papal infallibility and published at Metz in 1658. The thesis of papal infallibility, the censure stated, is "falsa, temeraria, scandalosa et in Fide pericolosa."[97] More consistently after 1682, books like that of de Vernant were condemned and suppressed in France. The Gallican ecclesiopolitical system entailed in practice numerous controls by the royal government over Church matters, and churchmen tended to accept these as normal elements of the age-old partnership of Church and Crown. They *expected* the public authorities to assist in the preservation of the faith and good order of the Church as understood in French tradition. Their request of Louis XIV to enforce the four articles is a very clear example of this. In 1695 the Parlement of Paris, as Bossuet suggested in a *mémoire* to the king, forbade the distribution in France of a major treatise upholding papal supremacy by Juan Tomàs Rocaberti, a Spanish Dominican.[98] In 1724 the parlement suppressed a book by Mathieu Petitdidier, *Traité sur l'autorité et l'infaillibilité des papes*. This rash book defending papal infallibility, said the decree, would tend "to disquiet spirits, sow the seeds of division, and cause dangerous novelties to break out."[99]

---

96. Antoine Charlas, *Tractatus de libertatibus ecclesiae gallicanae* (Liège: Matthias Hovium, 1684). Charlas, a priest of the diocese of Pamiers and friend of Bishop Caulet, gave a trenchant critique of many leading promoters of Gallicanism. Martimort, in *Gallicanisme de Bossuet*, 606–621, describes at length Bossuet's reaction to Charlas's book.

97. Text as given in Durand de Maillane, ed., *Les libertés de l'Eglise gallicane*, 4:10. Jacques de Vernant was the pseudonym of a Carmelite theologian, Bonaventura Hérédie. On this episode, see Martimort, *Gallicanisme de Bossuet*, 237–254. Gres-Gayer stresses that the faculty did this of their own accord, and not under pressure from the Crown, "The Magisterium of the Faculty of Theology," 425–426.

98. Juan Tomàs de Rocaberti, O.P., *De romani pontificis auctoritate*, 3 vols. (first published Valencia: 1691–1694). Actually, Bossuet suggested several options in dealing with this book, outright suppression being only one of them; see text of his note to the king in the Lachat edition of Bossuet's works, 22:617–630.

99. Text as given in Durand de Maillane, *Libertés de l'Eglise gallicane*, 5:29.

These examples could readily be multiplied just from the collection offered in Durand de Maillane. Besides these controls over books in France, the Gallican system entailed comprehensive controls over communications from the Roman curia. These were regulated by the French government, pursuing a policy dating back at least to a decree of Louis XI in 1475. If a document from Rome did not receive the approval referred to as the *placet,* then it was not published in France.[100] These regulations were not at all unique to France; they were the common policy of Catholic governments generally.[101] This means that the "enormous power" of the papacy was in concrete reality not as formidable as suggested by Bishop Choiseul in his position paper of March 17, 1682.[102]

The Present Study

The term *consensus Ecclesiae,* central to our entire study, will be rendered throughout as "the consensus of the Church." There may be a few times when "consent" would seem a good English translation of *consensus,* but it seems desirable to observe complete consistency in our usage. When *consentement de l'Eglise* occurs in French texts, it also will be rendered as "the consensus of the Church," for *consentement* can mean agreement as well as consent. The terms *sensus fidei, sensus fidelium,* or *consensus fidelium* will not appear in this work, for they do not occur in the treatises dealt with here, either Gallican or papalist. Moreover, these terms really involve some theological issues that are

---

100. Concerning these controls over the Church in France, see Latreille et al., *Histoire du catholicisme en France,* 2:355–378, esp. 363–367, and Roland Mousnier, *The Institutions of France under the Absolute Monarchy, 1598–1789* (Chicago: University of Chicago Press, 1979), 2:311–316. Another succinct, informative summary is given by Charles Lefebvre et al., *Les sources du droit et la seconde centralisation romaine,* in *L'époque moderne (1563–1789),* tome 15, vol. 1 of Gabriel Le Bras and Jean Gaudemet, eds., *Histoire du droit et des institutions de l'Eglise en Occident* (Paris: Cujas, 1976), 44–46.

101. A clear and instructive summary of these policies in a number of Catholic countries is given by Oskar Köhler, "Foundations and Forms of the Established Church in the Bourbon States of the Seventeenth and Eighteenth Centuries," in *The Church in the Age of Absolutism and Enlightenment,* vol. 6 of Hubert Jedin and John Dolan, eds., *History of the Church* (New York: Crossroads, 1981), 329–342.

102. See Richard F. Costigan, S.J., "Papal Supremacy: From Theory to Practice," *Vital Nexus* (Halifax, Nova Scotia) 2 (September 1996): 9–17.

different from the ecclesiological and institutional issues of the Gallican/papalist controversy.

Ecclesia in this book always means the episcopate, that is, the bishops of the Church collectively considered. It is the hierarchy, and not the whole community of clergy and lay faithful. We shall note this particularly in the most important Gallican authors, Bossuet and Tourney. The papalist authors also usually mean the episcopate, though they sometimes like to imply that the Gallican agenda is calculated to introduce democracy into the Church. We need to be clear that the mainstream Gallicanism of our authors, which is that of the Declaration of 1682, is not democratic. Thus it is definitely not the ecclesiology of Edmond Richer (1559–1631), a doctor and then syndic of the Faculty of Theology of Paris, who published in 1611 a small book entitled *De ecclesiastica ac politica potestate libellus*. For Richer, Christ conferred authority on the whole community of the faithful, who then delegate it to the bishops and pope, who thus have (only) a ministerial function. Congar appropriately calls Richer's theory "Gallicanisme presbytérianiste," and it was indeed very popular for a long time among many of the rank and file of the French clergy.[103] Less appropriately, Léopold Willaert, S.J., says that Richer is the principal and dominant codifier of ecclesiastical Gallicanism for the seventeenth century.[104] As will be seen, certainly neither Jacques-Bénigne Bossuet nor Honoré Tourney, nor the many who concur with their ecclesiology, would agree with this.

The word *reception* will occur a few times in this book, and it could be used more frequently. It is evident that this concept, when applied to papal statements addressed to the Church, is closely related to the consensus of the Church as discussed in this historical study.[105]

---

103. Yves Congar, O.P., *L'Eglise de saint Augustin à l'époque moderne* (Paris: Cerf, 1970), 394. For the popularity of Richérism among French clergy, see François Lebrun, ed., *Histoire des catholiques en France du XVe siècle à nos jours* (Toulouse: Privat, 1980), 157–158; also Louis S. Greenbaum, *Talleyrand, Statesman Priest: The Agent-General of the Clergy and the Church of France at the End of the Old Regime* (Washington: Catholic University of America Press, 1970), 129–130.

104. Willaert, *Après le concile de Trente: La restauration catholique, 1563–1648*, 388.

105. Among many good works on reception in recent years, it should suffice to

In some situations they are the same thing, as is clearly the case if the consensus is subsequent: that is, when the episcopate accepts (receives) a statement of the pope on some doctrinal or disciplinary matter after he has issued it. But also when the consensus can be called concomitant or antecedent, the basic ecclesial idea is the same: the Church "receives," or agrees with, the papal statement because it recognizes in it the historic faith of the Catholic Christian community. The Gallican idea of consensus can be properly thought of as a version of reception, and Yves Congar, in an important 1972 article, includes insightful comment on some concerns of Gallican leaders that are evident in their version.[106] The papalist view does not recognize in the Church any such thing as reception or consensus when a papal pronouncement is issued, if these terms mean anything more than docile assent and obedience to the statement.[107] The Roman Pontiff has full power by virtue of his office to decree the faith, and neither the episcopate nor the community as a whole has any competence to evaluate or judge his decrees. For this reason there is no reception or consensus as understood by Gallican or any other authors. This doctrine of the papalist authors was strongly asserted in

---

mention a few. Gilles Routhier, in *La réception d'un concile* (Paris: Cerf, 1993), offers a lengthy explanation with abundant references in his first chapter, "La 'réception'" Histoire du thème et usage du concept," 15–65. See also Frederick M. Bliss, *Understanding Reception: A Backdrop to Its Ecumenical Use* (Milwaukee: Marquette University Press, 1993). Two other good treatments are Francis A. Sullivan, S.J., *Magisterium: Teaching Authority in the Catholic Church* (New York: Paulist, 1983), 50–51, 84–87, 109–177; and Patrick Granfield, O.S.B., *The Limits of the Papacy* (New York: Crossroad, 1987), 134–168. James Coriden, in "The Canonical Doctrine of Reception," *Jurist* 50 (1990): 58–82, offers a very informative treatment of the use of the term in legal history, and specifically in canon law. In addition, an entire recent volume of the *Jurist* is devoted to reception: 57, 1 (1997). Thomas Rausch, S.J., in "Reception Past and Present," *Theological Studies* 47 (September 1986): 497–508, summarizes much useful information on reception, especially in an ecumenical context.

106. Yves Congar, O.P., "La 'réception' comme réalité ecclésiologique," *Revue des sciences philosophiques et théologiques* 56 (July 1972): 369–403, at 398–390. An abbreviated version of this article is available in English: "Reception as an Ecclesiological Reality," in Giuseppe Alberigo and Anton Weiler, eds., *Election and Consensus in the Church*, vol. 77 of *Concilium* (New York: Herder, 1972), 43–68.

107. See the excellent article on this by Hermann Josef Pottmeyer, "Reception and Submission," *Jurist* 51 (1991): 269–292.

the *ex sese* clause of *Pastor Aeternus,* which surely rejects reception along with the consensus of the Church.

The order of chapters in this book is not particularly one of logical sequence, for they could have been alternatively arranged. That is, each presents the thought of one author (except for the one on Bailly and Bergier) as a self-contained whole, and there is really no appreciable dialogue between the authors of the two sides. Also, there is no really discernible development in the thought of the several authors of either camp over the time span covered in the book. Several could usefully have been linked together; for example, Orsi expressly devotes himself to a critique of Bossuet, and La Luzerne focuses his critique on Orsi. Or one could have alternated chapters on Gallican and papalist authors. But it seemed simpler and perhaps most useful to put all of them in the straight chronological order of the publication of the treatise (or principal treatise) of each author. All the authors of Gallican books are of course French, and we will make no effort to deal with authors of other countries who shared their concern for consensual and collegial values in ecclesiology. All the authors on the papalist side are Italian, even though the papalist ecclesiology is strongly upheld by some authors of other countries, such as Spain.

CHAPTER 2

Jacques-Bénigne Bossuet
1627–1704

Bossuet and Ecclesial Controversy

The study of the primary sources in the background of the First Vatican Council's proclamation of papal infallibility is as illuminating as the need for it is evident. For example, Hans Urs von Balthasar, surveying some people in the history of the Church who had expressed even slight reservations about the absolute supremacy of the Roman Pontiff, says that the Gallicans wanted "to qualify every papal decision, be it by an appeal to a council or by a stipulation that the directives must be accepted by the whole Church (bishops and flock) to be valid."[1] He does not cite any source for this and could not do so, for Gallicanism does not stipulate the consent of "the flock" to papal pronouncements, only that of the episcopate. Nor does von Balthasar cite any Gallican source in calling Bossuet "sincere" though grossly mistaken in teaching Gallican views,[2] nor when he says that the *ex sese* clause of Vatican I was necessitated by the "equivocation" and "one-sided insistence on rights on the part of the Gallicans."[3] Von

---

1. Hans Urs von Balthasar, *The Office of Peter and the Structure of the Church* (San Francisco: Ignatius, 1986), 68.
2. Ibid., 67.   3. Ibid., 217.

Balthasar is typical of authors alluding to Gallicanism: they simply do not cite Gallican sources and seemingly see no need to do so.[4] But careful study of these sources is very instructive, and ignoring or misrepresenting what they really say about a matter like the consensus of the Church is not helpful in understanding the divergent historic viewpoints on papal infallibility. The fact is that Bossuet's views on this ecclesial question are much more nuanced than those attributed to him or to other Gallicans by critics like von Balthasar.

Jacques-Bénigne Bossuet, bishop of Meaux from 1681, was one of the leading prelates of the Church of France in the seventeenth century. One of the relatively few bishops of France who were not of the aristocracy, Bossuet was born in Dijon into a very substantial family deeply involved for generations in law and the judiciary. His father, Bénigne, was a counselor of the Parlement of Metz. He attended a Jesuit school in Dijon and then in 1642 the College of Navarre in Paris, where his teachers included a number of distinguished scholars. Ordained priest in 1652, he also earned his doctorate in theology that year. In 1670 he became the bishop of Condom and was also chosen by Louis XIV to be tutor of the dauphin, the crown prince of France. In that same year he was admitted into the French Academy, and in 1682 he became bishop of Meaux. Remembered today perhaps mainly as a great orator, "the Eagle of Meaux," he was also an author of serious theological and historical works and a very important exponent of the ecclesiology of Gallicanism.[5]

Probably the one book of his that is still read is *Discourse on Universal History* (1681), which is considered a pioneering work in the philosophy—really, of course, theology—of history. Herbert Butterfield

---

4. On this, see chapter 1, note 10.

5. The comprehensive scholarly study of Bossuet's thought on all matters relevant to ecclesiology remains Aimé-Georges Martimort, *Le gallicanisme de Bossuet* (Paris: Cerf, 1953). This work also contains much information on the life and works of Bossuet. Among articles on Bossuet in standard reference works, two are major studies: A. Largent, in *DTC*, 2.2:1049–1089 (1932), and E. Levesque, in *DHGE*, 9:1339–1391 (1937). See also the brief entry of Richard F. Costigan, S.J., "Bossuet, Jacques-Bénigne," in *Biographical Dictionary of Christian Theologians*, ed. Patrick W. Carey and Joseph T. Lienhard, S.J. (Westport, Conn.: Greenwood, 2000), 86–88.

says, "Apart from being a magnificent expression of the spirit which informed literary work in the France of Louis XIV, it is quite imposing as an outline of history and an example of seventeenth-century scholarship."[6] Bossuet, he adds, "represents a high spot in the history of modern Catholicism." Ultramontane writers liked the way Bossuet stressed the unbroken continuity of religious leadership from Innocent XI back to St. Peter and from there back to Moses, the patriarchs, and the beginning of the world.[7] Nineteenth-century Catholic apologist Jaime Luciano Balmes (1810–1848) extols the *Discourse* as "the first and best book ever written on this subject" and reminds his Catholic readers that "Bossuet was a Catholic, and moreover one of the most trenchant adversaries of the Protestant Reformation."[8]

Really Balmes is somewhat mistaken in referring to Bossuet as simply a trenchant adversary of Protestantism, for he wrote at least two significant books showing interest in some kind of dialogue, or at least peaceful relations, with Protestants. *Exposition de la doctrine catholique sur les matières de controverse* (1671) offers a clear explanation of Catholic doctrines with the hope of clearing up misunderstandings that had developed during the century and a half since the era of Luther and Calvin. This book seems to have been respected and appreciated by many.[9] Some years later, in 1688, Bossuet published his *Histoire des variations des Eglises protestantes*. This work's perceptions of Protestantism are admittedly negative, for it pursues the guiding principle that perpetuity in the same unchanging principles is a sign of truth, and variation is a sign of error. Thus the many splits of the Protestants into a great number of churches show that they are in error. This does not sound very ecumenical to us today, but Bossuet

---

6. Herbert Butterfield, *The Origins of History* (New York: Basic Books, 1981), 216. Orest Ranum has published a new edition of the *Discourse on Universal History* (Chicago: University of Chicago Press, 1976).

7. Bossuet, *Discourse* (Ranum edition), 289–290.

8. Jaime Luciano Balmes, *Protestantism and Catholicity Compared in Their Effects on the Civilization of Europe* (Baltimore: John Murphy, 1851), 418.

9. On the reception of this book see Martimort, *Gallicanisme de Bossuet*, 330–349.

seems to have hoped that some Protestants might be led to reconsider their religious commitment. Catholics at least thought it was a fine book.[10]

Among Bossuet's books the one most relevant to ecclesiology, and the only one dealt with in this study, is his massive *Defensio declarationis cleri gallicani* (1,372 octavo pages), published after he died. Since he was the main redactor of the Declaration of 1682, his discussion and defense of it is uniquely authoritative, and it is also a work of great erudition and interest in its own right.

With the partial exception of this one area of ecclesiology, Bossuet certainly has been recognized as an eminent Roman Catholic author, writing in the historic mainstream of Catholic thought. Gustave Lanson said of him in 1891: "Catholic, severely orthodox, he professes on all points the doctrines that the councils and the uniform tradition of the Church have authorized; his theology is Catholic theology."[11] Patrick Riley notes how Bossuet defended that Roman Catholic orthodoxy against Protestant and rationalist thinkers of many kinds.[12] George Salmon, in his major study of infallibility in 1888, is all in all correct in terming Bossuet "the most trusted champion of his Church."[13] He exaggerates somewhat when he says, referring to the fact that Bossuet's views on papal infallibility were strongly rejected at Vatican I, "Consequently, Bossuet is treated by the predominant Roman Catholic school as no better than a Protestant."[14] But the exaggeration is not so great in the case of papalist (Ultramontane) authors, who had for a long time tended to see Bossuet and other Gallican theologians as being so unfaithful to absolute papal ortho-

---

10. On this book see Largent's *DTC* article, 1066–1067. Owen Chadwick offers learned comments in *From Bossuet to Newman: The Idea of Doctrinal Development* (Cambridge: Cambridge University Press, 1957), 1–20.

11. Gustave Lanson, *Bossuet* (Paris: Lecène, Oudin, 1891), 321. The 4th edition of this book was reprinted by Arno, New York, 1979.

12. Patrick Riley, in the introduction to his translation of Bossuet's *Politics Drawn from the Very Words of Scripture* (New York: Cambridge University Press, 1990), xiv.

13. George Salmon, *The Infallibility of the Church* (London: John Murray, 1923; first published in 1888), 87.

14. Ibid., 88.

doxy as to be not *much* better than Protestants. This was despite the recognition by such leading papalists as Bellarmine and Ballerini that papal infallibility was not a dogma of faith.[15]

The case of Joseph de Maistre is instructive and important, given his prominence as a leader of the Ultramontane Movement in the nineteenth century.[16] His landmark work *Du pape* (1819), asserting papal sovereignty and infallibility in forceful and trenchant terms, entails much scornful criticism of Gallicanism, a critique he continues in its sequel, *De l'Eglise gallicane dans son rapport avec le souverain pontife* (1820).[17] Deep ambivalence about Bossuet comes through vividly in the five chapters in *De l'Eglise gallicane,* in which he discusses and laments the role of Bossuet in the Declaration of 1682 and in the *Defensio*. He understands very well that the bishop of Meaux is like himself a man of order, stability, and orthodoxy, so much so that he would not even want to convoke an assembly in which any questioning of authority might take place (205). He states as a "grande vérité," all in italics: "Never has authority had a greater or above all a more upright defender than Bossuet" (259). "The idea of calling into

15. See Pietro Ballerini, *Appendix de infallibilitate pontificia in definitionibus dogmaticis* (1768), as published together with Ballerini's *De potestate ecclesiastica summorum pontificum et conciliorum generalium* (Rome: Typis S. Congregationis de Propaganda Fide, 1850), 231; and Robert Bellarmine. S. J., *Tertia controversia generalis: De summo pontifice,* 4, 2, in *Opera omnia,* ed. Justin Fèvre (Paris: Louis Vives, 1870), 2:80. Both authors, while stating that all Catholics really should believe in papal infallibility, recognize that it had never been defined.

16. Among numerous treatments of the role of Joseph de Maistre in the Ultramontane Movement, three brief but authoritative ones areYves Congar, O.P., *L'Eglise de saint Augustin à l'époque moderne* (Paris: Cerf, 1970), 414–416; Roger Aubert, "La géographie ecclésiologique au XIXe siècle," in Maurice Nédoncelle et al., *L'ecclésiologie au XIXe siècle* (Paris: Cerf, 1960), 17–19; and Yves Congar, "L'ecclésiologie de la Révolution française au Concile du Vatican, sous la signe de l'affirmation de l'autorité," in the same volume by Nédoncelle et al., 81–85. For a longer discussion of de Maistre's ideas on the Church and the papacy, see Richard F. Costigan, S.J., *Rohrbacher and the Ecclesiology of Ultramontanism* (Rome: Università Gregoriana Editrice, 1980), 20–36. All these have numerous references to the literature.

17. The edition of *De l'Eglise gallicane* used here is Joseph de Maistre, *Du pape, suivi de l'Eglise gallicane dans son rapport avec le souverain pontife,* 2 vols. (Brussels: H. Goemaere, 1852). *De l'Eglise gallicane* is in volume 2, so all page numbers, hereafter given in the text, refer to that volume.

question the authority of the pope at a meeting in the Catholic Church, of treating in a national meeting points of doctrine that could only be discussed by the universal Church" was foreign to him (205). De Maistre thinks that Bossuet attended the meeting hoping to serve as a moderating influence (207).

It is in his lengthy and troubled discussion of the *Defensio* that de Maistre regretfully but harshly decides that Bossuet lacked the strength of character to resist the royal demand that he write a full-scale defense of articles that he really despised in his heart (210), articles that really were "Protestant in their essence" (216). This accounts for the fitful and foot-dragging way in which he wrote the *Defensio* (209), his weak comment that the French had not dreamed of making the articles a dogmatic definition (210–211), his unwillingness to publish it when he had completed it (220–221), and his unfulfilled desire to revise it (222). De Maistre summarizes: "The four articles present incontestably one of the saddest monuments in ecclesiastical history. They were the work of pride, of resentment, of party spirit, and above all of weakness, to put it mildly." If implemented, they would make "the government of the Church difficult or impossible" (235). This being the case, "[t]he defense of the articles cannot be better than the articles themselves" (236). De Maistre's great conviction is that a clergy devoted to absolute papal sovereignty in all things would not comply with the demands of any national monarch. To his mind, the Gallican clergy's subservience to Louis XIV in the Declaration of 1682 proves the thesis: the king ordered it like a watch or a carriage, and they, Bossuet among them, spinelessly complied (ibid.). Noting that great men sometimes reach a "fatal point," after which they sadly decline, de Maistre says, "Bossuet should have died after the 'Sermon on Unity,' like Scipio Africanus after the battle of Zama" (265).[18]

---

18. The "Sermon on Unity," preached by Bossuet at the beginning of the Extraordinary General Assembly of the French Clergy on November 9, 1681, was widely admired by Ultramontanes as well as Gallicans for its reverent appreciation of the role of the pope in the universal Church. In the text of this sermon, in volume 11 of Bossuet's *Oeuvres complètes*, ed. F. Lachat (Paris: Louis Vives, 1862–1866), see esp. 592–609.

Félicité Lamennais, who by the mid-1820s had emerged as the most vigorous spokesman of the Ultramontane viewpoint, continued the fierce criticism of Gallicanism with indignation fueled by the experience of the France of that time.[19] He and a growing number of younger clergy and some laity scorned the bishops who complacently accepted the Bourbon Restoration's continuance of the historic Gallican system's royal controls over the Church, reinforced by new ones added by Napoleon.[20] His *De la religion considérée dans ses rapports avec l'ordre politique et civile* (1825–1826), a scathing exposé of the whole Gallican system, includes severe comments on Bossuet. It was the "lamentable destiny of this great bishop" that he cooperated in this cause.[21] Bossuet, Lamennais believes, did not share the "vile passions" of the other prelates of 1682, who acted out of resentment of the Sovereign Pontiff (164). Indeed, he attempted, especially with his "Sermon on Unity," to be a mediator between his confreres and the Church (by "Church" meaning evidently the papacy). He forgot that the Church does not accept such mediation. "Having nothing to cede, she never deals" and never accepts any alteration of her doctrine (164).

Lamennais devotes seventy pages to a critique of the four Gallican

---

19. A very good book on Lamennais in English is Alec Vidler, *Prophecy and Papacy: A Study of Lamennais, the Church, and the Revolution* (London: SCM Press, 1954). A briefer treatment is Adrien Dansette, *Religious History of Modern France* (New York: Herder, 1961), 1:207–226. A major modern work is Jean-René Derré, *Lamennais, ses amis, et le mouvement des idées à l'époque romantique, 1824–1834* (Paris: C. Klincksieck, 1961). On Lamennais's religious thought, see Louis LeGuillou, *L'évolution de la pensée religieuse de Félicité Lamennais* (Paris: Armand Colin, 1966).

20. On this development see Costigan, *Rohrbacher,* 39–70; and by the same author, "The Ecclesiological Dialectic," *Thought* 49 (June 1974): 134–144, and "Lamennais and Rohrbacher and the Papacy," *Revue de l'Université d'Ottawa* 57 (July–September 1987): 53–66. The Gallican system did entail very extensive royal controls over Church matters. On this, see André Latreille et al., *Histoire du catholicisme en France,* 2nd ed. (Paris: Spes, 1962), 2:355–378, esp. 363–367, or Roland Mousnier, *The Institutions of France under the Absolute Monarchy, 1598–1789* (Chicago: University of Chicago Press, 1979), 1:311–316.

21. Félicité Lamennais, *De la religion considérée dans ses rapports avec l'ordre politique et civile,* as in *Oeuvres complètes de F. de la Mennais* (Paris: Daubrée et Cailleux, 1836–1837; Frankfurt: Minerva, 1967), 7:103. Subsequent page references to this work will be given in the text.

Articles. He devotes most attention to Article 1, which states that the Roman Pontiff has no power over kings in temporal matters. This he professes to see as exempting governments from any moral norms or judgment and thus as undermining all public morality (165–194). As for the other three articles, he maintains that they "equally overturn the fundamental principle of the Church" (194). Article 2 states adherence to the conciliarist doctrine of the Council of Constance, Article 3 asserts that the Roman Pontiff should govern the Church according to the canons of tradition, and Article 4 states that dogmatic definitions of the pope are not irreformable apart from the consensus of the Church. He discusses and rejects Article 2 at some length and never moves clearly into Articles 3 or 4, except for a very long footnote that criticizes on logical and practical grounds the "dispersed infallibility of the Gallicans" (203n–207n). His real argumentation throughout, like that of de Maistre, does not work from Scripture or tradition, but rather is logical and political in nature. There *must* be a really sovereign religious power that can rule and order society by simply decreeing solutions to all religious, moral, or even political questions. What constitutes a society is a supreme power, so if the Church does not have a certainly supreme power, it is not even really a society (207).

The Mennaisian group, seeing the French episcopate pursuing a course of subservience to royal interests,[22] were not inclined to value the collective judgment of bishops, which is a basic assumption of the collegial and consensual ecclesiology of Gallicanism. Rather, they sought a supreme supranational spiritual leader who could simply assert and maintain Catholic principles no matter what the weaknesses of national clergies and hierarchies. In a spirit of great idealism, they projected onto the distant Holy Father in Rome the qualities seen as

---

22. This kind of critique of the French hierarchy is spelled out in greater detail in Richard F. Costigan, S.J., "Tradition and the Beginning of the Ultramontane Movement," *Irish Theological Quarterly* 48 (1981): 27–46, which draws on writings of three associates of Lamennais: Philippe-Olympe Gerbet, René-François Rohrbacher, and Thomas Gousset.

lacking in the bishops near at hand.[23] Low regard for bishops in practice led to a devaluation of the episcopate in theology, and as the Ultramontane current surged through the decades before Vatican I, very little thought was given to scriptural, patristic, or historical considerations about the role of bishops in the Church.[24] These latter considerations are central to Jacques-Bénigne Bossuet as he defends the fourth of the Gallican Articles, which upholds the role of the episcopate in the teaching of the faith.[25]

The Catholic Church and the Roman Church

One of the basic and most manifest lessons of Church history, Bossuet maintains, is that the Roman Church has at times been saved by the whole Catholic Church. The greatest and most instructive example of this is "the infamy of the tenth century," in which for many long decades "the most shameful encroachers occupied the chair of Peter," and the clergy of Rome seemed unable to do anything about it.[26] Clearly, the faith, staying power, and authority of the whole universal Church sustained the Roman Church in spite of unfit popes during those dark years (9, 220). "It is therefore the full and supreme

23. This aspect of the Ultramontane Movement, developed throughout Costigan, *Rohrbacher*, is summarized in the conclusion, 243–247.

24. See articles cited above by Aubert, "La géographie ecclésiologique au XIXe siècle," and Congar, "L'ecclésiologie de le Révolution française au Concile du Vatican."

25. The edition of the *Defensio declarationis cleri gallicani de ecclesiastica potestate* that is used here is the *Oeuvres complètes* edited by Lachat. The *Defensio* fills volumes 21 and 22 and totals 1,372 pages. The fact that the work was not published by Bossuet during his life led to some confusion, as different editors arranged the numerous books of the work in varying orders according to personal preference. In fact, Aimé-Georges Martimort has published a whole book discussing the various editions, *L'établissement du texte de la "Defensio declarationis" de Bossuet* (Paris: Cerf, 1956). Likewise, the alternative title, *Gallia orthodoxa*, is used in different ways in different editions. Lachat uses it for the 124-page *Dissertatio praevia* and places it before book 1.

26. *Defensio*, 9, 219. The principal areas of the *Defensio* in which Bossuet deals with Article 4 of the Declaration are books 8, 9, and 10, which are found in volume 22 of Lachat's edition. The *Dissertatio praevia* and books 1 through 6 are in volume 21, and the remainder are found in volume 22. It seems most useful to cite the work by book number and the page number of the volume. Subsequent references are given in the text.

and universal authority of the Catholic Church that supplies what is lacking even in the Roman Church" (9, 221). The same lesson is shown very graphically also in the Great Western Schism, when for forty years even good and saintly women and men did not know which pope should be recognized as the true one (9, 223). Bossuet believes that through this long and painful ordeal, Christ demonstrated two profound truths. First, "that by his inscrutable judgment the Roman Church could fall into this disorder and tumult from which it could not extricate itself, and depended [for a solution] on the authority of the Catholic Church." Second, "that under a doubtful and wavering pope, even under a false pope or no pope, there remains, even for a lengthy period, not only the unity but also the certain authority of the Catholic Church" (9, 223).

To Bossuet it seems clear that the universal Church, which can survive corruption, malfeasance, and stupidity in its Supreme Pontiffs, can and does also survive errors made by the pontiffs in the exercise of their teaching office. It is his conviction that "even if the Roman Pontiff defines something false, the Catholic Church and the Apostolic See remain" steady as they were constituted (9, 224). History, he believes, shows that "they are refuted who think that the Catholic Church would at once perish if any Roman Pontiff defined something false: as if this were the one thing that the authority of the Catholic Church could not supply." Not only the whole community of the Church but the Apostolic See, the papacy, "founded by God as the bond of Catholic society and communion," certainly endures through every crisis (ibid.). Can it be thought that during the Great Schism, when two and finally three popes contended for the allegiance of the Church, "the seal of Christian fraternity established by Christ in the communion of the Roman Pontiff was broken off? Hardly!" Rather, a deep-seated conviction that there should be reunion under one pope animated and guided all parties, who continued "to enjoy the communion of the Catholic Church and of the Apostolic See joined with it." In view of the abundant evidence of the resilience of the Church through such varied crises, "why should the Apostolic See or the Catholic Church collapse if the Roman Pontiff defines something false?" (9, 224) Is this the one case in which the Holy Spirit given by Christ fails the Church? Surely there is no case more necessary than the preservation of the faith. Does it make sense to say that if the pope preaches a false doctrine, "the Church is unarmed and devoid of all protection if he uses certain formulae and solemnities? What is more absurd than that?" (ibid.)[27]

Bossuet accepts without question that Jesus Christ, in conferring on Peter a special role in governing and teaching the Church, established a real primatial authority. Discussing the "Tu es Petrus" text, he says, "That office, that magisterium, that power moving to unity of faith, is the foundation of the Church, and cannot be taken away from the Church, or ever made to collapse by any force" (10, 38).[28] But the papalists err in insisting that every individual pope is an immovable rock. No, "that invincible and unshaken power is in him who is the principal and corner stone, namely Christ." The human leader of the Church certainly possesses real power: "There is undeniably power in the ministerial rock; it is the greatest and most important, but it is partial, and the whole is greater than the part, as we have often said" (10, 349). It is not the person of Peter but his office and the whole Church that have strength and authority from Christ: "[T]he ministerial rock, the Apostolic See, the head of the Churches, cannot be overturned, because it has the strength promised and given to the whole body of the Church" (ibid.). (Bossuet does not develop here or elsewhere the idea of "ministerial rock.")

Thus Bossuet accepts as perfectly valid and legitimate the distinction between *sedes* (the seat, see) and *sedens* (the incumbent, a specific pope) as an explanation for the endurance of the Church, and of the Apostolic See, through many episodes in which particular popes failed to use good judgment or even failed to preserve the doctrine of the Church. This distinction was consistently dismissed by papalist

---

27. Though referring to phrases like *ex cathedra* or other terms that could be used in a solemn definition, Bossuet does not name any in this passage.

28. "Magisterium" renders *magistratus*.

authors as just another Gallican device to evade the absolute obedience owed to every Supreme Pontiff.[29] But we use this distinction, Bossuet says, not to evade the authority of the pope, "but so that we can show that the Roman Church was instituted by Christ in such a way that if the *sedens* makes a mistake, the *sedes* still remains intact, the uninjured series of pontiffs remains, and a mistake made by one can be repaired by the diligence and faith of another."[30] The faith of the whole Church, or of the Roman Church, simply does not abruptly fail or cease when one pope makes a mistake. "The Roman faith does not perish when any one pontiff departs from it, nor does the Roman faith become void in vacancies or interregna even when they last for many years."

The case of Pope Liberius (352–366), whose lapse at one point in the Arian controversy has been much discussed, provided Bossuet with the first of several examples of popes whose errors in doctrinal questions did not impair the power of the Church and its primatial office to preserve the faith. He concludes a discussion of the case of Liberius with a comment that sums up admirably his main point: "Though Liberius altogether failed, the faith of Peter stood, the faith of Sylvester stood, and that of Mark, Julius, and the other Roman Pontiffs who had preceded Liberius" (9, 231). The presbyters of the Church of Rome, and many other persons at the time, upheld that faith, and the more they revered the Apostolic See the more they wanted it to be truly orthodox.

The case of John XXII (1316–1334), who publicly taught a doctrine regarding the beatific vision that was at variance with the traditional doctrine of the Church, has great significance for Bossuet. John XXII said in several sermons (1331–1334) that the just do not receive the beatific vision until the Last Judgment, but he was compelled on his deathbed at Avignon to recant. "You may say," Bossuet comments, "that it was a bold act for the French to teach the Roman

---

29. See, for example, Giuseppe-Agostino Orsi, O.P., *De irreformabili romani pontificis in definiendis fidei controversiis judicio* (1739) (Rome: Paulus Junchius, 1771), II, 4, 259–263.

30. *Dissertatio praevia [Gallia orthodoxa]*, chap. 85, 109–110.

Pontiff himself the faith." (When the papacy was at Avignon most of the cardinals and other leading prelates there were French.) In reality it was simply a matter of the Catholic Church acting to preserve the faith: this pope "no longer hesitating and wavering, was brought by the consensus of the Catholic Church to true and certain faith in the truth" (9, 257).

Preaching the faith from the eminent citadel of the papacy is certainly a central part of the apostolic office, continues Bossuet. The pope, he says, must not only define and anathematize but teach and preach the faith to the whole world. "John XXII plainly failed in this duty" (9, 257–258). Does the fact that he preached a falsehood mean that the faith of the Roman *Church* wavered, or that the *Apostolic See* preached something false or heretical? (9, 258; emphasis added) Or does it mean that "the Catholic Church did not resist the pope preaching this, or judging or defining this, or that it lacked the means to undo the false definition? Hardly" (ibid.). In referring to this pope's statements on the beatific vision as a definition, Bossuet is of course overstating the matter,[31] but he does seem correct in claiming that John was speaking on this issue of faith in his public capacity as pope and not simply as a private doctor (9, 255). The bishop of Meaux, in these final words of book 9, offers a good summary statement of his view on the consensus of the Church. "Let us understand, therefore, that what the Roman Pontiffs have preached, believed, and declared are not yet [the doctrine] of the Roman Church and Apostolic See until, having been promulgated by the Roman Pontiff and received by the whole Church, they have prevailed and solidified, and [so are recognized as] the Roman faith, the faith of Peter, and the faith of the Apostolic See, which cannot fail" (9, 258). The Church, in short, has the wherewithal to correct a mistake of the Supreme Pontiff. It will be noted that many of Bossuet's statements of the consensus of the Church fit the idea of "reception" in recent ecclesiological discussion.[32]

---

31. On this point, see James Heft, S.M., *John XXII and Papal Teaching Authority* (Lewiston, N.Y.: Edwin Mellen, 1986), 97–99.

32. See note 105 of chapter 1 for numerous scholarly treatments of reception.

Theocratic Claims of Gregory VII and Boniface VIII

But most prominent among the genuine concerns of Bossuet and of the French generally was the doctrine enunciated by several popes asserting that the Roman Pontiff has a sovereign power to judge and if need be to depose kings and emperors. The blunt rejection of this doctrine constitutes Article 1 of the Gallican Declaration, and Bossuet devotes some 416 pages (books 1 through 4) in the *Defensio* to a comprehensive critique of it. Not only, he maintains, was there no consensus in the Church undergirding such an idea when Gregory VII (1073–1085) enunciated it in the eleventh century, it was an idea completely new. It had "never even been thought of" in the first ten centuries (1, 149). When Gregory proclaimed it, its "newness stupefied the world" (1, 151). This pope and some of his successors "acted contrary to evangelical truth and to the most ancient tradition when they attempted to depose kings" (9, 239). It is true that they did not, despite their evident belief in the idea that such power belongs to the papacy, erect it into an ecclesiastical "dogma." However, in declaring and pressing this viewpoint, "they produced enormous resentment for the ecclesiastical power, provided grievances for schismatics and heretics, and led Catholics into error rather than confirming them in faith." The only reason why all this did not cause really irreparable harm was that "the Catholic Church never approved it, and never admitted it as a doctrine of faith" (9, 239). It was, in other words, not "received" by the Church.

One of those successor popes, Boniface VIII (1294–1303), did come very close, Bossuet believes, to proclaiming the power of deposition to be a "dogma of the Church" (9, 239).[33] Bossuet points out correctly that in the bull *Unam Sanctam* (November 18, 1302), written in the heat of his controversy with King Philip IV of France, Boniface certainly does say that the spiritual power is superior to the temporal and can judge it.[34] Bossuet says that Boniface seems to prepare

---

33. We will synthesize statements from both book 3 and book 9 in this section.
34. The Latin text of *Unam Sanctam* is given in DS 870–875. Brian Tierney, in *The*

the way in the "exposition," the body of the document, for a definition of the deposing power (3, 461). But in the concluding sentence, which certainly uses the phraseology of a definition, and which does emphatically assert that every human being, to be saved, must be subject to the Roman Pontiff, Boniface refrains from adding the phrase "etiam in temporalibus."[35] He seemingly wanted to say it, and this is a point that Bossuet stresses, but "at that point restrained himself, deterred by the newness and difficulty of the matter." He was aware that even after several centuries this idea still did not have broad support in the consensus of the Church. The French, Bossuet adds, did not assent to the Bonifacian view, well aware that "these new ideas were far from the ancient tradition of the Fathers and from the understanding [*sensus*] of the Gallican Church." They did this "so that the constitution of Boniface VIII could not harm" the Church (3, 461).

Bossuet says that some, unnamed but presumably more militant Gallicans, have said that the definition should be understood as proclaiming dogmatically the "manifest error" that had been spelled out in the exposition, and that therefore the whole document is indefensible. Others, also unnamed but presumably of the Ultramontane persuasion, maintain that everything in the document, proclaimed as it is by the Apostolic See, must be accepted as of faith (3, 240). Bossuet thinks of himself and the mainstream of the Gallican Church as standing in a *middle* ground, with most Catholics, in recognizing a primacy of the papacy in spiritual matters but not in temporal (3, 461). The age-old ecclesiology faithfully preserved by Gallican tradition, unlike that of Boniface VIII, Bossuet says in a summary comment, has stood the test of time. It is "a doctrine relying on Scripture, antiquity, and tradition, which by whatever name and by whatever authority it has been opposed, has remained established with eternal

---

Crisis of Church and State, 1050–1300 (Englewood Cliffs, N.J.: Prentice-Hall, 1964), 188–189, gives an English translation.

35. That concluding assertion is DS 875, which states: "Therefore, we declare, state, and define [*declaramus, dicimus, diffinimus*] that it is altogether necessary for salvation that every human creature be subject [*subesse*] to the Roman Pontiff."

and with unconquered strength in the Catholic Church" (3, 465). It is a basic belief of Bossuet that one major reason why the decrees of Boniface "did not harm the faith [meaning, apparently, did not ruin it] was that the Gallican Church, so great a part of the Catholic Church, while others remained silent, openly remonstrated and led Roman Pontiffs to temper the acerbity of the Bonifacian doctrine" (9, 240).

Near the end of book 4, Bossuet offers a summary in fourteen points of what he has said in defense of the first article of 1682. Point 14 is strongly worded and is an eloquent statement of the harm done to the fabric of the Church when its highest authority goes so far beyond the faith consensus of the ecclesial community. When the Roman Pontiffs claimed the power to depose kings, "this power was never recognized by any king, and never by the estates of any kingdom." Rather, kings and kingdoms resisted the claim, and the attempt to depose kings gave openings to ambition and pretexts for rebellion. All in all, this papal claim "was never useful to anyone and brought great harm" to many (4, 522). Pervading French thinking about Article 4 was the belief that the Church has no way of knowing that there will not be another Boniface VIII issuing another *Unam Sanctam*—and quite possibly presuming to define it as an dogma of faith.

Consensus of the Church and the Ecumenical Councils

The relative authority of pope and ecumenical council is not directly related to Article 4's concern with the assent of the Church to papal pronouncements and is indeed the subject of Article 2, which asserts the doctrine of conciliar supremacy. However, some things that Bossuet says in defending Article 2 are helpful in understanding the Gallican belief that supreme authority in the Church really rests with the consensus of the whole Church, by "Church" meaning always the whole body of bishops.[36] The recognition of the authority

---

[36]. Bossuet's main treatment of Article 2 is contained in books 5 and 6, which cover pages 543–758 in volume 21 of Lachat.

of the councils since the early centuries, Bossuet says, surely rests on the belief that they express the faith of the whole Church. When there is a general assembly of the bishops, the Church's known and accepted chief teachers, gathered from the whole world to settle a question of doctrine, then it is not a matter of this or that doctor or faction but of the voice of the Church. The great councils are recognized as having "certain and ineluctable authority" because they "represent the universal Church" (7, 8). For this reason, "nothing has been regarded as infallible and irrefragable unless it has been confirmed by the consensus of the universal Church" (7, 9). The judgment of the Roman Pontiff can be retreated in a synod, "but after a synod, provided it is regarded as legitimate, nothing may be retreated, nothing may be discussed [again]" (7, 34).

Bossuet sees the Council of Chalcedon, with its reception of the letter of Pope Leo I at a critical point in the debate, as illustrating the thesis. It is the consensus of pope and bishops on the doctrine that gives it its "irrevocable strength," not the authority of the pope alone, "which then no one thought of." The fathers at Chalcedon "codecide and cojudge, and the *sententia* of the pope is the *sententia* of the council" (7, 37). They studied Leo's letter carefully and concurred in its doctrine. Their individual signatures (on the council's decree) were not a matter of "mere obedience" (7, 38). Going through the proceedings of Chalcedon, and some statements of Leo himself, Bossuet concludes that the bishops "judged, were persuaded, and understood that the faith expounded by Leo was the common faith of all of them" (7, 39)[37]

---

37. The famous exclamation of the fathers at Chalcedon, "Peter has spoken through Leo," receives diametrically opposed readings from Roman and Gallican authors. Papalist authors say that the council gratefully and obediently assents to the papal judgment. Bossuet and other Gallican authors say that the council recognizes, after studying it, that the epistle of Leo expresses the traditional faith of the Church. Thus, they "receive" it. The consensus of modern scholarship leans toward the latter interpretation. See W. de Vries, *Orient et Occident: Les structures ecclésiales vues dans l'histoire des sept premiers conciles oecuméniques* (Paris: Cerf, 1974), 140–141; and also Francis A. Sullivan, S.J., *Magisterium : Teaching Authority in the Catholic Church* (New York: Paulist, 1983), 67–68.

In book 8 Bossuet addresses the papalist claim that the authority of the Roman Pontiff is certainly superior to that of any and all councils. The adversaries, he says, without naming any of them, assert that the supreme power of the Apostolic See is so great that only those councils confirmed by it are to be regarded as legitimate universal synods, and that each legitimate synod has only as much authority as the Apostolic See decides (8, 104). In fact, they claim that "all the authority of bishops and of councils flows from Peter and his successors as from a font" (8, 105). Rejecting this claim, Bossuet maintains that "confirmation does not entail any papal infallibility or superiority" (ibid.). The word *confirm* does not have to mean the possession of superior power. Popes often confirm the decrees of their predecessors; does this detract from the power of these latter? Councils sometimes confirm, or reaffirm, decrees of other councils or of the Apostolic See. Thus "even from the strongest approbation, confirmation, or corroboration that words can express there cannot be inferred a superior power, as the adversaries contend" (8, 110). Concluding a survey of the first eight councils, he maintains that to the extent that these were confirmed by the Roman Pontiff this "did not provide their strength [*robur*], so that strength that was lacking in the decrees was added to them; rather it provided that what was in them might be more fully declared" (8, 118–119).

The Council of Jerusalem, as reported in Acts 15, stands for Bossuet as the model for all councils, and certain key words in that account really provide the basis for an authentic *theology* of the councils. In the history of the councils, he says in book 10, we find everywhere valid the apostolic dictum of Jerusalem, "visum est Spiritui sancto et nobis (Acts 15:28)" (10, 341; emphasis his). This clearly joins the "it has seemed good to the Holy Spirit" with the "and to us"; that is, the unity of the whole episcopal and apostolic order in teaching the faith is stipulated. This history, like the Scripture itself, certainly shows that "it is not, as they now claim, that councils have from the pope the ability to decide rightly, [they have it] from the Holy Spirit, and joined with it the authority and testimony of the universal Church" (10, 341).

Other New Testament texts are at times cited by Bossuet as undergirding a conciliar ecclesiology. He notes a comment by Bellarmine acknowledging the value of councils in the transmission of the faith. Bellarmine noted that "definitions of faith depend principally on apostolic tradition and the consensus of the churches," adding that there is no better way to ascertain what is the belief of the whole Church than a large meeting of bishops from all the provinces (8, 157).[38] But he erred, says Bossuet, in calling such a council a "medium humanum" that the Roman Pontiff may see fit to use. It is "not a *medium humanum,* but plainly *divinum,*" because Christ had addressed his disciples in the plural when he said "ego mitto vos (Jn 20:21)" and "ego vobiscum sum (Mt 28:19)" (8, 157; emphasis his).

Consensus Ecclesiae: What and How

It has often been said that Gallicanism demands a *consensus subsequens* to papal pronouncements.[39] That is, after the Roman Pontiff issues a doctrinal statement, the Churches in various countries study it, and if they believe it is authentic Catholic doctrine, give their consensus. The papal statement is not considered definitive or, to use a term current among both papalist and Gallican authors, irreformable, until it has been so received in all countries. It is assumed that the doctrine of *consensus subsequens,* if implemented, would result in a long, perhaps interminable, process, and moreover that this is probably the real intention of the Gallicans: obstruction of the pope's conduct of the teaching office. Article 4 of the Declaration of 1682 has commonly been understood to stipulate *consensus subsequens,* with the *nisi accesserit consensus Ecclesiae* clause taken to mean that chronologically the consensus is added to the papal teaching after the pope issues it.

38. Bellarmine, *Tertia controversia generalis: De summo pontifice,* IV, 7.
39. This habit of the older papalist authors continues in modern scholars; see, for example, Paul Nau, O.S.B., "Le magistère pontifical ordinaire au premier Concile du Vatican," *Revue Thomiste* 62 (1962): 207; Roger Aubert, *Vatican I* (Paris: L'Orante, 1964), 219; Klaus Schatz, S.J., *Kirchenbild und päpstliche Unfehlbarkeit bei den deutschsprachigen Minoritätsbischöfen auf den I. Vatikanum* (Rome: Università Gregoriana Editrice, 1975), 84, 218, 324, 490.

Gallican authors do indeed at times describe the consensus of the Church in these terms, and Bossuet is one of these. For example, near the end of book 8, summarizing what he has said about popes and councils, he says, "[N]or is even anything issued by the Holy See, or by the Fathers, or by the Roman Pontiffs, held to be irrefragable except after the consensus of the Church is added" (8, 153). Again, concluding a section on a controversy in the early centuries, he says: "This stands unmoved: Cyprian, Augustine, and others, in a question that they deem one of faith, if after a judgment of the Roman Pontiff there seemed some dissident Churches, awaited the judgment of the universal Church in order to achieve certitude" (9, 179).

But this is not the only, or principal, way in which Gallicans describe the *consensus Ecclesiae*. It is actually more complex and nuanced, and the focus is really placed most often on *consensus antecedens*, which is the underlying or pervasive agreement of the Church as a whole on the basic truths of faith. This comes through consistently in Bossuet's statements about the consensus of the Church. He consistently rejects the imputation that Article 4 is really disloyal to the Holy See, and that it is calculated to delay indefinitely the acceptance of a statement of the pope. He is irritated by snide questions about the mode of implementation of the consensus called for by the Gallican ecclesiology. Nicholas Dubois and other critics ask what are the instruments of the consensus. Would you send messengers and letters everywhere to investigate it, with immense labor and expense? Bossuet impatiently dismisses these "vain and inane little questions."[40] Critics ask, "how many churches, how many bishops, how many chapters, abbots, regions" are needed for the consensus? "Does it include the Indians and the Japanese?" "How much trouble, how much expense, how many messengers will be running all over" to try to discover a consensus that will satisfy the Gallicans?[41]

---

40. *Dissertatio praevia [Gallia orthodoxa]*, chap. 77, 100. Bossuet does not cite any text of Nicholas Dubois, a contemporary critic of the Gallican position; on Dubois, see Martimort, *Gallicanisme de Bossuet*, 531.

41. *Dissertatio praevia*, 77, 100.

These questions are dismissed by Bossuet as "vain and absurd," for Gallicanism does not think of consensus in these terms. Elaborating on this point elsewhere, he says that just as in any other kingdom, so in the kingdom of Jesus Christ the most effective ideas and norms are those that are not decreed by any specific act of authority but consist in the perennial sense and usage of all the people (9, 162). Vincent of Lerins, when he spoke of the faith which is "semper et ubique," was surely thinking of this kind of consensus and not of messengers and letters. "These deliria were reserved for our time." There are truths of the faith that Catholics everywhere have traditionally understood even apart from formal new statements of the magisterium. When the pope enunciates one of these, all Catholics, including the French, readily assent, so the critics should stop accusing us of making unreasonable demands regarding consensus (9, 163). One of Bossuet's best succinct statements of the nature of *consensus Ecclesiae* occurs in this same chapter 1 of book 9. "When the successor of Peter pronounces from the common tradition in such a way that all recognize the sense of their own faith in his statement, then there is that consensus which provides pontifical judgments with their firm and unbendable strength" (9, 162).

But the Gallican ecclesiology does not think in terms of some collective sentiment in which the faith consists simply of what the mass of people seem to believe. Much less does it consist of what individuals think the Catholic faith is. Gallicanism is emphatically not democratic, and it is not a charismatic or uninstitutional or antinomian form of Christianity. Gallican Roman Catholicism is as fully hierarchical as papalist or Ultramontane Roman Catholicism, but it places emphasis on the episcopate as a whole, always including the Roman Pontiff, and not simply on the sovereign power of the Supreme Pontiff alone. Bossuet had no use for the democratic church theory of Edmond Richer, which he rejects as "issuing from horrible and deeply imbibed errors" (6, 747).[42] For Bossuet, the *Ecclesia* in *consensus*

---

42. See works relating to Edmond Richer cited in note 103 of chapter 1.

Ecclesiae always means the episcopate. Robert Duchon notes that Bossuet "opposes every association of priests, of deacons, and of the faithful in the government of the Church."[43] But Duchon also shows at length how Bossuet differs from the more thoroughly episcopalist theory of Febronius, accepting a greater role for the Roman Pontiff than the latter.[44] His conclusion is apt: "Adversary of all multitudinarism and of all ecclesiastical democracy, Bossuet closes the door on the discussion, for he knows that the successors of the apostles are alone qualified to manifest the Church and to speak in its name."[45]

The bishops function as a community of teachers endowed with the full authority of the teaching office. To perform this function responsibly, Bossuet states, they need to know that what they are teaching is the traditional doctrine of the Catholic Church. Thus when they study a statement from Rome in order to "receive" it, they are *not* claiming authority superior to that of the Roman Pontiff, or even equal to his. They are simply acting as responsible teachers, ascertaining that the doctrine is an authentic belief of the Catholic Church. "Thus the bishops, when they receive a decree of the Apostolic See, after study, conjoin their *sententia* to his *sententia*, their judgment to his judgment, their authority, which has come from God, to the supreme authority of the Roman Pontiff, which has come from God" (9, 202). They do this not with any thought of replacing the authority of the Roman Pontiff but to fulfill their own role as teachers of the universal Church. In Bossuet's words, "[I]t is not that their judgment and authority equal the judgment and authority of the Apostolic See, but that they understand from the consensus and unanimity itself that full strength [*plenum robur*] exists" (ibid.). This surely shows plainly that Bossuet does not think mainly in terms of a simplistic *consensus subsequens*.

One event in the long, complex Jansenist controversy is cited by

---

43. Robert Duchon, "De Bossuet à Febronius," *Revue d'histoire ecclésiastique* 65 (1970): 416, citing the *Dissertatio praevia,* chap. 76, where the point is made, if not quite as clearly as Duchon says.
44. This is the main gist of the Duchon article.
45. Duchon, "De Bossuet à Febronius," 422.

Bossuet as a good example of "the reception [*acceptatio*] of pontifical constitutions that we are talking about."⁴⁶ In 1653 French bishops received the decree *Cum occasione* of Innocent X (Giambattista Pamphili; pope September 15, 1644–January 7, 1655) against the "Five Propositions" of Jansenism.⁴⁷ That is, on reading it and discussing it, they recognized its doctrine as sound Catholic tradition and readily indicated their concurrence. The Roman Pontiff, as head of the whole Church, has a supreme power to teach. "Since this chief [*princeps*] of ecclesiastical communion wants by his definition to promote nothing other than what he knows all the Churches think, when everything is done truly and in order, the consensus that follows attests" that he is right.⁴⁸ "Experience shows that this doctrine and practice do not infringe at all on the authority and power of the apostolic decree." "Where in the world more than in Gallia were the constitution of Innocent X and others in the Jansenist matter received with greater veneration, or with greater vigor implemented." Certainly the Jansenist sectaries, "even if they appealed a thousand times to ecumenical councils, would not be heard anywhere, for the very constitution, once published and everywhere accepted, obtained the strength of an irrefragable judgment," for the Roman Pontiff and the bishops had acted in concert.⁴⁹

Bossuet and the Historical Church

Several modern authors have commented that Jacques-Bénigne Bossuet was too devoted to the past, specifically the ancient past, and that he was unprepared to recognize that development and evolution inevitably and properly pervade and characterize all human history. Owen Chadwick begins his *From Bossuet to Newman* by saying that

---

46. *Dissertatio praevia*, chap. 78, 101.
47. On this episode see Martimort, *Gallicanisme de Bossuet*, 202–215, esp. 213–214; or a briefer treatment in *The Church in the Age of Absolutism and Enlightenment*, vol. 6 of Hubert Jedin and John Dolan, eds., *History of the Church* (New York: Crossroad, 1981), 37–40.
48. *Dissertatio praevia*, chap. 78, 102.
49. Ibid.

"Bossuet had declared the axiom that variation in religion is always a sign of error."[50] Chadwick is referring, of course, to Bossuet's critique of Protestantism in his *Histoire des variations des Eglises protestantes* and does not deal with the ecclesiological issues that are our concern here.[51] Yves Congar sees in Bossuet "a nuance of fixism" on the "ancient discipline" of the Church, "a certain forgetting of the *human* life of the Church, a certain closure to what opens the ways of the future."[52] Aimé-Georges Martimort, writing in the 1950s, criticizes Bossuet and his colleagues for the "anachronism" of clinging to an "ancient doctrine that they found in books."[53] In his conclusion also he faults Bossuet for being too attached to an idealized past.[54] He thinks that it was Bossuet's strong personal need for stability and continuity that made him "react against the Ultramontanes who, in his perception, admired without discernment all the novelties and changes" in the doctrine of absolute papal monarchy.[55] Raymond Thysman, in an article in 1957 dealing with the influence of Bossuet on Henri Maret, a leading opponent of papal infallibility at Vatican I, says that Bossuet was too devoted to Christian antiquity and not attuned to the proper growth of the Church institution.[56] Bruno Neveu, who has engaged in massive research on the history of French scholarship, thinks that Bossuet and other Gallicans admire early Christianity too much and seems irritated that they prefer it to the more centralized Church of modern times.[57]

Bossuet does consider the Ultramontanes guilty of creating a new

---

50. Chadwick, *From Bossuet to Newman*, 5.
51. Chadwick makes only passing mention of the *Defensio* in an endnote on p. 198.
52. Congar, *L'Eglise de saint Augustin à l'époque moderne*, 400; emphasis his. Congar's section on Bossuet in this work is good in its appreciation of the values actually sought by Bossuet (397–400) and by Gallicans generally (391–402). He says that Bossuet was guided by a "theological vision" of the Church, not simply by social or political considerations (397). Congar makes similar comments in "La 'réception' comme réalité ecclésiologique," 378, 389–391.
53. Martimort, *Gallicanisme de Bossuet*, 474.
54. Ibid., 704.   55. Ibid., 707.
56. Raymond Thysman, "Le gallicanisme de Mgr. Maret et l'influence de Bossuet," *Revue d'histoire ecclésiastique* 52 (1957): 443–447.
57. Bruno Neveu makes these points in many of the fascinating studies in his *Eru-*

doctrine. He ends the *Dissertatio praevia* by asking how, if papal infallibility is a necessary doctrine of the faith, the Church could have lived for seventeen centuries without knowing about it. "Certainly in the Catholic Church we are living in the seventeenth century, and there is not yet agreement on that infallibility among the orthodox and pious." "Holy and learned men resist it." Therefore we should locate the certainty that the faithful need in the consensus of the whole Catholic Church and not in a dubious papal infallibility. That infallibility *is* dubious, "for if Christ had granted it [to the pope], he would also have revealed it to his Church from the beginning, and not left it in doubt."[58] Elsewhere he says, "[I]t would seem incredible and absurd if such a great gift as infallibility were bestowed by Christ on the pontiff and not revealed to the Church" (corollarium to book 11, 437).

One could comment that Bossuet does not seem to allow for evolution in the implementation of the Petrine primacy in the course of centuries. But we also need to keep in mind that these comments, like the whole *Defensio*, were occasioned by a flurry of Ultramontane polemical works published after the issuance of the Declaration of 1682. The first chapters of the *Dissertatio praevia* indignantly complain about several authors who attacked the Gallicans and impugned their orthodoxy. One of these was José Saenz Aguirre, who caustically questioned whether the Gallicans really accepted even the authority of the councils.[59] Others were Thyrso Gonzalez[60] and—one who especially exercised Bossuet—Juan Tomàs Rocaberti, who published both a lengthy and trenchant treatise on papal supremacy and a huge,

---

dition et religion aux XVIIe et XVIIIe siècles (Paris: Albin Michel, 1994). One especially interesting one is "Mabillon et l'historiographie gallicane vers 1700," 175–235. He criticizes Bossuet on 210–211. See also Donald R. Kelley's very informative chapter, "Canon Law and History: Charles Dumoulin Finds a Gallican View of History," in his *Foundations of Modern Historical Scholarship: Language, Law, and History in the French Renaissance* (New York: Columbia University Press, 1970), 151–182.

58. *Dissertatio praevia*, 97, 128.

59. José Saenz de Aguirre, O.S.B. (1630–1699), a Spanish Benedictine cardinal, published *Auctoritas infallibilis et summa cathedrae sancti Petri extra et supra concilia quaelibet atque in totam ecclesiam denuo stabilita*. (Salamanca: Lucas Perez, 1683). These questions about the French and the councils occur on 532–535 in this large book.

60. Thyrso Gonzalez de Santalla, S.J. (1624–1705), general of the Jesuits (1687–

twenty-one-volume collection of works upholding papal supremacy.[61] Rocaberti, "by far the most acrimonious of all, has declared war on a France not deserving [to be so attacked]."[62] Rocaberti accuses us of "error, schism, and even heresy," and "if we bear this accusation in silence, the pristine honor of a France always orthodox will disappear."[63] Thus Bossuet states that his reason for undertaking the *Defensio* is to show the true orthodoxy of the doctrine of the Parisian school: "[T]hat doctrine was not excogitated [in 1682] but from the very beginning of Christianity flows from common decrees and from the principles of the Christian nations."[64]

Later Ultramontanes like de Maistre and Lamennais, dominated by their experience of the ongoing subjection of church to state in the Napoleonic era and the Bourbon Restoration, and by their idealistic devotion to the supranational papacy, were not prepared even to try to understand a less pope-centered ecclesiology. Their whole focus was on the urgent, imperative need of an utterly sovereign Church power that would stand above all national and dynastic—and episcopal—concerns. They did not have a high regard for the French bishops whom they knew, perceiving them as being simply sub-

---

1705), published a lengthy and vigorous critique of the Gallican Articles entitled *De infallibilitate romani pontificis in definiendis fidei et morum controversiis* (Rome: Felicis Caesaretti, 1689).

61. Juan Tomàs de Rocaberti (1624–1699), a Spanish Dominican, followed his *De romani pontificis auctoritate*, 3 vols. (Valencia, 1691–1694) with the great collection that he entitled *Bibliotheca maxima pontificia* (1695–1699).

62. *Dissertatio praevia*, chap. 5, 10.

63. Ibid., chap. 1, 6. This is the very first paragraph of the *Dissertatio*.

64. Ibid., chap. 12, 20. Bossuet states in chapter 6 of the *Dissertatio* that the Declaration of 1682 did not purport to be a dogmatic definition, but only the considered judgment of serious French theologians (13–15). He thinks of himself throughout as defending the ecclesiology of the "schola Parisiensis." In fact, his title for the long essay cited in this chapter as *Dissertatio praevia* is "Gallia orthodoxa, sive vindiciae scholae parisiensis totiusque cleri gallicani adversus nonnullos." Martimort treats the Parisian ecclesiology at length, *Gallicanisme de Bossuet*, 13–125. In reality, the "Faculté de Théologie de Paris," the body of several thousand men who had doctorates from the Sorbonne, always included many of the Ultramontane or Roman view. Jacques Gres-Gayer, in a major study, offers a wealth of information on a large number of *romains* in those years: "Gallicans et Romains en Sorbonne d'après le nonce Bargellini (1670)," *Revue d'histoire ecclésiastique* 87 (July–December 1992): 682–744.

servient to emperor and king. They had no interest in any historical roots of a less centralized form of church governance and no inkling that there could be any legitimate reasons for adhering to a more collegial and consensual ecclesiology.

The most valuable work to date on the meeting of French clergy that produced the Gallican Articles is that of Pierre Blet, whose massive archival research (already noted in chapter 1) sheds much light on the ideas of the participants.[65] He maintains that the ecclesial views expressed in the articles were the genuine long-held beliefs of French clergy and were not simply dictated by the Crown.[66] Regarding Bossuet personally, he reaffirms Martimort's finding that the four articles were Bossuet's "own theology [*propre théologie*] on the relations of priesthood and empire and on the relations between the bishops and the pope."[67] Blet summarizes: "[W]hen Bossuet evokes the ancient canons, consecrated by the veneration of the whole universe, he spoke a language equally familiar and agreeable to the prelates of France; there was no need for Louis XIV and Colbert to make them accept it."[68] There was, of course, nothing particularly French about the idea of a Church more collegial and consensual in structure, for the Church actually was less monarchical and less centralized in earlier centuries.[69] "The Gallicans of the seventeenth century," Yves Congar has noted, "knew their history remarkably well."[70]

65. Pierre Blet, S.J., *Les Assemblées du Clergé et Louis XIV de 1670 à 1693* (Rome: Università Gregoriana Editrice, 1972). For an appreciation of this work, see the extended review article by R. Darricau, "Lumières nouvelles sur l'histoire du Clergè de France sous Louis XIV," *Revue d'histoire ecclèsiastique* 69 (1974): 93–102.
66. This is summarized in Blet, *Assemblées du Clergé et Louis XIV,* 348–362, esp. 350–351 and 360–361.
67. This is Blet's wording (ibid., 348), citing Martimort, *Gallicanisme de Bossuet,* 451–452 and 549–563.
68. Blet, *Assemblées du Clergé et Louis XIV,* 350.
69. Much modern research on the evolution in the Church toward a more monarchical structure is succinctly and clearly synthesized in Patrick Granfield's chapter, "The Pope as Monarch," in his *The Papacy in Transition* (Garden City, N.Y.: Doubleday, 1980), 34–61. Also, Robert B. Eno, S.S., summarizes a wealth of scholarship on this in *The Rise of the Papacy* (Wilmington, Del.: Michael Glazier, 1990).
70. Yves Congar, O.P., "Gallicanisme," in G. Jacquemet, ed., *Catholicisme* (Paris: Letouzey, 1956), 4:1735.

In a chapter on the documentation of the *Defensio*, Martimort notes that Bossuet had a very large library of ecclesiastical literature, including the essential primary sources, and that he utilized it with great diligence in defending his theses.[71]

Though Bossuet is obviously not a detached, impartial historian, it is really not correct to portray him as dedicated mainly to impeding or blocking the papal teaching authority, or as simplistically wedded to a past thought to be "free" of a real papal primacy. His ideas on the consensus of the Church are embodied in an ecclesiology of collegiality that is historically informed and coherent and intended to integrate both the pope and the body of bishops in one Roman Catholic Church. If he could read Pope John Paul II's recent encyclical on ecumenism, *Ut Unum Sint* (May 25, 1995), Bossuet would probably maintain that the most basic thesis that he was trying in his time and in his way to defend is affirmed in the new encyclical. John Paul II says that the ministry of the bishop of Rome, including the teaching ministry, exists "within the college of bishops."[72] He adds: "When the Catholic Church affirms that the office of the bishop of Rome corresponds to the will of Christ, she does not separate this office from the mission entrusted to the whole body of bishops, who are also 'vicars and ambassadors of Christ.'"[73] Bossuet does think of himself as defending this same vision of Church throughout the 1,372 pages of the *Defensio:* Christ appointed not one but twelve apostles to lead the Church; the ministry of the twelve should not be submerged in that of Peter. He sees a genuine need to show in Church history how the successors of the twelve shared in the ministry of guiding and teaching the community of faith. In any case, present-day scholarship needs to look attentively at the primary sources in a controversy, to try to ascertain as accurately as possible what people were saying, and to understand their motives and goals.

---

71. Martimort, *Gallicanisme de Bossuet*, 564–577.

72. John Paul II, *Ut Unum Sint* (May 25, 1995), #94 [as in *Origins*, 25 (June 8, 1995), 69]. The phrase occurs twice in this paragraph.

73. Ibid. #95 [text in *Origins*, 69]. The quoted phrase is from *Lumen Gentium*, #27.

CHAPTER 3

Honoré Tournely
1658–1729

Tournely and the Church

Honoré Tournely rose from humble beginnings to become one of the outstanding theologians of his day.[1] As a young boy in Provence he tended pigs for his farmer parents, but a priest uncle arranged for him to pursue studies in Paris, where he proved to be an excellent student. He earned his doctorate in theology at the Sorbonne in 1686, taught theology at the University of Douai from 1688 to 1692, and in the latter year was invited back to the Sorbonne, where he was professor of theology from 1692 to 1716. A leader of those opposed to Jansenism, Tournely strongly urged the acceptance of the bull *Unigenitus* issued by Pope Clement XI in 1713. Controversy over this bull ebbed and flowed, and in 1716 Tournely and twenty-one other doctors were ousted from the faculty. During the next five years he occupied several prestigious positions, including several at the royal palace. In 1721 he enjoyed the great satisfaction of being accepted back at the Sorbonne. Honoré Tournely was widely admired as man of

---

1. Johann Mayr offers some biographical information about Tournely in *Die Ekklesiologie Honoré Tournelys* (Essen: Ludgerus-Verlag Hubertus Wingen, 1964), 1–2.

great ability, learned and articulate, and also attractive in his personal manner. H. Hurter says, "He was a man of admirable virtue, [and] great docility toward the judgments of the Church, which he always strenuously defended."[2] It will be noted throughout our review of his thought here that while he earnestly opposed certain Roman claims about papal authority, he consistently opposed both Jansenism and Protestantism. Indeed, in the latter respect he was actually compared by some to Robert Bellarmine, his adversary in ecclesiology but fellow defender of Catholicism.[3]

Among his numerous treatises in theology one in particular is an important work of ecclesiology. His *Praelectiones theologicae de ecclesia Christi* (first published in 1726) provides an excellent delineation of the central current of Gallican thought on the Church and the papacy. M. Dubruel, correctly describing him as "one of the most moderate, but also one of the most learned" and influential Gallican theologians, uses him as a representative exponent of Gallican ecclesiology in his DTC article on Gallicanism.[4] Regarding the consensus of the Church, Tournely adheres seriously to Article 4 of the Declaration of 1682, seeing it as a quite valid expression of much traditional Catholic thought on the nature of papal teaching authority. His detailed and nuanced study of this point has been neglected even by the few modern scholars who have written on Tournely.[5]

Many years of research and reflection are clearly evident through-

2. H. Hurter, S.J., *Nomenclator literarius recentioris theologiae catholicae* (Oeniponte: Libraria Academica Wagneriana, 1893), 2:1073. Hurter also gives a very brief biographical sketch of Tournely's life.

3. Mayr, *Die Ekklesiologie Honoré Tournelys*, 2.

4. M. Dubruel, "Gallicanisme," *DTC*, 6.1:1096–1137. Dubruel gives a lengthy summary of Tournely's ecclesiology (1097–1108) and of his Church-State thought (1118–1122). He deals with the topic of the consensus of the Church (1103–1107), but really makes only brief mention of Tournely's *extended* discussion of many aspects and nuances of this question. J. Carreyre's short *DTC* article on "Tournely" (15.1:1242–1244) does not go into any particulars of Tournely's ecclesiology.

5. Mayr, in his *Die Ekklesiologie Honoré Tournelys*, the one book-length study on Tournely, does deal with the consensus of the Church in two places: 125–133, concerning the infallibility of the Church, and 139–146, on the infallibility of the Roman Pontiff. But in neither of these does he discuss such important points as consensus antecedent or subsequent, express or tacit, to which Tournely devotes great attention.

out Tournely's extended analysis of authority in the Church, a topic pursued systematically and insightfully in his massive treatise *De ecclesia*, whose two parts total some seven hundred closely printed octavo pages. Tournely's deep ecclesial concern comes through very clearly in his "Praefatio," addressed to students of theology. Here he says that, amid many ongoing challenges encountered by the faith community, the individual will find in adherence to the church steady and reliable guidance.[6] The Church is custodian and sustainer of the faith and the supreme judge of controversies about it. Moreover, Tournely urges all his students to preserve communion with the successor of Peter, citing the Council of Florence on papal primacy.[7] The Church's firmness against schismatics and other challenges comes from its enduring unity in faith with its visible head (1, viii–ix).

At no time does Tournely tend to "omit" the papacy from the description of the Church or to depreciate its importance. Rather, the contrary is true at every point. Indeed, when he defines the nature of the Church, he actually, like Bellarmine, includes the Roman Pontiff in the definition of the Church. "The Church is rightly defined as an assembly of persons joined in the profession of one and the same Christian faith, and in the communion of the same sacraments, under the government of the legitimate pastors, and especially the Roman Pontiff" (1, 13).[8] Moreover, in discussing the notes of the Church, he maintains that the "Catholic Church of Christ truly is and should be

---

Indeed, the whole Mayr book is a rather perfunctory account of what Tournely says and shows little interest in discussing controversial topics. Ulrich Horst, O.P., has one and a half pages on Tournely and his *Konsensustheorie* in his *Unfehlbarkeit und Geschichte: Studien zur Unfehlbarkeitsdiskussion von Melchior Cano bis zum I. Vatikanischen Konzil* (Mainz: Matthias Grünewald, 1982), 124–126. Yves Congar, O.P., has a good paragraph on Tournely in *L'Eglise de saint Augustin à l'époque moderne* (Paris: Cerf, 1970), 400–401.

    6. Honoré Tournely, *Praelectiones theologicae de ecclesia Christi* (Paris, 1765), 1, i. All subsequent references to Tournely will be to this book, cited as *De ecclesia* and by part number and page, in parentheses in the text. The *De ecclesia* is divided into two parts, separately paginated, both contained in volume 5 of this 11-volume edition of his *Praelectiones*.

    7. *Decretum pro graecis*, DS 1307.

    8. As Congar notes in *L'Eglise de saint Augustin à l'époque moderne*, 400, Tournely, in adopting this definition from Bellarmine, omits only the words *unius Christi in terris*

Roman" (1, 108). This is because "the Roman or Apostolic See is the center and bond of Catholic unity and communion, and no one can be accounted Catholic except one who is joined in unity of faith and doctrine with it" (1, 112). This theme of the necessity of union with the Roman Pontiff, while undergoing many refinements of nuance, is maintained consistently throughout the work.

Addressing the issue of authority in the Church, he asks first, "Who is the supreme judge of controversies of faith?" (1, 138) Through eight pages he says that it is not Scripture alone (1, 140–148). Nor is it the individual inspiration of the Holy Spirit, for "in every well-ordered and well-constituted state it is necessary that there be judges, who interpret the law" for all (1, 148). So also, "the law of faith must be public and known, given the nature of the Church as a visible society" (ibid.). Again, the secular prince cannot be recognized as the judge in matters of faith. He is indeed the guardian and maintainer of the laws of the Church and of the dogmas of religion, "but he is not the arbiter or supreme judge of controversies of faith" (1, 150). In this passage expressing a traditional view of the role of the Christian king, Tourney does not see fit to mention the *placet, lettres patentes,* or the Gallican system's other royal controls over communication within the Church of France and between the Holy See and France.[9]

Thus, clearly it is the *Church* that is the judge of doctrinal questions: "[O]nly the Church is the supreme and infallible judge of controversies of faith" (1, 152). For Tournely, Church, when there is question of authority, does not mean the whole community of faith, but only the hierarchy, "that is, the Supreme Pontiff and the bishops, whom the Holy Spirit has placed as bishops to rule the Church of

---

vicarius. (Congar neglects to include the words *in terris.*) See Robert Bellarmine, S.J., *Quarta controversia generalis: De Conciliis* 3.2, in *Opera omnia,* ed. Justin Fèvre (Paris: Louis Vives), 1:317.

9. On the workings of Gallicanism on the ecclesiopolitical level, see André Latreille et al., *Histoire du catholicisme en France,* 2nd ed. (Paris: Spes, 1962), 2:355–378, esp. 363–367, or Roland Mousnier, *The Institutions of France under the Absolute Monarchy, 1598–1789* (Chicago: University of Chicago Press, 1979), 1:311–316.

God, either in council or apart from a council" (ibid.). The Church, he says in a later connection, has a living, public authority competent to resolve questions and doubts, and this is the Roman Pontiff and the bishops. It is not the "populus Christianus" but the "rectores et pastores" of the Church (1, 218). Tournely's Church is a hierarchical one.

The Roman Pontiff

The term *the head of the Church,* Tournely says, has two uses. "There is a head of the Church that is supreme, essential and invisible, and this is Christ" (2, 1). And there is a "head that is ministerial, visible, and external, the Roman Pontiff, who is called the Supreme Pontiff par excellence because of the primacy of honor and jurisdiction that he possesses in the whole Church over the other bishops" (ibid.).

Speaking on behalf of mainline Gallican ecclesial thought, Tournely states unequivocally that Christ conferred on Peter a primacy over the other apostles (2, 2). Contrary to the accusation often made by papalist authors, that the Gallicans attributed to the papacy a mere primacy of honor, he affirms that "by the word primacy, we understand not only a prerogative of honor and dignity, but also a preeminence of power and jurisdiction" (2, 2).[10] This is the historic belief of the Church, he adds, and it is only in these "later times" that the primacy of Peter has been impugned, by Luther, Calvin, and the other Protestants (ibid.). It is agreed among all orthodox (Catholic) theologians that the Roman Pontiff possesses by divine privilege a primacy of jurisdiction and authority over the entire Church. "It is in assigning the limits and prerogatives of this authority and jurisdiction that they differ exceedingly with each other" (2, 26). In other words, Tournely says, we all agree on papal primacy, but the key question is, what are the *prerogatives* that come with the primacy? He lists and discusses three different positions on this found among Catholic theologians.

---

10. Tournely devotes eight pages to scriptural and patristic testimonies in support of this position, and another fifteen to answering objections to it.

The first he terms that of the "Ultramontanes." They consider that the Roman Pontiff is an absolute monarch, that the fullness of ecclesiastical jurisdiction resides in him alone, and that from him a certain portion of it flows down to the individual bishops. They believe that the Pontiff defining ex cathedra cannot err, and that he can be judged by no one, not even a general council. Finally, they regard him as "lord of the whole world," with power to depose kings and release subjects from their oath of fealty (2,2).[11] It is striking, Tournely notes incidentally here, how the Protestants have scored "many triumphs" by representing this as the "common doctrine of all Catholics" (ibid.).

A second position, virtually the opposite extreme from the Ultramontane, is the view of those who effectively deny a real primatial authority in the Roman Pontiff. The most prominent and widely read exponent of this view in seventeenth–eighteenth century France was Edmond Richer. In his De ecclesiastica ac politica potestate libellus (1611), in Tournely's words, "in order to extol the authority of the Church, he completely puts down [deprimit] the papal and violates the legitimate privileges of the primacy of the Roman See" (ibid.).[12] Richer, as Tournely reports, maintains that Christ conferred the keys of jurisdiction directly on the Church as a whole, and not on Peter or the Apostles. The pope and bishops receive such authority as they have from the Church, an authority that is instrumental and executive. Thus the pope is a symbolic and ministerial head, and not essential to the existence of the Church (2, 27). Tournely had no use whatever for Richerism, but it was a view popular among a number of rank-and-file clergy in France at that time.[13]

Tournely makes a point of noting that Richer's book was promptly condemned by the French hierarchy at a council at Sens the very

---

11. All this is stated in one paragraph. He does not cite any works of Ultramontane writers here.

12. See references on Richer cited in note 103 of chapter 1.

13. See, e.g., François Lebrun, ed., Histoire des catholiques en France du XVe siècle à nos jours (Toulouse: Privat, 1980), 157–158; and Louis S. Greenbaum, Talleyrand, Statesman Priest: The Agent-General of the Clergy and the Church of France at the End of the Old Regime (Washington, D.C.: Catholic University of America Press, 1970), 129–130.

year after it appeared. They branded its theses as "false, erroneous, and scandalous" and said they even "sound heretical and schismatic" (2, 27). For Tourney the Supreme Pontiff "is the true and proper visible and external head of the Church, not merely a symbolic and figurative one, as Richer said" (2, 28). Whether the pope should be termed a "ministerial head" depends on what is meant by this. "He is not a ministerial head in the sense of Richer, as if he received all his authority from the Church"; he is only the executive of the Church's will (ibid.). After all, Peter received the keys directly from Jesus Christ. "Nonetheless, the Roman Pontiff can be called the ministerial head of the Church in a right sense, both in relation to Christ and to the Church." Certainly he is a minister in relation to Christ, for Paul says in I Cor 4:1 that we are all "ministers of Christ and dispensers of the mysteries of God." He is a minister also in relation to the Church, "whose decrees he first of all is bound to observe, and by virtue of his office he is bound to be vigilant that they are observed by all" (2, 29).

Between these two extremes, says Tourney, there is a *sententia media,* a middle position, that upholds the primacy of the Roman Pontiff in carefully stated terms (2, 27–28). The pope, as head of all the (local) Churches, is solicitous for the observance of the canons in the universal Church. In questions of faith and morals he has the leading role ("praecipuas partes"), and his decrees apply to all the Churches. Although he is "not the sole judge of controversies" and is "not infallible," all the members of the Church should recognize that his words carry great weight and should assent to them. If there is a major and prolonged controversy, the Roman Pontiff has the power to summon all the bishops to a council. It is *here,* at an assembly of the entire episcopate of the universal Church, that there is the "supreme and infallible authority" needed to settle definitively a question that has agitated the Church (2, 28).[14]

In this passage Tourney does not apply the name *Gallican* to this "middle position" regarding papal primacy, which he clearly espouses

---

14. "Represents" renders *repraesentat.*

himself, but it *is* that of mainline episcopal or ecclesiastical Gallicanism as expressed in Articles 2, 3, and 4 of the Declaration of 1682. "What kind of regimen was established by Christ in the Church?" (1, 264)[15] It is agreed among Catholics, Tournely says, that the Church is not a democracy, in which the power of deciding doctrine and policy is accorded to the multitude. Rather, the Church is certainly a monarchy, for it has one Supreme Pontiff who has the primacy not simply of honor but of jurisdiction (1, 265).[16] But there are several kinds of monarchy. Granted that the Church is "truly monarchical," is it also "purely monarchical," which would mean that the whole Church "depends on the *arbitrium* [judgment] and *imperium* [power to command] of the Roman Pontiff alone?" No, the Church is not such an absolute monarchy. "The regimen of the Church is not purely monarchical but tempered with aristocracy, and the exercise of apostolic power is to be moderated through the canons established by the Holy Spirit and consecrated by the reverence of the whole world" (1, 266). This is the view, he says, which is properly asserted by Article 3 of the Declaration of the Gallican Clergy of 1682. The "aristocracy" is, of course, the episcopate, which is also of divine institution, and has according to both Scripture and tradition a true authoritative voice in deciding controversies of faith (1, 268–269).[17]

The system of absolute monarchy, he continues, may be appropriate and laudable in civil society but not in the spiritual. One cannot argue from the civil sphere to the ecclesial, claiming that the Church must pattern itself after the civil model. Rather, "the condition and state of the Church depends solely on the will of Christ in instituting it" (1, 280). There were good reasons why Christ did not want the Church to be purely monarchical. (1) Absolute domination could have incited and fostered pride in the primate and degenerated into tyranny. Thus Christ instituted a ministerial office, which is more conducive to humility. (2) The Church, as a spiritual communion,

---

15. This introduces a sixteen-page discussion in the latter section of part I.
16. He spells this out further on 1, 266–267.
17. He does not cite any sources here.

consists of free acts of faith and piety, and "cannot be ruled by force and external coercion through an absolute and monarchical power." (3) The "communion of saints" cannot be governed by the personal will of one man but by "common and catholic consensus" (1, 280). He recalls that Diego Lainez, a Jesuit theologian at the Council of Trent, said that the whole Church is the "servant of the Roman Pontiff." This is not only erroneous, Tournely comments, it "does not even merit refutation." The reverse is true: "[T]he Pontiff, while still head of the Church, is still the servant and minister of the Church," and his ministry consists of "conserving the children of the same mother in unity of faith, morals, and communion" (1, 280).[18]

The basic concern of the Gallican view comes through clearly and insistently in this section on the kind of regimen intended by Christ for the Church. Citing a number of popes from Julius I (337–352) to Nicholas I (858–867) who affirm that they govern the Church in accord with the canons, he concludes: "From so many outstanding testimonies of holy pontiffs emerges the axiom which we have always preserved from our ancestors with the greatest care: the Church is governed *by law, not by absolute power*" (1, 275; emphasis his) And this is "the very solid foundation of the liberties of our Gallican Church, firm and constant adhesion to the sacred canons of the ancient and common law, which have been founded by the spirit of God and consecrated by the reverence of the whole world" (ibid.).

Papal Infallibility and the Consensus of the Church

Tournely begins his hundred-page study of the question, "Can the Supreme Pontiff err in defining cases of faith and morals?" by quoting Article 4 of the Declaration of 1682, which states: "In questions of faith also the Supreme Pontiff has the principal role, and his decrees

---

18. Diego Lainez (1512–1565) was the second general of the Society of Jesus and a papal theologian at Trent. Tournely cites Sforza Pallavicino's history of the Council of Trent (tome II, book 18, chapter 15), where Pallavicino gives a lengthy summary of a discourse given by Lainez at the council. In it Lainez strongly upholds papal supremacy but really does not say that the Church is the servant of the pope, so Tournely must have seen that comment attributed to him elsewhere.

apply to all the Churches; but his judgment is not irreformable unless the consensus of the Church is present with it" (2, 63).[19] We want our students of theology in France, Tournely says, to understand clearly the several positions on this celebrated question so that they can intelligently defend this doctrine of the Gallican Church, always in such a way, of course, that the "sacred and legitimate authority of the Apostolic See remains intact" (2, 73).

In issuing the Declaration of 1682, Tournely points out, the Church of France did not violate Catholic orthodoxy or exceed its rights as a particular segment of the universal Church (2, 69). Papalist authors generally acknowledged begrudgingly that papal infallibility was not a defined dogma of faith. Pietro Ballerini, for example, writing a few years after Tournely, admitted this, as will be noted in the chapter on Ballerini. Tournely cites Robert Bellarmine as acknowledging reluctantly that the view denying papal infallibility, though "erroneous and proximate to heresy, is not properly heretical, since it is tolerated by the Church" (2, 69).[20] Tournely says, "Far more soundly and rightly, others think that this question is one of those about which there is, *salva fide*, dispute. For since there is nothing defined by the Church about this controversy, no party, whether affirming or denying, should be branded with the note of heresy" (2, 69). Furthermore, it has always been licit for particular Churches to follow one side in such situations. "Is it licit for Italians to be attached to one side, and not licit for French to be attached to the other?" A comment that he adds here interestingly reveals the general acceptance in the ancien régime of the involvement of the royal government in Church matters: "Is it licit for Italian theologians to claim in their

---

19. The original reads: *In fidei quoque quaestionibus praecipuas Summi Pontificis esse partes, eiusque decreta ad omnes et singulas ecclesias pertinere; nec tamen irreformabile esse judicium, nisi ecclesiae consensus accesserit.*

20. Speaking of the view that the pope, if he defines something apart from a general council, could possibly teach a heresy, Bellarmine says, "[W]e do not venture to call it properly heretical, for we see that those who follow this opinion are thus far tolerated by the Church; however, it seems altogether erroneous and proximate to heresy, so that it could deservedly be declared heretical by the judgment of the Church." *Tertia controversia generalis: De summo pontifice,* 4, 2, in *Opera omnia,* 2:80.

books the authority of the Roman Pontiff over the temporal affairs of kings, and not licit for kings and their ministers to prohibit such an opinion with their edicts, or for our theologians to refute it?" (2, 69)

One interesting comment that Tournely makes here was seized upon by Ultramontane authors as illustrating the subjection of French ecclesiology to the royal power in France and a regrettable lack of integrity in French theologians who adhered to the Gallican position. Tournely notes that it is difficult, in view of all the testimonies that Bellarmine and others have compiled, not to recognize a certain and infallible authority in the Apostolic See. "But it is far more difficult to reconcile them with the Declaration of the Gallican Clergy, from which it is not permitted to us to recede" (2, 72). Giuseppe-Agostino Orsi and René-François Rohrbacher cite this statement as showing that Tournely refrains from accepting papal infallibility simply because he is not permitted by the royal government to do so. In reality, it is surely clear that Tournely means that he is not "permitted" by the *merits* of the arguments on the issue, which he spends a solid hundred pages (!) in presenting and discussing.[21] Rohrbacher, incidentally, has high praise for most of Tournely's theology.[22] Writers like Orsi (presumably) and Rohrbacher (certainly) were unaware that the Declaration of 1682 was the result of initiatives of the French clergy, and not of the king, and represented their views on Church authority. (It may be noted parenthetically that when Orsi published his treatise on papal authority, he had recently been appointed prefect of the Sacred Congregation of the Index, which had as its whole reason for being the issuing of decrees stating that the reading of certain books was not permitted.)

The French clergy, Tournely says, made no pretense of defining a dogma in the Declaration of 1682 and have always upheld the true

---

21. Giuseppe-Agostino Orsi, O.P., *De irreformabili romani pontificis in definiendis fidei controversiis judicio* (Rome: Paulus Junchius, 1771), I, III, 250; René-François Rohrbacher, *Histoire universelle de l'Eglise catholique* (Paris: Gaume Frères, 1842–1849), 26:164. On this see Richard F. Costigan, S.J., *Rohrbacher and the Ecclesiology of Ultramontanism* (Rome: Università Gregoriana Editrice, 1980), 230–233.

22. Rohrbacher, *Histoire*, 26:155–165.

authority of the Roman Pontiff against its detractors (2, 70). But the key question on this whole issue, as Tournely sees it, is: What provides the firm certitude, the irreformability, of a statement of the pontiff speaking ex cathedra? Does this come from the consensus and reception of the Church or from a divine privilege conferred on the Roman Pontiff, enabling him to define the faith single-handedly? The Ultramontane school strongly holds for the latter, saying that the pope, speaking ex cathedra, is infallible before and independently of the consensus of the Church. Not only is the consensus of the Church totally unnecessary to the papal teaching function, it is actually not permitted for the Church, the episcopate, to refrain from concurring with a papal pronouncement (2, 67).[23]

The view of the Gallican Church is distinctly opposed to the papalist, for it thinks that the judgment of the Roman Pontiff in cases of faith and morals is subject to error and is not certainly irreformable, unless the consensus of the Church is present with it. "Therefore, before that consensus, it does not consider the judgment of the First See irreformable" (2, 72). The Church must be able to recognize in the papal pronouncement the belief of the historic community of faith, and for this there must be a wide involvement of the episcopate as a whole.

What is necessary, in Tournely's view of the consensus of the Church, is recognition of the genuine role of the episcopate in teaching the faith. He does not propose any single way in which this role of the episcopate is implemented. The consensus of the Church (episcopate) may be antecedent, concomitant, or subsequent, and it may be express or tacit (2, 84). It is antecedent if the papal doctrine has already become rather widely known—for example, from having been worked out at several councils. It is concomitant when the bishops are in council with the pope and there decide upon the position to be taken. Tournely stresses that a general council does not receive authority from the Supreme Pontiff, but rather has received im-

---

23. This view of papal authority is attributed to the Ultramontanes generally, without citation of particular authors.

mediately from Christ himself the gift of teaching the faith without error. The consensus is subsequent if the pope sends his statement either to a universal synod or to the bishops dispersed in their dioceses. In either case, the latter add their judgment to the judgment of the Supreme Pontiff (2, 85).

Whatever the manner in which the bishops receive the papal decree, "they always use their right and authority received from Christ to judge cases of faith: in accepting the decree they add their judgment and consensus" (2, 85). Sometimes the matter is so clear and well known that the bishops can and do concur in the papal statement without need of further study or discussion. This is what happened, Tournely thinks, in the case of Jansenism. The bishops of France received the bull *Unigenitus* readily and without feeling the need for further analysis and discussion (2, 85). He says in an earlier reference to this episode that the bishops received the bulls against Jansenism "not in blind obedience, but with prior understanding and judgment of the matter" (1, 272).[24] Tournely stresses that in this situation, the bishops are not acting "only as executors" of the pontifical will, "but are fulfilling and carrying out the role of judges" (2, 85). In this reception they are not extolling themselves as judges of the Supreme Pontiff, "but only exercising the right entailed in the episcopal dignity" (1, 272). Individual bishops, of course, cannot subject the judgment of the Supreme Pontiff to their own judgment. Only the universal Church, "when assembled in general council, can subject the statement of the Roman Pontiff to a new examination and judgment, or even annul it" (2, 85).

The consensus of the episcopate may be express or it may be tacit and "interpretative" (2,85). The latter may be said to happen when the papal pronouncement has been adequately published and made known, and bishops do not remonstrate against it. As for the numerical or quantitative aspect of the consensus, Tournely states that it is not necessary to have the consensus of *all* the bishops. It is enough to

---

24. See on this Yves Congar, O.P., "La 'réception' comme réalité ecclésiologique," *Revue des sciences philosophiques et théologiques* 56 (July 1972): 390.

have the concurrence of "the greater number, whereby the Church is sufficiently represented" (2, 86).[25] If there are a few who do not want to concur, they should consider themselves bound to do so. In case of a major division in the episcopate, in which there are many bishops standing with the Roman Pontiff and many disagreeing with him, "certainly one should adhere to the side which is conjoined with the head, for it should be considered the better and sounder part." This is true even if these seem to be numerically fewer, though Tournely does not think that God in his providence would allow this to happen. This is because "the Church is a visible body united with its head the Roman Pontiff, and the Roman Pontiff himself is the center of unity and ecclesial communion" (2, 87). Clearly, despite frequent comments to the contrary in papalist authors, Tournely's attitude toward the papacy is *not* adversarial. He simply wants to maintain what he considers the rightful and traditional role of the episcopate.

The very conservative nature of Tournely's whole outlook on the Church comes through further as he inquires: Are the faithful bound to assent to a papal pronouncement on faith or morals as soon as it is issued (and promulgated in their country) and before it is clear that the bishops have confirmed it with their consensus? (2, 145) He answers with an unequivocal Yes, they are bound to assent to it, even though it is not yet strictly irreformable. The reason for this is that people should obey the authority of a legitimate superior even when it is still, strictly speaking, subject to error. The presumption is always in favor of the superior authority, and it is not up to individual members of the Church to try to judge the rightness or wrongness of the authority's act (2, 146).

In the concluding pages of his discussion of papal authority, Tournely makes some penetrating comments in response to papalist arguments based on the Roman Pontiff's role in convoking and confirm-

---

25. Thus, what Jacques Gres-Gayer says about Gallican doctrine demanding unanimous approbation by the bishops does not apply to Tournely; see "The *Unigenitus* of Clement XI: A Fresh Look at the Issues," *Theological Studies* 49 (June 1988): 276.

ing councils. Granting that it pertains to the pope to convoke a council, he asks, "What does that right [*ius*] have in common with the privilege of inerrancy?" (2, 161) Emperors used to convoke councils, and archbishops convoked provincial councils. Do they need infallibility to do that? The Roman Pontiff confirms councils. "Does he in doing this confer by himself alone strength, force, and firmness on the councils? Certainly not, for they have this immediately from Christ, [who said,] I am with you all days." The pope's confirmation adds to the council his and the western Church's consensus, without which a council is not considered fully and truly ecumenical. "For thus all the members join in unity of faith; thus the body of the Church is perfectly represented, which consists of head and members" (2, 161).

Tournely disagrees profoundly with the pervasive assumption of the Ultramontane view that the possessor of supreme administrative authority must have the power to determine the faith itself in decrees that are absolutely final, irrevocable, and irreformable, that is, unable to be in error. Like the pope, every bishop performs these functions of teaching and clarifying doctrine and policy. Does this make every one of them infallible? "Are we bound to obey only superiors whom we know to be unable to err?" No, we obey all those who have legitimate authority from God and who perform this function for Christ (2, 162). Tournely is a very articulate spokesman for the view that Jesus Christ conferred the authority to teach the faith on all twelve apostles, not simply on one man, however devoted that one man may be to his primatial responsibility. This view believes that when Jesus said to Peter, "Confirm your brothers," he did not mean for him simply to replace the other eleven. The mainstream Gallican view expressed by Honoré Tournely is essentially what is today called collegiality.

CHAPTER 4

Giuseppe-Agostino Orsi, O.P.
1692–1761

Orsi and His Objectives

A major comprehensive reply to Bossuet was offered in 1739 by Giuseppe-Agostino Orsi, O.P., a learned and prolific theologian and author of books on a number of theological subjects. Orsi, a native of Florence, had studied literature at a Jesuit school there, as well as law in Pisa, before joining the Dominicans at the convent of San Marco in Florence in 1709. He became known for his extensive knowledge of Church and doctrinal history and was assigned to be a professor at Santa Maria sopra Minerva in Rome in 1732. Three successive popes gave him very important honors. Clement XII in 1738 made him secretary of the Sacred Congregation of the Index, Benedict XIV appointed him master of the Sacred Palace in 1749, and Clement XIII made him a cardinal in 1759.[1]

---

1. The main and best source for both the life and work of Giuseppe-Agostino Orsi remains the *DTC* article by M. M. Gorce: *DTC*, 11.2:1612–1619. There is a thirteen-page "Vita" of Orsi by an unidentified author at the beginning of the first volume of his *De irreformabili romani pontificis*. In addition, a brief article on him is given in Gaetano Moroni, *Dizionario di erudizione storico-ecclesiastico* (Venice: Emiliana, 1840–1861), 49:144–145; and a longer account in Angelo Fabroni, *Vitae italorum doctrina excellentiorum qui saeculis XVII et XVIII floruerunt* (Pisa, 1785), 11:6–36.

It was Orsi's works in ecclesiology that gained him a measure of recognition beyond his own lifetime, particularly the book that we will mainly study in this chapter, *De irreformabili romani pontificis in definiendis controversiis fidei judicio*.[2] His books on the papacy were admired and recommended by several leading Ultramontane authors in the nineteenth century. In particular, both Joseph de Maistre and Félicité Lamennais referred their readers to Orsi's work. De Maistre cites Orsi in both *Du pape* and *De l'Eglise gallicane*.[3] In the latter work especially, he considers Orsi's comments about Bossuet apt and effective—for example, when he says that Bossuet resembles the Protestants in his approach and methods.[4] In other places he notes with satisfaction how Orsi puts Bossuet in his place on certain topics.[5] Lamennais, in his *De la religion considérée dans ses rapports avec l'ordre politique et civile*, recommends Orsi's work on papal authority as a good complete presentation of Catholic tradition on papal supremacy.[6] Hermann Josef Pottmeyer notes the influence of Orsi, whom he terms "a sharp enemy of Gallicanism," on two other nineteenth-century Roman authors, Clemens Schrader and, especially, Carlo Passaglia.[7]

Both his confreres and his own statements indicate that gratitude to Clement XII for making him the secretary of the Sacred Congregation of the Index gave him the keen desire to defend the honor

---

2. *De irreformabili romani pontificis in definiendis fidei controversiis judicio*, 3 vols. (Rome: Paulus Junchius, 1771). A briefer version in Italian was entitled *Dell'infallibilità e del autorità del romano pontefice sopra concilii ecumenici*, 2 vols. (Rome: Pagliarini, 1741).

3. Joseph de Maistre, *Du pape, suivi de l'Eglise gallicane dans son rapport avec le souverain pontife* (Brussels: H. Goemaere, 1852). *Du pape* is volume 1 of this edition. In it he cites Orsi on 33 and 45.

4. *De l'Eglise gallicane* (volume 2 in this edition), 215.

5. Ibid., 238–241, 271.

6. Félicité Lamennais, *De la religion considérée dans ses rapports avec l'ordre politique et civile*, in *Oeuvres complètes* (Paris: Paul Daubrée et Cailleux, 1836–1837; Frankfurt: Minerva, 1967), 7:194n; Lamennais cites the Italian résumé of Orsi, *De infallibilità, et dell'autorità del romano pontefice sopra concilii ecumenici* (Rome, 1749).

7. Hermann Josef Pottmeyer, *Unfehlbarkeit und Souveränität: Die päpstliche Unfehlbarkeit im System der ultramontanen Ekklesiologie des 19. Jahrhunderts* (Mainz: Matthias Grünewald, 1975), 334 (Schrader), 324 (Passaglia).

and authority of the Holy Father against all his many adversaries.[8] It would be hard not to sympathize with Clement. Even when, as Cardinal Lorenzo Corsini, he became pope in 1730, concluding an acrimonious four-month conclave, he was an old man of seventy-eight, in poor health and losing his eyesight. For the last eight years of his ten-year pontificate he was completely blind and frequently bedridden. In addition, the papacy during these years was singularly ineffective in both ecclesiastical and political matters.[9] As has been noted elsewhere, papal decrees even on doctrinal and other Church matters were not accepted in the Catholic countries unless they received the *placet* from the royal governments. For example, even the Breviary readings for the new feast of St. Gregory VII, who in 1076 tried to depose a head of state, Henry IV of Germany, evoked indignation in France and were prohibited by the Parlement of Paris (1728, 1730).[10] Regarding political matters, von Pastor comments at the beginning of his account of the pontificate of this pope, "When Clement XII, out of veneration for Clement XI, [1700–1721] took that Pontiff's name, he could hardly have foreseen that the Catholic Powers would treat him even worse than the Albani Pope."[11] For example, he could do nothing when Emperor Charles VI asserted suzerainty over Parma and Piacenza, which had for centuries owed allegiance to the Holy See. The Papal States were overrun by Spanish armies, the people of Rome revolted against the forcible recruitment of troops by the Spaniards, and Clement repeatedly had to make various concessions to the Spanish and other powers. Hans Kühner puts it vividly: "De-

---

8. Dedication to Clement XII at the beginning of *De irreformabili,* twelfth (last) page. The pages of the dedication are not numbered. The "Vita" of Orsi is after the dedication, xxxii.

9. On the whole pontificate of Clement XII, see Ludwig von Pastor, *History of the Popes* (St. Louis: B. Herder, 1902–1953), 34:356–400; two very brief accounts are Burkhart Schneider, S.J., "The Papacy under the Increasing Pressure of the Established Church," in *The Church in the Age of Absolutism and Enlightenment,* vol. 6 of Hubert Jedin and John Dolan, eds., *History of the Church* (New York: Crossroads, 1981), 563–566; and J. N. D. Kelly, *Oxford Dictionary of the Popes* (New York: Oxford University Press, 1986), 295–296.

10. On this episode, see von Pastor, *History of the Popes,* 34:155–157, 272–274, 431.

11. Ibid., 355.

fenseless, the 80-year old graybeard in the Quirinal had to watch helplessly as ruin finally engulfed him."[12]

Orsi does not mention either these problems or Clement's infirmities in his very devout and flowery dedication at the beginning of *De irreformabili*, "To the most holy lord, Clement XII, Pontifex Optimus Maximus." A deeply religious vision inspires Orsi to say in the opening sentence: "Among the many gifts and privileges with which the See of Peter is adorned and his Roman Pontiff successors in it are decorated, none, Most Blessed Father, is more august and none more divine than that it is the immobile foundation of the universal Church and the column and firmament of truth."[13] Nothing, he continues, "lifts man more beyond the condition of human nature, and shows him to be similar and proximate to God," than reverent obedience to papal doctrinal decrees.[14] Admitting that it would be "idolatry" to say such things about a man if we did not know that papal teachings are God's own truth, he asks what greater show of reverence for the eternal wisdom and goodness of God could there be "than subjecting one's reason to him [the pope] and rendering one's intellect into captivity in obedience to him [the pope]."[15] The successor of Peter teaches truths from God, and "we do not perceive anything human in them, but revere the divine [element] and venerate and look up to his authority."[16] This is why is it so disturbing to see how "certain transalpine theologians" treat papal authority. There is no minor problem and no irrelevant point that they will not bring up to detract from the respect due to the Holy Father. "The lapse of Liberius, the imprudent dissimulation of Honorius, the scandals of the tenth century" fill their pages.[17] It is in response to the many carping criticisms of these disloyal authors and to reaffirm the true

12. Leonard von Matt and Hans Kühner, *The Popes: Papal History in Picture and Word* (New York: Universe Books, 1963), 199.
13. Dedication, first page.
14. Ibid., second page.
15. Ibid. Consultation with classics scholars has clarified that "him" in both places refers to the pope rather than to God.
16. Ibid.
17. Ibid., fourth page.

authority of the Roman Pontiff that Orsi has produced the present work.

Orsi's "Praefatio" following the dedication to the Holy Father targets the impiety and audacity of the Gallicans from its first sentence. The French clergy, in their Declaration of 1682, "after seventeen centuries prescribe limits to papal authority, which was circumscribed by no limits by Christ himself, the wisdom of almighty God," when he founded the kingdom that is the Church.[18] The Gallican Fathers have the nerve to set up limits that the Roman Pontiffs may not transgress. Among the defenders of the Gallican Declaration, there could hardly be a more formidable writer than "the most illustrious Bossuet, celebrated for so many published works, famous for literary achievements, conspicuous for many victories and triumphs" (iv). Orsi says that he heard many, even in Rome, say that they feared that Bossuet could not be effectively answered, and that defenders of papal authority would be more prudent to refrain from the attempt (v).[19] After some reflection, Orsi decided that Bossuet could and should be refuted: "It must be shown that not probably but certainly the successors of Peter are endowed with divine authority to end controversies about the faith, and that their decrees must be accepted like oracles of the Holy Spirit as certain and irretractable rules of the Catholic faith" (ibid.). The task of proving this decisively required that he relentlessly follow Bossuet's footsteps point by point, ploughing through the same materials that Bossuet used in his *Defensio* and giving the true reading of the data (ix).

Orsi concludes the "Praefatio" with comments on the importance of Article 4 of the Gallican Declaration. He thinks it is clear that the validity of the other articles of the declaration depends on the validity of the fourth. "For if the judgment of the Roman Pontiff and the Apostolic See is subject to the judgment of the universal Church, and

---

18. *Praefatio*, i. Pagination begins with the praefatio. Subsequent page references will be given in the text.

19. The author of the "Vita" makes similar comments on the very formidable challenge that Bossuet seemed to offer.

if the universal Church has the right of retreating and reforming it, the clear consequence is that an ecumenical council, representing the universal Church, has greater authority than the Roman Pontiff and the one Apostolic See." In reality, asserts Orsi, the Roman Pontiff's authority is "by the institution and divine law of Christ himself the highest by itself, and unchangeable, and subject to no other judgment" (xi). Since Articles 2 and 3 are so related to the fourth, the logical order seems to be to refute the fourth proposition first and establish the doctrine that it assails. He will do this in a spirit of moderation, both because of the great merits of Bossuet and because all disputes, even those with heretics, should be conducted without rancor and polemic. Would that the French would act this way in their writings against the rights of the Apostolic See (ibid.).

Proceeding into the body of this work, one begins to wonder why Ultramontane authors would recommend this book of Orsi rather than Pietro Ballerini's *De vi ac ratione primatus romanorum pontificum*, for the papalist ecclesiology in the latter is much more accessible. Ballerini's treatise is better organized and more clearly written. Orsi's *De irreformabili* is more difficult reading, mainly but not solely because of his methodology. His decision to follow Bossuet's footsteps and attempt to reply point by point to the "Most Illustrious Adversary" gives the whole work a rather disjointed quality. It also leads to some repetitiveness, for similar concerns do recur at different places in Bossuet's work. Moreover, Orsi unfortunately does not identify which edition of the *Defensio* he is using. There had been two by 1739, one published in 1730 and one in 1735, and neither of these presents Bossuet's books and chapters in the same order as the more widely used later editions.[20] In addition, Orsi really does not write very clearly most of the time, and reading him is a tedious, laborious

---

20. The edition appearing in 1730 was published clandestinely in Luxembourg by Andrea Chevalier. The author of the "Vita" mentions (xxxii) that Orsi had this one available to him, which probably means that it is the one he used. The 1735 version was edited by Gabriel-Charles Buffard, place and publisher not given by Aimé-Georges Martimort in his entry on this in his *L'établissement du texte de la "Defensio Declarationis" de Bossuet* (Paris: Cerf, 1956), 65–66.

process. What follows is culled and synthesized from his discussion of topics related to our subject.

Be it noted, though, that Orsi does show impressive familiarity with a wide range of authors on the subjects that he is dealing with. He cites, to name a few mentioned just in the early chapters of the work, Pierre de Marca, Antoine Charlas, Christian Lupus, Etienne Baluze, Louis Thomassin, Honoré Tourneley, Jean de Launoy, André Duval, and many others. Orsi deserves credit for industrious research, both in authors of the papalist view and in those of Gallican and other differing views. Alfonso Prandi notes that Orsi appreciated and used contemporary advances in scholarship such as those in Italy associated especially with the names of Ludovico Muratori and Giovanni Domenico Mansi.[21] Prandi thinks that Orsi saw these advances as surely beneficial to the cause of the Church and of truth, even while his "apologetic" concern is the real determinant of his work. He was one of those, Prandi notes, who believed that one "finds in the work of erudition material to sustain a particular dogmatic and ecclesiological vision," a vision that one continues to maintain with the new scholarly contributions.[22] This is surely an apt and just way of characterizing the attitude and work of Giuseppe-Agostino Orsi, a man who devotes himself earnestly to expounding a pope-centered vision of the Church. Indeed, and this is the subject of the Prandi article, he undertook in the 1740s to write the whole history of the Church in order to counteract the Gallican-tinted *Histoire ecclésiastique* of Claude Fleury. Many in Rome were upset when an Italian translation of Fleury appeared in 1740 and thought it should be condemned. Warnings from the French Crown caused this idea to be

21. Alfonso Prandi, "La *Istoria ecclesiastica* di P. Giuseppe Orsi e la sua genesi," *Rivista di storia della Chiesa in Italia* 34 (July–December 1980): 430–450. Many more Italian scholars of the eighteenth century are named in Oskar Köhler, "The Established Church and the Enlightenment," in *The Church in the Age of Absolutism and Enlightenment*, vol. 6 of Hubert Jedin and John Dolan, eds., *History of the Church* (New York: Crossroad, 1981), 532–534. More recently, Dries Vanysacker has offered a great deal of interesting information on this in *Cardinal Giuseppe Garampi (1725–1792): An Enlightened Ultramontane* (Brussels: Institut Historique Belge de Rome, 1995).

22. Prandi, "La *Istoria ecclesiastica*," 441.

dropped,[23] so Orsi decided to write a history himself and produced twenty volumes(!), covering the centuries up to Gregory the Great.

Orsi offers a useful statement of terms at the very beginning of the work. He uses the word *infallibilis* at times but more often uses words he considers synonyms. The more recent term *infallibile*, he says, and terms used by the ancients, such as "immobile, irreformabile, irretractabile, irrefragabile, . . . all mean one and the same thing" (I, 1, 1).[24] In each case, Orsi's sense is that a doctrinal statement of this kind is definitive and final and thus not subject to change. The word *irretractabile*," which he likes, specifically means that the doctrine cannot be "treated" again; that is, debated again with any idea of changing it.

Scriptural Basis for Papal Supremacy

It is clear that for Orsi the Catholic Church is an absolute monarchy. Its ruler is an absolute monarch, just like the great kings and emperors of the world, except that his authority is of a higher and more sacred order. For Orsi the New Testament teaches plainly that any and all power, authority, and jurisdiction in the Church come from the Roman Pontiff or depend on him. This is obvious from the very notion of monarchy or kingdom and is taught wherever Christ refers, as he often does, to the Church as a kingdom. "For the monarchical regimen requires that not only the various magistrates but the whole system of the kingdom are under the king, that they depend on him, and whatever authority and jurisdiction there is in them is referred to the king as to its beginning, fount, and origin" (I, 2, 154). Therefore, the Roman Pontiff is, in the kingdom that is the Church, the highest king and is endowed with monarchical power, and whatever authority there is in it comes from him. "We do not need to demonstrate that those things belong to [the Church's] constitution that are required in the constitution of other kingdoms: it flows by it-

23. On this episode, see "Orsi," *DTC*, 11.2:1617–1618.
24. I, 1, 1 denotes tome I, part 1, page 1. This method of citing the work will be used throughout. Tome I, part 1 and tome I, part 2 are separate volumes. Tome 2 is in effect a third volume.

self from the very notion of kingdom." The adversaries would need to show that the kingdom established by Jesus was to be different from other kingdoms. We can show from Scripture texts relating to Peter's primacy that "there is no power which can retreat the judgments of the Roman Pontiffs and is able to recall their solemn decrees on the faith to examination and judgment" (ibid.). Besides this basic and paramount image of kingdom, Orsi offers three other Gospel images that plainly teach papal monarchy: shepherd, home, and body.

Shepherd and flock. Jesus handed over to Peter to be fed not only the lambs but the sheep. He placed him as the supreme shepherd over the flock. Who could think that flock has the right to judge the shepherd? "Should the shepherd be ruled and governed by the flock? Are not sheep fed and governed by the shepherd? The name pastor means jurisdiction, flock means subjection" (I, 2, 154). Christ did not say for the sheep to feed the shepherd, but for the shepherd to feed the sheep. Thus the universal Church is related to the Roman Pontiff as a flock is related to the shepherd.

Householder and house. Christ asks in Luke 12, "Who do you think is the faithful and prudent householder whom the Lord placed over his family?" Orsi answers, "These words refer to St. Peter." That is, "the Roman Pontiffs are supreme in the house of God, which is the Church" (I, 2, 156). Just as there is no one in the Church for whom Christ has not shed his blood, so there is no one whatever who is not subject to the care of Peter and his successors. It is also clear that no one in the house can judge the householder. "Not only individual domestics and servants, but the entire family that is together in it, have no power over the householder, who cannot be judged by it, judgment being reserved to God alone as the supreme Lord." Surely all would agree that there is no family in which it is licit for the inferior servants, even all gathered together, to punish or expel the householder, even if he is bad, for that power belongs only to the Lord of all (I, 2, 157).

One Body. The Church is one body, and its head is the Roman

Pontiff. Now, the head rules and governs not only the individual members but the entire body composed of them. The head is definitely not ruled and governed by the members. "Therefore it is not for the Church to judge the Roman Pontiff, and direct and govern him by its authority; rather it belongs to the Roman Pontiff to rule not only individual bishops but the universal body consisting of all the bishops put together like so many members, and [also] to rule and confirm with supreme power an ecumenical council in which the Church is represented" (ibid.). Orsi does acknowledge at this point that the bishops at a council judge doctrines and pronounce anathemas with authority from Christ and the Holy Spirit. But all must recognize that "Christ communicates the Spirit to the Church in a certain order, and pours it through the head to the rest of the body, so that it is destitute of the Spirit unless it is subject to the head" (I, 2, 158).

All three of these images reinforce the idea of kingdom, which Orsi considers ideal for expressing the supreme monarchical power of the pope. In another place he says that just as authority flows from the king down to lower officials, "so teaching and instruction of sacred dogmas flow from the Roman Church to all the other churches like rivulets from a primitive spring" (I, 2, 91).

Councils and the Roman Pontiff

For Giuseppe-Agostino Orsi, Petrine supremacy is perfectly clear at the Council of Jerusalem (Acts 15), and this council is paradigmatic for all the councils of Church history. Any council, including an ecumenical council, is certainly subordinate to papal power. "When Peter stated his view, all disputation ceased then and there." Thus the New Testament itself, Orsi asserts, provides "the clearest proof that the judgment of Peter in matters of faith was regarded as irretractable and unchangeable" (I, 1, 22). Peter's pronouncement did not need any confirmation from the community assembled around him: "The statement of Peter, as soon as he uttered it, was efficacious, and no consensus of the sacred assembly was awaited so that it would have its force" (I, 1, 23). The Council of Jerusalem was the pattern for all councils. That council had its validity because of Peter's authorizing presence. Since then, "because of Peter still speaking in the Roman Pontiff, the ecumenical or general councils have their force; and thus once [a matter] has been judged in Rome, nothing after that can be retreated" (I, 1, 24).

Though Orsi, like other papalist authors, believes that a council is never strictly speaking necessary, he still recognizes that "ecumenical councils can at times be of the greatest utility, and sometimes even necessary, even though we believe that the Roman Pontiff by himself has enough authority to terminate any controversy whatever." Peter at Jerusalem judged it useful and expedient to gather the faithful in a synod so as to settle effectively the controverted matter in the name of the community. But the Gallicans do not grasp the plain meaning of the Council of Jerusalem. Peter allowed others to speak and they did, but not with any thought of overturning, revising, or weakening the view of Peter. But the authors and defenders of the Gallican Declaration grant the bishops the right, after the Roman Pontiff has spoken, "not only of confirming his statement of faith, which was done at the Council of Jerusalem, but of retreating and reforming it, or even, if they want, of completely rejecting it[!]"(I, 1, 26).

Like Peter at that first council, popes have judged it appropriate to convoke councils at various times in history, and there can be good reasons for holding a large assembly of the episcopate to deal with a controversy. The whole power and authority of the Church really "are in a way contained in the Supreme Pastor and head of the universal Church." But if the whole body speaks in council, it has more power to move weak minds, to draw them to one and the same view, and to strengthen and keep them together (I, 1, 100). Thus he seems to be saying that councils have what could be called a psychological value in the ongoing life of the Church.

Furthermore, those who are faithful to the Holy See, states Orsi, do not say what Bossuet accuses them of saying: namely, that the bishops at a council are there only as councilors of the pope, not true judges of doctrine. Rather, "we acknowledge that they, together with the Roman Pontiff and under him as members under the head, judge heretics, impose anathemas on them, and prescribe the laws and canons of the universal Church" (I, 2, 152).[25] But even in this context Orsi cannot resist stressing the paramount role and character of papal headship. We think, he continues, that "the supreme and irreformable judgment of the Roman Pontiff on matters of faith is richer, fuller, and more excellent in the head alone than the authority in the rest of the body, all of which jurisdiction and authority of the bishops derive from the Roman Pontiff." Indeed, "whatever authority is established in the body of the Church depends on the majesty and authority of the head" (ibid.).

The Pope and the Consensus of the Church

Authors who discuss Article 4 at length generally devote considerable attention to the question of how the consensus of the episcopate might be implemented during the long periods between councils, when the bishops are dispersed throughout the world. For example, is the consensus stipulated by the Gallicans and rejected by the papalists to be antecedent or consequent, that is, expressed or made known before or after the pope issues the pronouncement? There are also practical questions such as how to secure the opinion of the bishops within a reasonable period of time. Also, how many are needed: must it be unanimity, near unanimity, or some majority? Orsi does not see a need for discussion of such issues. They are all nonissues, given that for him the supremacy of the Roman Pontiff, as a monarchical teacher of the faith, is certain and self-evident.

Orsi does discuss at length one question that is related to the *consensus Ecclesiae:* Does the pope need to consult, and presumably get some kind of consensus or support from, any persons or groups, such as the cardinals, bishops, or learned doctors, before he defines something? The question is sometimes phrased: Does he need the concur-

---

25. He does not give an identifiable reference to Bossuet.

rence of the Church, meaning mainly clergy, of Rome? This is obviously a far cry from the consensus "of the Church" as usually understood on both sides of the debate about papal infallibility, where "the Church" means the whole body of bishops around the world, but comments Orsi makes here do serve to illustrate further this very monarchical papalist ecclesiology. Does the pope, as a necessary and essential condition, need a prior consultation with the Roman clergy, on whose concurrence or consensus the validity of the decree would depend? The implication that the Roman clergy are learned enough, or somehow important enough, to make such a difference might seem like Roman presumptuousness, except that, as Orsi notes, Irenaeus and other Fathers stressed that all the other churches should concur in faith with the *Roman Church,* where the eminent clergy have preserved the faith most reliably (II, 264).[26] Also, "if he does not need the Roman clergy, must he consult at least some Catholic bishops or doctors before he can solemnly and ex cathedra pronounce on a dogma or controversy of faith?" (ibid.) Orsi answers, "It seems to me that the Roman Pontiff can define something solemnly, and that he can propose the definition to all the Churches as an irreformable rule of faith, even if he has done no prior consulting with his Roman Church." And moreover, that "the definition of the Roman Pontiff is unretreatable does not depend at all on their consensus." However, the pope really *should* consult the cardinals on important matters. He "should omit none of the things that human industry prescribes, so that he has considered and explored the living apostolic tradition in the Catholic Church on the controverted dogma" (ibid.). But it must always be remembered that the prerogative of unfailing faith possessed by the Church of Rome comes to it from its head, the pontiff, and not to him from the clergy, including cardinals, of Rome (II, 267). In another place, Orsi discusses at length the regrettable failure of Pope Honorius I to follow these wise norms in the case of the Monothelete controversy (I, 1, 190–201).[27]

---

26. See Irenaeus, *Adversus haereses,* 3.2.
27. Honorius I (625–638) wrote two letters in which he sanctioned the position

It really must be stressed, Orsi believes, that Christ provided that Peter would possess at all times all the needed power and gifts to teach authoritatively and decisively. That's because if we ever permit the heretics, or any dissidents, to call into question whether the judges of the Church used essential diligence and care in making a doctrinal decision, then who is so blind as not to see that soon all judgments of popes and councils would be shaken (II, 268)? If we ever doubt the diligence of the judges, then there will always be more demands for a review of decisions. It is interesting that while Orsi reaffirms several more times in this discussion that the pope does not strictly *need* to consult the cardinals or anyone else before solemnly defining a doctrine, he is modest enough to say that this is his considered opinion. "That I may say candidly what I think, I see no reason" why the pope cannot do this (II, 269). A few pages later, in a major summary statement, he says, "It seems sufficiently clear to us at this time that the Supreme Pontiff, whenever in teaching the universal Church he solemnly defines, is not subject to error, whether [or not] he has consulted with the clergy of Rome or the Eminent Fathers [cardinals], or with other bishops, whether with many or few, whether publicly and in juridical form, or privately and alone; for we judge that this is a consequence of Christ's promises, which were absolutely made to him [Peter] alone" (II, 274). But we do not say that we consider every pope suitable to attempt to define any and every doctrine alone. Rather, a pope "should undertake to define alone only those controversies that he feels himself sufficiently moved and enabled by the Holy Spirit to define" (II, 275).

Faith in the promises of Jesus to Peter provides full spiritual security to Catholics who adhere to papal teachings. The Roman Pontiff's final and supreme judgment on a matter of faith provides the end to a controversy. Thus we "owe to his judgments on the faith the kind of obedience that not only assumes the rightness of the judg-

---

of the Monotheletes, who said that there is only one will in Christ. It has been debated whether he was really clear about the doctrinal implications of the letters, but he was formally condemned at the Third Council of Constantinople in 680.

ment but also excludes absolutely all doubt; it is not mere trust but full and most absolute faith." Gallican claims obviously undermine the security that all have a right to expect. "How can there be an ultimate and final judgment that is subject to doubt, inquiry, retreatment, and examination?" How can you impose a conclusion on a controversy if that conclusion can be called into question and can be freely debated? "The adversaries play games and abuse words" when they say that the pontiff is the chief teacher of the faith, but also that his statements can be retreated or appealed. "It belongs to a judge to compel obedience, and to a judge of the faith to compel obedience of faith" (II, 281). The judgment by the supreme judge in the Church imposes obedience that has to be accepted as final.

For Giuseppe-Agostino Orsi, all these questions about authority in the Church begin and end with the gracious and generous act of her almighty divine founder in conferring on blessed Peter the supreme power to teach the faith. This power "demands the obedience of the mind that is due to the highest and divine authority in the Church," by which "the mind is reduced to captivity in obedience to Christ" (II, 298). Peter and his successors derive their "divine authority" from the promise of Christ, and Christ always keeps his promises. "This pledge of Christ, moreover, is that which promises that the faith of Peter will never fail, that it is simple and absolute, not depending on the judgment and consensus of others, since it was given to Peter so that he might confirm others in the faith, and not that his faith might be confirmed by others" (II, 298–299). It is this promise that assures that "the Roman Pontiffs and their decrees of faith have the highest and divine and ineluctable authority, although no judgments of bishops have preceded them." The Gallicans simply do not recognize the paramount importance of this promise of Christ. Papal decrees do not, "as the adversaries contend, require for the firmness of their apostolic definition, or for their supreme, divine, and unchangeable authority, that the consensus of other churches be added to the judgment of the Roman Church." Rather, "the other Churches must accede to the judgment of the Roman Church, because it, from the most firm promise of Christ, rests on the highest divine and ineluctable firmness" (II, 299). Faith in the loving Savior certainly means devout and complete faith in the Holy Father to whom Jesus entrusted the Good News. This faith in the successor of Peter must be unconditional, which means that you cannot say that you love Jesus and then also say that the Supreme Pontiff needs to have the consensus of the Church with him when he teaches.

CHAPTER 5

Pietro Ballerini
1698–1769

A Very Rigorous Theologian

Pietro Ballerini, a priest of the diocese of Verona, produced many works of erudition, particularly in collaboration with his brother Girolamo.[1] Their father was a professor of surgery at the University of Verona. Very little is recorded of their youth other than they attended a local Jesuit school and then the diocesan seminary. Pietro, the older of the two by several years, was ordained priest for the diocese in 1722. He began teaching Christian doctrine and literature and this stimulated interests that led to his first book, which he intended to introduce students to St. Augustine, *Il metodo di S. Agostino negli studi* (1724). Over several years he devoted much attention to moral theology, in which area he soon became known for great rigorism and relentless opposition to any ideas that might encourage moral laxity. Though educated by Jesuits in his youth, he strongly opposed the probabilism associated especially with Jesuits, considering it really tantamount to

---

1. Biographical information on Ballerini is given by Tarcisio Facchini in his *Il papato principio di unità e Pietro Ballerini di Verona: Dal concetto di unità ecclesiastica al concetto di monarchia infallibile* (Padua: Il Messagero di S. Antonio, 1950), 33–39.

laxism. One of his books was a very critical history of probabilism.

During a controversy over usury, he wrote a book strongly reasserting the Church's traditional rejection of any taking of interest on a loan, a position that Pope Benedict XIV affirmed in his encyclical of 1745, *Vix pervenit*. Impressed by Ballerini's intelligence and learning, this pope asked him to produce a new and definitive edition of the works of Pope Leo I. The Ballerini brothers accepted this ambitious project and their edition of Leo's works (published 1753–1759) was highly regarded and later incorporated by Jacques-Paul Migne in the *Patrologia latina*.[2] Besides his publications Ballerini was entrusted with several significant tasks by Church leaders in Rome, Verona, Venice, and elsewhere. Ballerini was generally respected for his religious and moral integrity, an integrity that he sometimes took to extremes. Some contemporaries of his said that because of his very strict sense of morals, "he could not bear the burdensome task he had undertaken to hear confessions; he was afraid he might compromise his conscience." This seemingly means that he feared that he might tempted to leniency if he listened to people's personal stories.[3] Despite the rigorism of his moral views, he was by all accounts a mild, courteous man in his personal manner who tried to avoid polemical language when discussing controversial topics.

Pietro Ballerini wrote two major treatises on papal authority: *De vi ac ratione primatus romanorum pontificum, et de ipsorum infallibilitate in definiendis controversiis fidei* (Verona, 1766) and *De potestate ecclesiastica summorum pontificum et conciliorum generalium* (Verona, 1768). Of these, *De vi ac ratione* most expressly represents his determination to produce "un opera sistematica contro le teorie gallicane."[4] Systematic it

---

2. See A. de Meyer, "Ballerini, Girolamo et Pietro," *DHGE*, 6:400.

3. Facchini, *Il papato principio di unità*, 35, citing an early-nineteenth-century source, Luigi Federici, *Elogi storici de' piu illustri ecclesiastici veronesi* (Verona: Ramanzini, 1819), 3:116.

4. The phrase is Facchini's (*Il papato principio di unità*, 52). Regarding this motivation, Facchini (52–57) draws on letters and other personal papers of Ballerini. He does not, incidentally, cite here or elsewhere any works by or about any Gallican authors, and mentions Gallican authors only once, in passing, on 70.

definitely is, and Giuseppe Alberigo aptly attributes much of Ballerini's influence on later authors to the rigorously methodical way in which he crafts the formulae that became "practically definitive" on papal supremacy and infallibility.[5] This influence can readily be traced in *Pastor Aeternus* itself, as Tarcisio Facchini in particular has shown in great detail, both by citing terms and phrases in the council document and by noting how some of the council fathers cited Ballerini by name in the council discussions.[6] Hermann Pottmeyer calls Ballerini a "key figure" in the campaign against Gallicanism in the eighteenth century and says that his great influence clearly extends up to the First Vatican Council.[7] An important cardinal, Giuseppe Garampi, nuncio (1772–1785) to Poland and then to Austria, was one special promoter of Ballerini's books on papal authority. He led a network of people across Europe dedicated to the cause of Ultramontanism and he considered Ballerini's works the best of the many that he sent to these people.[8] Candido da Remanzacco justifiably comments that the banner of papal infallibility unfurled by Pietro Ballerini was raised by the fathers at Vatican I "on the very pedestal that Ballerini had constructed."[9] One will keep in mind, of course, that the monarchical papalist ecclesiology of Ballerini is essentially the same as that of Bellarmine, Orsi, and other authors of this school.

---

5. Giuseppe Alberigo, *Lo sviluppo della dottrina sui poteri nella Chiesa universale: Momenti essenziali tra il XVI e il XIX secolo* (Rome: Herder, 1964), 288. Alberigo devotes twelve pages to Ballerini, 288–300.

6. Facchini devotes special attention to tracing the influence of Ballerini at Vatican I, in a chapter (*Il papato principio di unità*, 201–213) and in an appendix (245–249), where he examines texts of *Pastor Aeternus* showing the language of Ballerini. See also on this Yves Congar's concluding essay in Bernard Botte et al., *Le concile et les conciles: Contribution à l'histoire de la vie conciliaire de l'Eglise* (Paris: Cerf, 1960), 302–303 and 305n.

7. Hermann Josef Pottmeyer, *Unfehlbarkeit und Souveränität: Die päpstliche Unfehlbarkeit im System der ultramontanen Ekklesiologie des 19. Jahrhunderts* (Mainz: Matthias Grünewald, 1975), 44–45.

8. Dries Vanysacker, *Cardinal Giuseppe Garampi (1725–1792): An Enlightened Ultramontane* (Brussels: Institut Historique Belge de Rome, 1995), 111–112.

9. Candido da Remanzacco, O.F.M. Cap., "Vita e opere di Pietro Ballerini (1698–1769)," *Studia patavina* 9 (September–December 1962): 487.

The Nature and Force of the Primacy

Pursuing the reasoning in Ballerini's stern dismissal of Article 4 of 1682 is quite illuminating, showing why there is no place for the *consensus Ecclesiae* in his vision of the Church.[10] Ballerini states plainly in the preface to *De vi ac ratione* that he is going to take issue with those Catholic authors who say that they accept a primacy of jurisdiction but who dissent regarding the faculties or prerogatives that belong to the primacy.[11] They evidently do not understand either the true "ratio" (nature) of the primacy or the "vis" (force) of its jurisdiction. The Catholic adversaries acknowledge, even in the fourth Gallican article itself, that the Roman Pontiff has the leading role in the issuance of dogmatic decrees, but they balk at agreeing that these are per se irreformable or infallible (xv). The adversaries say that they agree with the principle that there should be unity of communion and of faith with the Roman Pontiff by reason of the primacy. What they fail to see is the conclusion that follows strictly from this: that the primacy itself contains the force ("vis"), the coercive force, to preserve both kinds of unity, and especially the unity of all believers in the faith of the Roman Pontiff (xvi).[12] Spelling this out in rigorous systematic

---

10. None of the scholars who deal with Ballerini do more than mention what he says about the consensus of the Church. Facchini includes a perfunctory summary of Ballerini's treatment of the topic (*Il papato principio di unità*, 98–104) but does not discuss it, nor does he draw on Ballerini's *Appendix de infallibilitate*. Incidentally, throughout several chapters mentioning mistakes of Bossuet, there are *no* citations of any work by Bossuet (!). Ulrich Horst, O.P., in twenty-five pages (52–77) on Ballerini in *Unfehlbarkeit und Geschichte: Studien zur Unfehlbarkeitsdiskussion von Melchior Cano bis zum I. Vatikanischen Konzil* (Mainz: Matthias Grünewald, 1982), deals briefly with the consensus of the Church (65–67), but does not go into detail and does not draw on the *Appendix*. Michael Place, in *The Response Due to Papal Sollicitude in Matters of Faith and Morals: A Study of Selected Eighteenth-Century Theologians* (Ann Arbor: University Microfilms International, 1978), in a section on teaching authority in Ballerini (104–120), mentions but does not discuss the consensus of the Church. Candido da Remanzacco, in "Vita e opere di Pietro Ballerini," mentions but does not discuss the *consensus ecclesiae* (477–478), and does not deal with the *Appendix*.

11. Pietro Ballerini, *De vi ac ratione primatus romanorum pontificum, et de ipsorum infallibilitate in definiendis controversiis fidei* [Verona, 1766], ed. E. W. Westhoff (Monasterii Westfalorum: J. H. Deiters, 1845), xiii. This book of 397 pages will be cited hereinafter in the text.

12. The consistent translations for these key words, followed throughout here, are

fashion will be the task of his book, and since it is a rigorous system, Ballerini asserts, it is necessary to study the whole system (xviii, xix). An admirer of Ballerini like Candido da Remanzacco extols the strict logic of the system: "[F]rom a few principles he deduced with insuperable logic a complex of truth including papal infallibility."[13] But it needs to be noted also that the work embodies much painstaking research in not only Catholic works and authors but also Protestant and some others.

The whole work does proceed in clear and logical fashion, each chapter setting forth and demonstrating a single, precisely phrased proposition. Chapters 1 through 7 enunciate such basic propositions as that Peter received the primacy, a primacy that is one not simply of order but also of jurisdiction, and that is personal, of divine right, and based on Gospel testimony. But it is the *purpose* of the primacy, addressed in proposition 8, that is supremely significant in Ballerini's conceptualization of papal authority, for everything is *deduced* from Christ's *intention* in establishing the primacy. This must be understood clearly, he says, in order to clarify the precise force and jurisdiction of the primacy. The reason for the primacy, as even the Gallican Declaration agrees, is "the unity of the Catholic Church" (32). Christ assigned to the chief pastor the duty of preserving the unity of the Church, and he "foresaw and provided everything that was necessary to guard and conserve his Church and its unity" (39).

Proposition 9, asserting that the primacy must have "coercive force for catholic unity," bases itself on the guiding assumption that "God never commits an office to anyone without bestowing on him

---

as follows: *vis* is always rendered as "force," *potestas* as "power," and *auctoritas* as "authority." Thus, Ballerini's favorite phrase, *vis coactiva ad unitatem fidei,* is always rendered as "coercive force for the unity of faith." Though it may sound rather harsh, "coercive force" is the literal meaning of *vis coactiva,* and he does have available to him, and occasionally uses, the alternative words, *potestas* and *auctoritas.* It may be noted that both Facchini and da Remanzacco consistently render *vis coactiva* in Italian as "forza coattiva."

13. Candido da Remanzacco, "Vita e opere di Pietro Ballerini," 470. That logic he elsewhere calls "inexorable," 472.

the faculties suitable for accomplishing it" (40). Thus Jesus Christ certainly conferred on Peter the full power needed to achieve the end of the primacy, and this is the strictly coercive force to form and maintain unity of faith (41). The power must be certainly coercive. It must be that "force of compelling" (vis cogendi) that is proper to "jurisdiction," which "cannot be understood without the coercive force that obliges the subjects" (42). It would have done no good to give Peter the role of merely representing unity "if the force of compelling to unity had not been added to it" (44). Peter had to have, necessarily, the full power to impose the faith on his subjects, the members of the Church.

In addition to unity of faith, unity of charity and communion is also essential for the Church, and the Savior provided for that need also in the power he gave to Peter, as is spelled out in proposition 10 in chapter 10. In view of the need for complete unity of the Church, the primacy "was endowed with special and coercive force to preserve and keep firm the unity of both faith and charity" (52). In equally blunt language, proposition 11 states that the primacy is endowed with "force compelling [all] to unity of charity and communion, and faith" (53). The next three propositions and chapters, some 170 pages, present a detailed study of scriptural data and a quite extensive array of patristic testimony relating to papal primacy.

It is in his forty-page chapter 14 that Ballerini replies most directly and fully to the doctrine of Article 4. Tarcisio Facchini, as noted above, does not cite any Gallican sources in his book on Ballerini, but Ballerini himself shows extensive reading in Gallican literature and in records of meetings of the French clergy, including that of 1682. He has also read Bossuet's defense of the Gallican Declaration and devotes ten pages to a discussion of it (236–246). These Catholic adversaries, he says, do indeed see the principle of the primacy and profess that they accept it, but somehow fail to see its strict consequences. The great and pervasive error of their Gallican stance is the insistence on *imposing conditions* on the acceptance of papal authority. They say that one need assent to definitions of the Roman Pontiff only if it is evident that he is defining from the common faith and tradition of the apostolic Church, or if there is added at least the tacit consensus of the Church, from which one learns that it is the common faith (246).

Ballerini, in reply, will show that the necessity of assenting to papal definitions is not subject to any such conditions (247). Bossuet should be reminded of what he said in the *Variations* when he criticized Melanchthon for clinging to various pretexts for declining to accept papal authority. If each one, Bossuet there notes gravely, may appeal to his own reasons for considering papal authority oppressive, then the Church authority would become subject to the whim of all (252).[14] Any such conditions, Ballerini asserts, are incompatible with the unity of the Church. The power of the primacy must be deemed "absolute" (absoluta), for if it is to be a force apt and efficacious to preserve unity of faith, then it "must not be tied to any condition of human judgment or will" (ibid.). (It is characteristic of papalist authors to assume that the Roman Pontiff speaks with divine judgment and the episcopate with mere human judgment.) If we are not going to say that Christ provided badly for unity of faith when he established the Roman cathedra, then we must say that the Roman Pontiff has in his primacy "absolute force, which is not subject to any condition" (ibid.).

The Roman Pontiffs, when they assert a doctrine, certainly "proclaim from the common tradition the faith common at once to all the Catholic Churches" (253), and there cannot be any doubt about this. It is both superfluous and wrong to talk about any provisions being needed to judge the pope's exercise of the teaching office. The adversaries claim that definitions of the Roman Pontiff are not irreformable "nisi accesserit consensus Ecclesiae." If this condition were valid, says Ballerini, then "all the coercive force for unity of faith," which we have been attributing to the Roman Pontiff, "would

---

14. Ballerini correctly cites Bossuet's *Histoire des variations des Eglises protestantes*, 5:24 (Versailles: J. A. Lebel, 1817), in which four-volume edition the passage cited is found on 1:298.

be void" (255). The stipulation in Article 4 really denies the coercive force of papal definitions because it claims that they do not compel to unity "except after the consensus Ecclesiae is added" (ibid.). (The Gallican text, of course, pointedly omits such a chronological term as "after.") According to Scripture and the Fathers, Christ endowed the primacy with force that is by itself suitable and efficacious for obtaining its end, which is the unity of the Church. It has force enough "to compel the universal Church to unity" (256). But if that power depended on the *consensus Ecclesiae,* then "the force and the right to compel [*ius cogendi*] would not be a proper and personal prerogative of the primacy, but rather of the Church, whose consensus would bestow the force of compelling on the definitions." Moreover, it would be difficult in practice, and time-consuming, to obtain such consensus and easy for adversaries to impede it. "Accordingly, it is false that the power of compelling to unity, which Christ bestowed on Peter and his successors in the primacy, was tied to the condition of the consensus of the Church" (ibid.). When he committed to Peter the role of confirming the brethren in dissensions regarding the faith, "he committed it so that he [Peter] should compel them to assent, and hold them in unity, and did not derive the force of compelling from their consensus" (257). Clearly, for Ballerini the supreme power conferred by Christ on Peter is a divine given that is assumed to be perfectly well known to all faithful Catholics, and it should not even need to be defended.

The duty of filially obeying papal definitions certainly applies to bishops also, emphatically including any bishops who, on receiving a decree from Rome, feel that they want to examine it and judge the matter defined. "In Catholic bishops assent out of obedience is always to be assumed" (260). If there is some "liberty" to examine and study a papal decree, this "does not liberate them from the submission and assent that all owe out of obedience." The only liberty of examination or judgment that is "conceded" to Catholic bishops is that which was vouchsafed to the Fathers at Chalcedon after the promulgation of St. Leo's dogmatic epistle on the errors of Eutyches. They were not allowed ("non licuit") to dispute the definition. They were allowed, on reading over his definition, to add their judgment to the pontifical, exclaiming, "Peter has spoken through Leo!" so as to help persuade any dissidents to return to unity (ibid.).[15]

If bishops in their sees conduct any examination of a papal statement, they weigh the traditions of their own Churches and compare them with the apostolic definition. If their own concurs with it, they rejoice to have their tradition confirmed, happy to be reassured that their Church has retained the "true faith." If theirs differs from the Roman definition, they are admonished that they diverge from the truth, because the Roman faith is the touchstone. There is always the presumption of consensus in Catholic bishops. This includes those who receive papal decrees with some examination, who are always fewer, as well as the greater number who receive them with pious obedience (261).

Councils are not necessary in the life of the Church, but they can be useful aids to clarifying and promulgating the doctrines of the Roman Pontiff. They show that "the faith proposed and defined by the Roman See is at the same time the faith of the whole Catholic Church" (263). Moreover, there is no need for Roman synods or for expressions of the consensus of the Roman clergy, though popes sometimes issued doctrinal statements at such synods. "For the whole coercive force [of the synods] for the universal Church . . . takes its origin from the personal primacy and jurisdiction of the pontiff alone" (264). Ballerini does not generally give examples of what he considers ex cathedra papal definitions, but he does at one point offer several: Innocent I against Pelagianism, Celestine I against Nestorian-

---

15. The famous exclamation of the fathers at Chalcedon gets diametrically opposed readings from papalist and Gallican authors. Ballerini here offers the papalist reading: the council gratefully and obediently assents to the papal judgment. Gallican authors (e.g., Tournely, 2, 80) see the council as recognizing, after studying it, that the epistle of Leo expresses the traditional faith of the Church. Thus, they "receive" it. The consensus of modern scholarship leans toward the latter interpretation; see W. de Vries, *Orient et Occident: Les structures ecclésiales vues dans l'histoire des sept premiers conciles oecuméniques* (Paris: Cerf, 1974), 140–141; and see also Francis A. Sullivan, S.J., *Magisterium: Teaching Authority in the Catholic Church* (New York: Paulist, 1983), 67–68.

ism, Leo I against Eutyches, and Agatho against Monotheletism (293). He does not mention here that in all these instances the popes were speaking in conjunction with councils.

No Human Conditions

After Ballerini published *De vi ac ratione* in 1766, he wrote a much shorter treatise on papal infallibility, which he published in conjunction with his *De potestate ecclesiastica* in 1768. The shorter work, *Appendix de infallibilitate pontificia in definitionibus dogmaticis*, he describes in a prenote as a "compendium" of what he had said at greater length in *De vi ac ratione*.[16] In actuality, the *Appendix* is not simply a briefer version, for in it he says some things not in the earlier work. Even more rigorously deductive than *De vi ac ratione*, the *Appendix* affords further vivid insight into the whole conceptualization of papal authority that pervades the Roman ecclesiology, with particular reference to the reason for its very blunt and absolute rejection of any idea of reception or consensus of the Church.

Ballerini proceeds through a series of propositions, all strictly deduced from the starting concept enunciated in proposition 1: "Papal authority, established for the purpose of conserving unity, especially unity of faith, must be sufficient by itself for the obtaining of this end" (*App.* 209). God, when he establishes an office for some purpose, provides appropriate and sufficient means for certainly obtaining that purpose. This means, asserts proposition 2, that papal authority must be full jurisdiction, which is endowed with coercive force (*App.* 210).

Proposition 3 states emphatically the principle that rules out any notion of the consensus of the Church, and does so, incidentally, in language different from that of *De vi ac ratione*. If any authority is to be *per se sufficiens*, it must be such as not to need the support or help

16. Pietro Ballerini, *Appendix de infallibilitate pontificia in definitionibus dogmaticis*, as published together with Ballerini's *De potestate ecclesiastica* (Rome: Typis S. Congregationis de Propaganda Fide, 1850), 207. This brief work, totaling thirty-three pages (207–240 in this volume), will be cited hereinafter in the text as *App.* with page number.

of any other authority (ibid.). This proposition "overturns the condition of the consensus of the Church, which the adversaries demand," for if the apostolic authority to define matters of faith is endowed with suitable and sufficient power to preserve unity, then it must not need the consensus of the Church (*App.* 211). To say with the adversaries that the authority is sufficient, *if* the consensus of the Church is added to it, is to deny that it is apt and sufficient in itself. Papal authority does not need any support such as the consensus of the Church, a condition invented by the adversaries, "a new invention that was unknown in antiquity" and in Church history (ibid.). Indeed, such a condition would undermine any authority in Church or state: "Woe to the authority of superiors, even princes, if their precepts and laws do not have the force of obliging unless the consensus of the subjects is added" (*App.* 212).

It is at this juncture that Ballerini most strongly invokes the famous dictum of Irenaeus, doing so in terms that throw additional light on his basic understanding of papal teaching authority. Irenaeus, he says, certainly rejects any suggestion that the Roman See in any way depends on the consensus of the Church. Irenaeus says of the Church of Rome that "it is necessary for every Church to concur with this one because of its more potent principality."[17] In Ballerini's treatment of it, this is no longer simply a statement of a second-century author, but a mighty near-divine proclamation of papal supremacy, which seems almost to stand right beside the "Thou art Peter" of Matt 16 and the "Feed my sheep" of John 21. It is a statement not only authoritative in the strictest sense in itself, but one from which one can deduce a whole array of corollaries about the sovereign papal power.

Irenaeus, according to Ballerini, teaches that there is a necessity imposed on all the faithful in all Churches to concur with the Church having the primacy. "The primacy, which by its own force imposes this obligation, by its own force requires the consensus"

---

17. Irenaeus, *Adversus haereses*, 3.3.2.

(*App.* 212).[18] By virtue of its *potentior principalitas,* the Roman Church by itself alone is endowed with so much force "that it imposes on all the Churches the necessity of unity and consensus. When this one faith is known, the consentient tradition and faith of all the others is at once known" (*App.* 213). For Ballerini, the brief statement of Irenaeus is a powerful rejection of Article 4 of the Gallican Declaration. "Therefore, Irenaeus did not deduce the force of compelling all to unity from their consent, which he thought there is no need to inquire about or to learn; but rather deducing this consent from the coercive force of the Roman faith and primacy, he attributes to the Roman faith and primacy a force *per se sufficiens* to oblige all" (ibid.).

The next four propositions of the *Appendix* spell out further corollaries of this. Number 4 asserts that the authority of the Roman Pontiff, since it is sufficient to preserve unity in the entire Church, necessarily binds *all* Christians, singly and collectively, of whatever rank or station, including the episcopal. Proposition 5 adds that the authority that unifies the whole Church in faith imposes the obligation not only of external compliance but also of the inner assent and obedience of the mind. Such is the nature of faith. And "let no one think that bishops are excepted" from this duty of mental obedience, for they are obliged to obey no less than the rank and file of the clergy and laity (*App.* 216). Moreover, continues proposition 6, assent to papal definitions must exclude all doubt and all questioning as to whether the pontiff may have erred. "The internal assent proper to faith, by which the intellect is captured in the compliance of faith, cannot be conjoined with doubt; and accordingly simple doubt about a dogma is enough to violate faith" (*App.* 218).[19] This also follows rigorously from the starting principle: the authority necessarily *gives full certitude,* because otherwise it would not be sufficient to preserve the Church's unity of faith.

Hence also there must not be any talk about a need to check with the faith of any other parts of the Church. As Irenaeus has plainly

---

18. These are, of course, the words of Ballerini.
19. "Captured" renders *captivandus est.*

said, "the faith of all the other Catholic Churches must be the same as the Roman faith, which is the same as to say that the Roman faith is the same as the faith of all the Catholic Churches, that is, of *the Catholic* Church itself" (*App.* 219; emphasis added). Since this is so, "to ascertain the true Catholic faith, there is no need to inquire what is the faith of the other Churches; inquiring about and learning the Roman faith is sufficient" (ibid.).

Papal authority, states proposition 7, must be termed "infallible." Ballerini says that he deduces this from the infallibility of the whole Church, which according to the promises of Christ cannot err in the faith (*App.* 220).[20] Surely the primatial authority, which has the role and power to teach and ensure the unity of that faith, must also be infallible. As has been indicated throughout, there cannot be any conditions attached to this authority. "Hence unity with the Roman faith is absolutely necessary. Accordingly, the prerogative of infallibility that must be attributed to it is an absolute prerogative, and the coercive force for the unity of faith is equally absolute; just as the infallibility and the coercive force of the Catholic Church itself are absolute, which [Catholic Church] must adhere to the Roman faith, as we learn from Irenaeus" (*App.* 221–222).

Despite the very forceful way in which Pietro Ballerini asserts this monarchical conception of papal primacy, and despite the fact that he clearly considers it to be certainly true, he does not claim that it is a dogma of faith. Rather, he expressly acknowledges that it is not. In the latter part of the *Appendix,* he addresses the question whether papal infallibility must be believed with the assent of faith. He answers, "I do not say that it must be believed as a matter of Catholic faith that the pope in deciding controversies of faith is infallible" (*App.* 231). As a scholarly theologian writing in the 1760s, he knows that this has not been defined. "Something is not a dogma of faith that is controverted among Catholics and that has not yet been expressly defined by the Church. Thus the otherwise Catholic adversaries, who uphold the opinion contrary to papal infallibility, are not regarded as

---

20. He does not give references here.

heretics" (*App.* 251). Ballerini is aware that the brief *Inter multiplices* of Alexander VIII in 1690 simply stated that the Gallican Articles were "null and void." Thus he agrees, perhaps reluctantly, with the majority of the committee of theologians who studied the articles for several years in Rome, that they could not be termed "heretical."

Nonetheless, though not a defined dogma of faith, papal infallibility should be considered as certainly true, because it has been demonstrated by strict theological reasoning from certain premises. The adversaries are prevented only by their prejudices from recognizing this. But really it is wrong to dissent not only from statements that are defined of faith but also from "propositions that are validly deduced from certain theological principles and clearly demonstrated" (*App.* 231). Ballerini warns the adversaries to ask how they can be excused of all guilt before God if they impugn papal infallibility just because it is not defined and incite people to slight that authority, thereby withdrawing them from unity of faith. "Is not this clearly to oppose oneself to the institution and plan of Christ the Lord?" (*App.* 232)

It is puzzling how the idea gained currency that Ballerini bases his ecclesiology on the idea of "communion," for he really does not, though several authors have said that he does. Ulrich Horst says that Ballerini really hoped and expected, "by building his ecclesiology on the idea of *communio*, to reach a common ground with the Gallicans."[21] Though he surely wanted them to be convinced by the rigor of his argument, he had to be aware that this would be a simple conversion to his Roman view, not a "gradual meeting of minds."[22] Both Giuseppe Alberigo and Yves Congar also attributed this idea to Ballerini, and more recently William Henn has echoed it.[23] But Ballerini really did not build his ecclesiology on the idea of *communio*. His

21. Horst, *Unfehlbarkeit und Geschichte*, 58.
22. Horst uses this phrase ("allmähliches Einverständnis") in ibid., 77.
23. Alberigo, *Lo sviluppo*, 289; Yves Congar, O.P., "De la communion des Eglises à une ecclésiologie de l'Eglise universelle," in Yves Congar, O.P., and B. D. Dupuy, O.P., eds., *L'épiscopat et l'Eglise universelle* (Paris: Cerf, 1964), 259; William Henn, O.F.M. Cap., *The Honor of My Brothers: A Brief History of the Relationship between the Pope and the Bishops* (New York: Crossroad, 2000), 135.

starting point is Christ's establishment of the primacy to ensure unity in the Church, and communion is introduced only later, as a duty or obligation of the subjects. It is a duty that they cannot evade, because the Roman Pontiff is "endowed with power to compel them to unity of charity or communion as well as of faith" (53).[24]

It never occurs to Pietro Ballerini that there is anything anomalous about *compelling* people to unity of charity and communion. Christ taught his followers to love one another, and he really meant it. Thus to make sure that they do this he gave Peter the full and absolute power to force all of them to love each other (!) Likewise, the problem of unity of belief is in this ecclesiology also simply solved. Jesus provides one supreme teacher who is empowered to teach the Good News and to maintain the unity of faith of the community. They believe because he has the power to tell them what to believe, and if need be to force them to believe it. Certainly, there is consensus on the essential beliefs of the Church, but it is the consensus of obedience: all the members and pastors of the Church obey the supreme teacher to whom Jesus gave the power to teach these beliefs of the community. True Catholics are filled with great and reverent gratitude to the divine Son of God who graciously and benevolently bestowed this power on Peter. For Ballerini, to suggest that the Supreme Pontiff needs to have the consensus of the rest of the episcopate with him when he proclaims a doctrine means that you do not understand the clear promises of Christ to Peter. Or, much worse, that you think that Christ did not keep his promises, and did not confer on Peter the power that he said he would. This would seem to mean that you do not really believe in Jesus, and do not really believe in the divine institution of the papacy. This perception of any adversaries of papal infallibility is what fuels the urgency in Ballerini's determination to refute them decisively by showing that papal authority, being divinely instituted, is absolutely monarchical. Any talk of the consensus of the Church must be rejected as an attempt to impose human limitations on the divine work of God.

---

24. This is in the heading of chapter 11 of *De vi ac ratione*. *Communio*, incidentally, is not mentioned in the *Appendix*.

CHAPTER 6

Louis Bailly and Nicolas-Sylvestre Bergier

Louis Bailly and Nicolas-Sylvestre Bergier were admired in their own time as dedicated apologists for the Roman Catholic Church. Both defended papal primacy against the criticisms of Protestant and secular writers, but both also earnestly maintained the mainstream Gallicanism of the Declaration of 1682. Their books were for many years among the most widely used in French and other seminaries and in the small libraries of parish priests.

Louis Bailly, 1730–1808

A native of Bligny, Côtes-d'Or, Louis Bailly was a doctor of theology who taught dogmatic theology at the seminary of Dijon for twenty-five years, from 1763 until the Revolution. He spent the years of upheaval in exile in Switzerland, and on his return was offered the post of vicar-general in Dijon. But he declined to accept it and spent the rest of his life ministering to the poor at a hospice in Beaune, where he came to be greatly beloved and venerated by the people.[1]

---

1. Information about the life of Louis Bailly is sparse. Besides the very brief entry on him by E. Dublanchy in *DTC*, 2.1:37, there is J. Dedieu's entry in *DHGE*, 6:263–264, and an interesting account in

During his academic years he wrote several books that became major textbooks used in French seminaries for many years. His *De vera religione* was greatly admired as a defense of the Catholic faith against all adversaries. First published in Dijon in 1771, it went through three more editions within fifteen years.[2] His publisher noted with satisfaction that it was being used all across France not only in seminaries but at universities and by pastors.[3] Bailly dedicated this book to Bishop Apchon of Dijon, who was admired as an exemplar of "all the virtues of the bishops of the primitive church"; he once rushed into a burning house and rescued two children just before the house collapsed.[4]

Two of Bailly's books are major treatises in mainstream Gallican ecclesiology. His most important work was his eight-volume *Theologia dogmatica et moralis*, first published in 1789 and reissued and reprinted at least eighteen times over the next fifty years.[5] It was a very widely used seminary textbook during these decades, both in France and elsewhere.[6] In fact, it was used in about three-fourths of the seminaries of France well into the nineteenth century, until it was supplanted by papalist treatises. Austin Gough gives an interesting account of the popularity of this book and of the shock caused in France when Pius IX personally ordered that it be placed on the Index in 1852. Even many priests and prelates of the Ultramontane per-

---

René-François Rohrbacher, *Histoire universelle de l'Eglise catholique*, 3rd ed. (Paris: Gaume Frères, 1857–1859), 27:366–374.

2. *Tractatus de vera religione* (Dijon: E. Bidault, 1771). It consists of two very small volumes and was reissued in 1772, 1776, 1784, and again in 1841.

3. "Avertissement du libraire," at the beginning of Bailly's *Tractatus de ecclesia Christi* (Dijon: E. Bidault, 1771), ix.

4. Rohrbacher, *Histoire universelle de l'Eglise catholique*, 27:366.

5. *Theologia dogmatica et moralis*, 8 vols. (Dijon: E. Bidault, 1789). The many editions (or printings) included ten between 1835 and 1852. The later editions included some revisions in response to the progress of the Ultramontane viewpoint; that is, they played down Gallican tendencies and promoted the papalist viewpoint.

6. See Edgar Hocedez, S.J., *Histoire de la théologie au XIXe siècle* (Paris: Desclée de Brouwer, 1948), 1: 69, 71; also J. Audinet, "L'enseignement 'De ecclesia' à St. Sulpice sous le Premier Empire et les débuts du gallicanisme modéré," in Maurice Nédoncelle et al., *L'ecclésiologie au XIXe siècle* (Paris: Cerf, 1960), 118.

suasion, and also the papal nuncio Garibaldi, were well disposed toward it.[7] This multivolume work contains in its second volume a lengthy treatise on the Church, which in its main lines contains the same ideas as his earlier *Tractatus de ecclesia Christi*, first published in 1776. Both earnestly defend the ideas of the Gallican Church, specifically as set forth in the Declaration of 1682.

While Bailly's ecclesiology is clearly set forth in both of these works, it seems most advantageous for us to study its main lines in the later *Theologia dogmatica et moralis (TDM)*, adding at a few points things that occur only or more interestingly in the earlier work.[8] *TDM* is a work of great erudition, with profuse though not really comprehensive citation of sources, and presented in the manner of scholastic manuals, that is, in syllogistic form, beginning always with a question, his response to the question, usually in a proposition that he defends, then objections and responses.

There is certainly in the Church, Bailly asserts, a supreme and infallible judge of controversies, for Jesus Christ did not omit what every well-ordered society (*republica*) requires: an authority that can provide peace in the community by settling controversies in a decisive way (372–373). In the Church this authority must be recognized as infallible, for otherwise a controversy about the faith could drag on indefinitely. This essential infallible authority is not Scripture, nor is it any person's belief in the inspiration of the Holy Spirit. It is the Church. "The Church is endowed with active infallibility, [that is,] the *Ecclesia docens*, in matters that pertain to faith, morals, and general discipline, has been endowed by Christ with the privilege of infallibility, and consequently it is the supreme judge of controversies of the faith" (383).

Ecclesia docens consists strictly of the whole body of bishops together with the pope. It does not include the rank and file of priests,

---

7. Austin Gough, *Paris and Rome: The Gallican Church and the Ultramontane Campaign, 1848–1853* (New York: Oxford University Press, 1986), 195–198.
8. For *TDM* we are using throughout the edition of 1826. Since we going through his work on the Church, which is the second volume of this eight-volume set of textbooks, all references, hereafter given in the text, are to volume 2.

nor the laity, nor civil rulers (411–426). "The multitude of bishops joined with the Supreme Pontiff, with [at most] a few adhering to a different view, cannot err in judgments of faith, and thus is the rule of truth, even in time of persecution" (427). Bailly clarifies that complete unanimity of all the bishops is not needed. It is sufficient if a very large majority, enough to consider "moral unanimity," concurs on the doctrine in question (429). Throughout both books Louis Bailly defends Roman Catholic doctrine on papal primacy against Protestants, schismatics, and any other adversaries who deny it. He asserts that the Church is a monarchy, that the pope has real primacy of jurisdiction and not just of honor, that this is by divine law, and that the pope is the chief teacher of the faith. He also upholds, explicitly against Ultramontane authors, the essential beliefs of the Gallican Church and of others who do not believe in absolute monarchy in the Roman Catholic Church.

In *De ecclesia Christi,* he notes some forms of government that are found among various societies in the world. The government of the Church is not democratic, for Jesus Christ did not give to the people *(plebs)* any authority to govern or to teach the Church.[9] Rather, the Church's government is monarchical, though it is not an absolute or pure monarchy as the Ultramontanes claim. The Roman Pontiff is certainly "the head and chief of the entire Church (243), but his is a monarchical rule "tempered by aristocracy." By "tempered," Bailly means that "the rule of the Supreme Pontiff is not absolute, nor completely independent; the body of the *optimates,* that is the bishops, of the Church exceeds him in authority" (244). Bailly also rejects the idea, asserted by some papalist authors, that pure monarchy is in itself the most excellent of all forms of government, and that therefore Christ must have chosen it for the Church.

In his fifty-page treatment of papal primacy in *TDM,* Bailly unequivocally asserts that the Roman Pontiff has inherited the full authority of St. Peter. "By divine law blessed Peter had primacy of hon-

---

9. *De ecclesia,* 242. We are using the 1780 edition of this work.

or and of jurisdiction over the entire Church" (461). He supports this assertion with ten pages of traditional proofs from Scripture and early Church history (461–470). Contrary to this faith of Catholics, Protestants simply deny any papal primacy, "Greek schismatics" contend that all the bishops were made equal by Christ, and Edmond Richer claims that the keys of the kingdom of heaven were given to the community to be delegated to the pope and the bishops (471). "Against all these all [Catholic] orthodox teach that the Roman Pontiff obtained primacy of jurisdiction in the universal Church" (ibid.)[10]

Bailly's description of the pope's primacy of jurisdiction is actually very similar to that of papalist authors. Peter and his successors necessarily received all the authority needed "to serve unity of faith and integrity of discipline for the utility of the Church," and the primatial office cannot achieve this end unless it is endowed with some power and jurisdiction over the particular Churches (474). He adds a summary of things that jurisdiction entails as illustrated in Catholic Church history, a summary that is probably the most useful to be found in any of our authors, whether Gallican or Ultramontane. From the beginning of the Church, he says, the Roman Pontiffs have frequently exercised without significant vocal disagreement such acts as the following. They have reproved bishops who made mistakes, as Stephen corrected Cyprian in the controversy over rebaptizing persons baptized by heretics. They have often deposed bishops, though respecting the rights of the province concerned. They have prescribed laws and issued decrees on the faith for the whole Christian world. They have for good cause dispensed from canons passed by councils. They have often rightly used the right of excommunicating offenders throughout the world. They have been consulted about controversies of faith by people from all regions. They have convoked councils and presided over them either in person or by legates. They

---

10. Bailly does not cite any sources for his references to Richer or to the Greek schismatics, whom he does not identify as orthodox.

have received appeals from the judgments of other bishops. These acts of popes are all widely known and they are all acts that can be termed jurisdiction. This record surely shows that the Roman Pontiff has been continually recognized in the Catholic Church as having a primacy of jurisdiction (474–475).

Moreover, this primacy of jurisdiction belongs to the pontiff *iure divino*, by divine right or institution, and not by a concession from the Church. There is no trace in the historical record, says Bailly, of any such concession of authority from the community, either in the early centuries or since (475). The *Ecclesia gallicana*, he adds, concurs with the rest of the Church on this point (476). Also, the pope can even be called "universal bishop," if this means that he has authority in all parts of the Church, though not if it means that the bishop of Rome is the only bishop properly so called, with all others being simply his delegates (479). The idea of the pope as universal bishop was one of the points successfully pressed by the papalist majority at Vatican I and added to the dogmatic constitution *Pastor Aeternus*.[11]

Thus a number of genuine prerogatives belong to the papacy, for the pontiffs necessarily have all those without which the primacy of honor and jurisdiction cannot exist and function. Bailly lists some of these, all of them asserted against the Protestants. (1) The pope, having the *sollicitudo omnium ecclesiarum*, must be vigilant for the propagation of the faith and the execution of the canons. (2) He has the right to make laws in matters of faith, morals, and discipline that pertain to all the Churches, if the body of bishops does not seriously object. (3) Though he is not superior to a general council, he can dispense from the decrees of a council in some circumstances, for there are times when people need to be able to get redress from an unreasonable or inapplicable decree. (4) The primacy means that the pope is the center of Catholic unity in what concerns the faith and the sacraments (483–484). From all this it follows that the Catholic

---

11. DS 3060. This paragraph of *Pastor Aeternus* says that the pope's power over the entire Church is "vere episcopalis," though the expression "universal bishop" is not used.

Church is "Roman," that is, it is necessarily conjoined with the chair (*cathedra*) of Peter in communion of faith and sacraments (485). In his *De ecclesia* he comments that if you are not joined with the See of Peter, you are a schismatic.[12]

But the many genuine prerogatives belonging to papal primacy do not, contrary to the claims of the Ultramontanes, include infallibility. The pope can make a mistake in asserting a doctrine. "If the Roman Pontiff, what we think is scarcely possible and which is to be hoped will never happen, proposes an error on some article [of faith], and departs from the doctrine of the Church, then on that article he would not be the bond of Catholic union" (485). But even then the Apostolic or Roman *See* would still be the center of Catholic unity, for that Holy See can never defect from the true faith. If an individual pope made a serious mistake, either he would soon correct it himself or he would shortly be removed by the Church and replaced by another. Thus "the dignity of being the center of ecclesial communion, for which the Roman Pontiff is known, does not entail his inerrancy in matters of faith" (486). From the standpoint of Bailly and other Gallican leaders and authors, for the pope to make a mistake in a doctrinal statement would not be the unthinkable, perhaps apocalyptic, catastrophe that it would be for Ultramontanes like Muzzarelli. The Church is resilient enough, and has the resources, to take it in stride.

Bailly devotes a fourteen-page section of a chapter to maintaining the proposition: "The Roman Pontiff, even teaching ex cathedra, is not infallible in matters of faith, that is, his decrees are not irreformable, unless the consensus of the Church is present with them. Thus the fourth article of the Declaration of the Gallican Clergy" (487).[13] He asserts this against Ultramontane theologians, of whom he mentions by name Bellarmine, Cano, and Cajetan, though with-

---

12. *De ecclesia*, 168.
13. "Unless ... is present with" renders *nisi accesserit*. In *De ecclesia*, 180, he says "donec" instead of "nisi," suggesting consensus subsequens. "Nisi" is of course the word used in Article 4 itself.

out citing their works. He says that if Jesus Christ had wanted the Roman Pontiff to have this easy and handy means of eliminating controversies of faith, "surely the apostles would have expressed it in plain words, just as they expressed the infallibility promised to the Church and the whole college of apostles in open and very clear words" (487–488). If they had done this, then there would not have been any doubt about the infallibility of the pontiff, nor would there have been so much dispute among Christians on this matter (488).

In his brief summary of some historical data, Bailly cites instances of papal statements being restudied, or retreated, by councils before being accepted. The Fathers at Chalcedon, for example, seriously discussed the letter of Leo I on the doctrine of Eutyches before they decided that Leo had written a good statement of the true faith of the Church (489–490). Also undermining the papalist claim of infallibility, Bailly believes, are examples of popes "acting ex cathedra" in proclaiming the deposition of kings and the releasing of subjects from their oath of obedience. He cites Innocent IV at Lyons I in 1245 issuing a sentence of deposition against Emperor Frederick (490).[14] Even an infallible authority could not exercise a power that it did not possess, and popes who attempted to depose kings and emperors "usurped a power that did not belong to them at all" (491). Certain medieval popes not only overstepped themselves in trying to depose rulers, but presumed to teach the faithful an error in doctrine: namely, that they really possessed such an almighty power (491).

Papalist authors cite papal confirmation of councils as a proof that popes are infallible. They say that councils are considered ecumenical and infallible only when their pronouncements are approved by the pope. This must mean that papal power is the really infallible and supreme power from which the council receives its authority (495).[15] "Nothing," replies Bailly, "is more futile than this argument, in which the Ultramontanes put so much stock; for to confirm councils is not

---

14. He actually cites the wrong pope, saying Innocent VI. The phrase "acting ex cathedra" is not a standard expression.
15. He does not give any references to Ultramontane authors.

to judge and weigh them, and confer power on them, but to assert and defend them as firm" (ibid.).

But nonetheless, Bailly continues, the Roman Pontiffs have earned through many centuries a special and unique place in the preservation and continuity of the Catholic faith: "[A]lthough not gifted with the privilege of inerrancy, they still can be likened to a rock, because they receive richer graces to remain stable in the faith, and to confirm in the faith the whole flock of Christians whose shepherd they are; and truly the Roman Pontiffs have outshone all others in faith and dignity in the various centuries of the Church" (494).

Though he includes in the proposition that he is defending in this section the *nisi accesserit* clause of Article 4, Bailly does not discuss here the consensus of the Church. We find it in several other places in *TDM* and in his *De ecclesia*. He does not comment on the options of antecedent, concomitant, and subsequent consensus, but he does devote a chapter to the question of the tacit consensus of the bishops to papal statements. In it he asserts a lengthy and rather unwieldy proposition: "A dogmatic constitution of the Roman Pontiff, sent to all Churches with the name Catholic, accepted expressly either in pastoral mandates or in other writings by the bishops in the area where the controversy began, with the other bishops around the world silent, is an irrevocable judgment of the Church; or what is the same thing, the silence of the bishops in that case is an indication of tacit consensus, and true approbation" (439). This is especially true, he adds, if it is a situation in which they would have had to speak out if the papal statement did seem to contain some error regarding faith or morals or the general discipline of the Church (441). It is the combination of papal judgment and that of the episcopate that gives a doctrinal statement its "irrevocable" character.

It is the Church's bishops, by virtue of their authority to teach and maintain the faith, who have the responsibility to speak and act if a papal statement seems in some way deficient. The faithful, including the rank and file of the priests, Bailly says in *De ecclesia,* should not presume to judge papal statements. Indeed, even "if there has been an error, an individual should not speak out until the Church, or body of bishops, has declared its mind; he should wait for their judgment."[16] But the bishops, since the deposit of faith has been entrusted to them, and since they are constituted judges by Christ, if they see an error should speak out and urge their fellow bishops to take some corrective action. In the meantime, the members of the Church should profess the faith of the Apostolic *See,* that is, of the popes taken collectively, and also of the present pope as regards his teachings on other topics up to the present. The papacy itself remains always the bond of union and the center of ecclesial communion, even during periods of controversy on particular points of doctrine (219). Considering all his strong affirmations of the paramount role of the Roman Pontiff in the Church, Bailly surely would have been genuinely hurt if he could have heard Pius IX refer to him, by name, as an "enemy of the Holy See."[17]

Some Ultramontane authors claim, Bailly notes in *TDM*, that the greater number of bishops in Christendom believe in papal infallibility, and they sometimes allege that the bishops of Italy, Spain, Germany, and Poland think this. In response, Bailly says that nothing has ever been defined on the present controversy, and such a doctrine, whatever Ultramontanes may say, does not belong to the faith. "Thus it is a matter of a mere opinion, about which various theologians and bishops have different ideas; moreover, it can happen that a false opinion is more common among theologians, for Christ promised that he would be with the greater number of bishops in what pertains to the faith [and] is defined or handed on as dogma, not in what is a matter of mere opinions." He adds that it is not at all certain how many bishops believe in papal infallibility. "There are many in Spain, Germany, and Poland who hold the contrary opinion" (499).

---

16. *De ecclesia,* 220.
17. See the excerpt of a letter of Pius IX in Daniel Moulinet, "Un réseau ultramontain en France au milieu du 19e siècle," *Revue d'histoire ecclésiastique,* 92 (1997): 100n; also Gough, *Paris and Rome,* 198.

Nicolas-Sylvestre Bergier, 1718–1790

Even more than Bailly, Nicolas-Sylvestre Bergier became known as a learned, dedicated, and talented defender of the Catholic faith. His numerous books were all written with the intention of responding to attacks on the Church by the rationalist and secularist thinkers who dominated intellectual life in the eighteenth (and the nineteenth) century in France. Born the son of a schoolteacher in the small town of Darney, which at that time was in the diocese of Besançon, Bergier had a great zest for studies in many subjects from his earliest years.[18] He attended a local school and then the university in Besançon, obtained a doctorate in theology, and was ordained priest in 1744. He then pursued further studies in Paris. Whether the bishop of Besançon appreciated his scholarly ability is unclear, for he appointed him pastor of a country parish at Flangebouche. Bergier served humbly in this position for sixteen years, and is said to have earned the love and esteem of the people. In 1764 he was made director of a college in Besançon that had been a Jesuit school until the expulsion of the Society of Jesus from France in 1763, and it was during his five years here that he began the steady stream of books for which he is known. In 1769 the archbishop of Paris invited him to be a canon of Notre Dame. He spent his last years at Versailles as a confessor of several members of the royal family, and died there on April 9, 1790.

18. For the life and work of Nicolas-Sylvestre Bergier, see the entry on him by E. Dublanchy in *DTC*, 2.1:742–745. There are much briefer entries on him by R. Chalumeau, in G. Jacquemet, ed., *Catholicisme* (Paris: Letouzey, 1956), 1:1464; and A. de Meyer, in *DHGE*, 8:4771–4772. Closer to Bergier's own time are two admiring and informative pieces. An author whose name we do not know wrote a "Notice historique sur l'abbé Bergier," published at the beginning of Bergier's posthumously published *Plan de la théologie par ordre de matières* (Besançon: Outhenin Chalandre, 1831), 1–23. Rohrbacher includes a lengthy section on Bergier in *Histoire universelle de l'Eglise catholique*, 27:374–391. A valuable more recent work adds greatly to our knowledge of Bergier: Ambroise Jobert, ed., *Un théologien au siècle des lumières: Bergier, correspondance avec l'abbé Trouillet, 1770–1790* (Lyon: Centre André Latreille, 1987). Jobert gives a thirty-page introduction on the life and work of Bergier, not dealing, however, with ecclesiological issues.

The author of an interesting "Notice historique" on Bergier says: "In the middle of a century of unbelief he picked up the gauntlet thrown down by irreligious philosophy, and consecrated all his strength and talent to the defense of the faith."[19] In the face of the Enlightenment's dismissal of religion as obscurantism and superstition, his books reaffirm Catholic beliefs and traditions and show considerable erudition and literary style. They include *L'origine des dieux du paganisme et le sens des fables découvert par une explication* (2 vols., Paris, 1767), *Le déisme réfuté par lui-même ou examen des principes d'incrédulité répandus dans les divers ouvrages de J. J. Rousseau* (2 vols., Paris, 1765), *La certitude des preuves du christianisme, ou réfutation de l'examen critique des apologistes de la religion chrétienne* (Paris, 1767), and *Apologie de la religion chrétienne* (2 vols., Paris, 1769), intended as a refutation of d'Holbach's *Christianisme dévoilé*.[20] These books earned great respect for Bergier as a defender of the Catholic faith in his time. Louis Ducros, for example, says that he was "the most laborious and celebrated Christian apologist of the eighteenth century."[21] R. R. Palmer calls him "the most prominent champion of Catholicism in the latter half of the [eighteenth] century."[22]

For the longer term, Bergier's fame rests particularly on two major works. One was his *Traité historique et dogmatique de la vraie religion, avec la réfutation des erreurs qui lui ont été opposées dans les différents siècles* (12 vols., Paris, 1780). This work was soon translated into Italian and German. In this work, says the "Notice," Bergier "has assembled the sundry principles of the impious of all the centuries, and formed a kind of body of their doctrine in order to discuss methodically the reproaches that they make against religion."[23] This work includes

19. "Notice historique sur l'abbé Bergier," 1.
20. The dates given in each case are the first publication of the book; most of them went through several editions.
21. Louis Ducros, *Les Encyclopédistes* (Paris, 1900; New York: Burt Franklin, 1967), 200.
22. R. R. Palmer, *Catholics and Unbelievers in Eighteenth-Century France* (Princeton: Princeton University Press, 1939), 46.
23. "Notice historique sur l'abbé Bergier," 9.

some ideas broadly related to ecclesiology that can be mentioned in passing here. Bergier describes three revelations, the "primitive," the "Mosaic," and the "Christian." His concern in the first of these is to show that belief in one God dates from the beginning of humanity and really antedates polytheism and idolatry. Thus Christianity can be considered the fulfillment of a single continual revelation, and the Church can be thought of somehow consisting of all the monotheistic believers in history. This idea influenced Lamennais's thought on the development of religion[24] and was adopted by Rohrbacher in his grand and universalistic vision of the Church.[25]

But probably the most famous and widely used book of Bergier is his *Dictionnaire théologique,* or *Dictionnaire de théologie,* originally published in 1788.[26] Readers found this comprehensive work, which offers articles on several hundred topics relating to religion, both informative and interesting. A striking and controversial aspect of this work is that it was included in the *Encyclopédie* of Diderot and his associates as the section on religion. Some thought that Bergier should not have done this, on the grounds that a Catholic theologian should not collaborate with the antireligious editors of the *Encyclopédie* and give the impression of approving their work. But before making this arrangement with them, he had seriously consulted with responsible Catholic friends and with the archbishop of Paris, who encouraged him to do it.[27] The author of the "Notice" comments that Bergier legitimately thought that if he did not supply the articles on religion, it would have been done by someone unfriendly to, and probably less

24. Louis LeGuillou, *L'évolution de la pensée religieuse de Félicité Lamennais* (Paris: Armand Colin, 1966), 29–32.
25. See Richard F. Costigan, S.J., *Rohrbacher and the Ecclesiology of Ultramontanism* (Rome: Università Gregoriana Editrice, 1980), 125–137. Actually, this very expansive idea of the Church has a long history in the concept of the *Ecclesia ab Abel,* in which the Church is considered to consist in some sense of all the just beginning from Abel. See Yves Congar, O.P., "Ecclesia ab Abel," in *Abhandlungen über Theologie und Kirche* (Dusseldorf: Patmos, 1952), 79–108.
26. The first edition, Paris, 1788, appeared in three quarto volumes and was soon followed by an eight-volume edition in 1789. The latter is the one used in the present study. Subsequent references to this work will be given in the text.
27. "Notice historique sur l'abbé Bergier," 10–14; *DTC,* "Bergier," 743.

informed about, Catholicism.[28] What is actually more surprising is that the Encyclopedists gave such a part in the project to a zealous Catholic apologist.

Bergier's Gallican ecclesiology can conveniently be seen in several articles of the *Dictionnaire*, articles that Ultramontane editors of later editions in the nineteenth century largely rewrote in a papalist direction.[29] Rohrbacher, though a very zealous Ultramontane, admired Bergier so much that he was willing to overlook his rejection of papal infallibility and stress his genuinely Catholic devotion to the infallibility of the Church against Protestants and unbelievers.[30] He says of Bergier that he was "the most laborious and the most complete of modern apologists," and "his writings are solid and estimable."[31]

Four articles in which Bergier's Gallican Church viewpoints are elucidated in the *Dictionnaire* are "Gallican," "Infaillible," "Infaillibilistes," and "Papauté, pape." In all four, Bergier's apologetic concern comes through clearly, for he consistently defends Roman Catholic beliefs and traditions against the accusations of the Protestants and the *incrédules* of modern times, and in some places the schismatics of the east. In particular he defends the papacy, both the doctrine of papal primacy and the historical record of popes, from the unjust accusations of these adversaries. In the article "Gallican" he states that the French, in trying to maintain the "liberties of the Gallican Church," are certainly not asserting some kind of complete independence from the rest of the Catholic Church or from the papacy. "On the contrary, no church has been more zealous in every age than that of France to preserve unity of faith and of doctrine with the Apostolic

---

28. "Notice historique sur l'abbé Bergier," 12–13. On this see also Jobert's introductory chapter in *Un théologien au siècle des lumières*, 27.

29. On these revisions of Bergier's articles, such as that by Thomas Gousset in 1838, see *DTC*, "Bergier," 743; Hermann Josef Pottmeyer, *Unfehlbarkeit und Souveränität: Die päpstliche Unfehlbarkeit im System der ultramontanen Ekklesiologie des 19. Jahrhunderts* (Mainz: Matthias Grünewald, 1975), 108–109. On the ecclesial significance of Gousset's work, see Richard F. Costigan, S.J., "Tradition and the Beginning of the Ultramontane Movement," *Irish Theological Quarterly* 48 (1981): 38–40.

30. Rohrbacher, *Histoire universelle de l'Eglise catholique*, 27:386.

31. Ibid., 27:374, 391.

See, and none has sustained with more force the authority and the jurisdiction of the Sovereign Pontiff over all the churches of the world" (3, 536). But she has always believed that that authority is neither despotic nor absolute, but rather that it is limited and regulated by the ancient canons, that is, "those of the first five or six centuries of the Church." The discipline of those earlier centuries is to be preferred to "that introduced later by virtue of the False Decretals of the popes, by which their authority over the Churches of the West was pushed much farther than in the previous centuries" (ibid.). (In the article "Papacy," he says that legitimate papal primacy was established long before the False Decretals, and also that the forgers were not instructed by the popes to do what they did [6, 203].)

It is also by virtue of our convictions that "we do not attribute personal infallibility to the Sovereign Pontiff, even in dogmatic decrees addressed to the whole Church, nor any power, even indirect, over the temporal [authority] of kings" (3, 536). The Church of France professed these beliefs in the Declaration of 1682, but "you should not believe that the contrary doctrine, commonly held by the theologians of Italy, is that of all the rest of the Catholic Church. The greater number of German, Hungarian, Polish, Spanish, and Portuguese theologians think about the same as those of France" (ibid.). He does not cite any names or sources on this.

In the article "Infaillible," Bergier upholds the Catholic doctrine of the infallibility of the Church. Against all the "heterodox sects" that do not believe that the "body of pastors" is infallible, he says, "Catholics maintain that this body, whether dispersed or assembled, is infallible" (4, 316). When a doctrine is taught by all the bishops, "the uniformity of their teaching is sufficiently known to all the Church by the profession that they make of being in communion of faith and doctrine with the Sovereign Pontiff" (4, 319). Heretics and unbelievers sometimes allege that every Catholic bishop claims to be infallible, but this is untrue. An individual bishop knows that he can be certain of teaching the truth "only as long as he remains united in belief and doctrine with the entire body of his colleagues" (4, 321).

"Infaillibilistes," Bergier says at the beginning of the next article, is a name sometimes given to those who say that the pope is infallible; that is, that when he addresses to the whole Church a dogmatic judgment on a point of doctrine it is not possible that this statement is in error. "This is the sentiment common to Ultramontane theologians; Bellarmine, Baronius, and others have maintained it with all their strength" (4, 323).[32] In this article, Bergier maintains the doctrine asserted in Article 4 of the Declaration of 1682. The French word he uses for "consensus" is of interest, though of probably only minor significance. In the wording of Article 4 that he offers here, a decree of the Roman Pontiff is not irreformable "until it is confirmed by the acquiescence of the Church" (4, 323). If *consentement* has a relatively juridical connotation, *acquiescence* could have a more general sense of "agreement." In any case, like other Gallican authors whom we have studied, Bergier does not really assert a doctrine of *consensus subsequens*, whereby the episcopate gives or withholds its agreement after the pope has spoken. A few pages later, he says that the needed acquiescence of the greater number of bishops may be either express or tacit. Tacit agreement of the bishops with the pope is sufficient to give a doctrinal statement "the same authority and the same infallibility as if it were passed by a general council" (4, 325). He does not explicitly discuss either *consensus antecedens* or *consensus concomitans*.

But Bergier is clear that the history of the councils from Jerusalem to Trent shows that "the force of the decisions [of a council] stems from unanimous agreement [*concert unanime*] or the plurality of votes," and not from the pope presiding over the council or confirming its decrees (3, 324). Moreover, if a pope had spoken on the question, "the bishops assembled in council did not believe themselves less entitled to examine it anew and to judge it" (ibid.). Bergier adds a perceptive reflection. "We say that the essential function of the pastors of the Church is to bear witness to the universal belief [of the

---

32. He does not give any references to Bellarmine or Baronius.

Church] and that the witness of the Sovereign Pontiff alone is not able to produce the same degree of moral certitude that results from a very great number of witnesses united" (3, 325).[33] He continues: "As the head of the universal Church the Sovereign Pontiff is without doubt well instructed in the general belief; he is the principal witness to it. But the witness that he bears to it, joined to that of the very great number of bishops, has a quite other force than when he is alone." Bergier believes in the "supernatural and divine infallibility of the Church," restating what he said in the previous article, but he earnestly thinks that "it is not possible to place on the same basis the infallibility of the Sovereign Pontiff" (ibid.). He thinks that the more collegial and consensual authority of the early centuries really is stronger, and has a stronger foundation in tradition, than a purely monarchical kind of authority in which everything depends on one man. He comments that the doctrine of papal infallibility is not needed to protect the Catholic faith from all danger. If it ever happened that "the Sovereign Pontiff made a mistake and proposed a false opinion, the Church, far from being led into error by this judgment, would strongly bear witness, through the speaking out of the body of pastors," to the authentic mainstream tradition of the Church (3, 324). For Bergier as for Bailly, the faith of the great Church community does not stand or fall on one man's judgment.

This article concludes with another interesting comment. Bergier says that the heterodox are uttering a "puerile sophism" when they claim that the Catholic doctrine of the infallibility of the Church is undermined by the dispute of French theologians with Ultramontanes about papal and conciliar infallibility. This controversy, though it goes on generation after generation, does not affect the Catholic belief in the infallibility of the whole Church. "Never has any Catholic theologian of any nation doubted that a general council that represents the whole Church is infallible; none has denied that the judgment of the Sovereign Pontiff, confirmed with the acquies-

---

33. Pottmeyer calls attention to this passage and quotes part of it, *Unfehlbarkeit und Souveränität*, 109n.

cence of the body of pastors, even dispersed, has the same authority and the same infallibility as a general council" (3, 325).

Bergier's earnest defense of the Roman Catholic Church against all unfriendly critics is especially clear throughout his twenty-eight-page article "Papauté, pape" (6, 184–212), in which he consistently and ably defends the papacy against the allegations of Protestant and secular polemicists. The Catholic belief in papal primacy is well known to the adversaries, but they habitually misrepresent and caricature it. "The Catholic belief is that St. Peter was not only the head of the apostolic college but the pastor of the universal Church, that the Roman Pontiff is the successor of the prince of the apostles, that he has like him authority and jurisdiction over the whole Church, and that all the faithful, without exception, owe him respect and obedience" (6, 184).[34] But theologians of all the "heterodox sects," hostile to any such belief in the papacy, allege that we make the pope the lord of the world and even a "kind of god on earth, and attribute to him despotic, arbitrary, and tyrannical power, the authority to make new articles of faith, to institute new sacraments, to abrogate the canons and ecclesiastical laws, [and] absolutely to change Christian doctrine" (ibid.). These are all obvious calumnies, says Bergier, for the powers allegedly claimed for the papacy are "directly contrary to the duties of a spiritual father and of a pastor of the faithful." The adversaries mistakenly confuse "supreme power with absolute, unlimited power not subject to any law" (6, 185). In Catholic theology the pope is infallible only when he teaches in union with the Church. Bergier offers a quite insightful comment when he says that the privilege given to Peter and his successors was given "not for their advantage but to render indefectible the faith of the Church; thus, it cannot be pushed farther than that indefectibility requires" (6, 193–194). A few pages later Bergier adds, still responding to Protestant critics: "The pastors [in the Roman Catholic Church] undergo

---

34. He cites the Council of Florence, without giving a reference. What he says does express the main substance of the "Decretum pro Graecis" on papal primacy; see DS 1307.

first the yoke that they impose on the faithful, for they recognize that it is not permitted to them to teach anything else than what they have received" (6, 196). The point he makes is, of course, deeply traditional, recognized by Vatican I also when it says in *Pastor Aeternus* that the help of the Holy Spirit was promised to the popes "not that they might make known any new doctrine but that, with his [the Holy Spirit's] assistance, they might devoutly guard and faithfully expound the revelation or deposit of faith transmitted through the apostles."[35]

In this lengthy article devoted to defending the papacy, Bergier urges that neither popes nor anyone else who lived in distant past times should be judged solely by today's norms (6, 199). If popes in some situations made statements that sound excessively strong today, it should be remembered that they did so in the stress of heated controversy, and moreover would ordinarily speak out only after being called upon to do so by some of the parties involved in the controversy (6, 198). Bergier says that since the Middle Ages, "[t]he power of the popes has become much more limited in the measure that things have changed, that order is established in the clergy, and in civil society" (6, 200). There is poignancy in this comment for he wrote it in 1788, the year before the beginning of French Revolution. He earnestly says that modern popes have returned to the "tender and paternal charity" of the first successors of Peter. "What just grounds of reproach," he asks, "have they given, even to their enemies, for more than a century?" (ibid.) It is unreasonable and "absurd in the eighteenth century to blame popes for faults committed by their predecessors seven hundred years ago" (6, 210). Bergier believes that truthfulness should be the rule for all participants in discussion and controversy, especially in theology, and certainly when studying the papacy. "The first duty of a theologian is to be just, and to seek the truth in good faith" (6, 208). Bergier's historical sensitivity shows the perspective gained in many years of study of Church and other history.

35. DS 3070.

Nicolas-Sylvestre Bergier and Louis Bailly were greatly respected in their own day as dedicated and effective defenders of the Roman Catholic Church, explicitly and strongly including the papacy. Both concur with the other Gallican authors studied in this book in accepting a real papal primacy of jurisdiction and not merely of honor. They also recognize the Roman Pontiff as the chief teacher of the faith, a chief teacher who should be respected as exercising genuine leadership in preserving the faith through countless controversies extending over many long centuries. They recognize that the papal magisterium is in a very real sense monarchical, and that a monarchical authority has a unique ability in many situations to preserve unity in a multinational community of faith. However, like Tournely and Bossuet and the other Gallican authors studied here, they do not believe that the monarchical papal teaching authority has the particular prerogative of infallibility in isolation from the whole body of the episcopate. There really is no reason to say that they voice this viewpoint only because of the one Declaration of 1682 and not because it is the fruit of their personal study of theology and Church history.

CHAPTER 7

César-Guillaume La Luzerne
1738–1821

A Respected Scholar-Bishop

One of the few greatly admired bishops of France in his time, César-Guillaume La Luzerne had a distinguished career in the Church before the Revolution, was for a while a leader in the Revolution before going into exile, and wrote several books on religious and political topics, including a closely reasoned defense of the Gallican Declaration.[1] A gifted member of a noble family of Normandy, La Luzerne became agent-general of the Clergy of France in 1765 only three years after ordination and was made bishop of Langres by Louis XV in 1770.[2] When the Revolution began, La Luzerne, though devoted through-

---

1. The one readily available source on the life and work of La Luzerne is L. Marchal's article in *DTC*, 8.2:2465–2466. H. Hurter, S.J., offers a brief entry on him in *Nomenclator literarius recentioris theologiae catholicae* (Oenoponte: Libraria Academica Wagneriana, 1895), 3:737–739.

2. Concerning the role of the agent-general of the Clergy of France, see John McManners, *Church and Society in Eighteenth-Century France* (New York: Oxford University Press, 1998), 1:150–154. Much interesting information on this is given in Louis S. Greenbaum, *Talleyrand, Statesman Priest: The Agent-General of the Clergy and the Church of France at the End of the Old Regime* (Washington, D.C.: Catholic University of America Press, 1970). See also Roland Mousnier, *The Institutions of France under the Absolute Monarchy, 1598–1789* (Chicago: University of Chicago Press, 1979), 1:367–368.

out his life to the traditional monarchy, concurred with many of the demands of the revolutionaries.[3] He knew that there had been many injustices and abuses of power and that France deserved and needed better government. Unlike many other monarchists, he understood that calling for the reform of abuses does not mean that one wants to undermine authority. Rather, to want reform means to want the authority "to be respected, blessed, cherished, and no longer the object of murmurs and the pretext of complaints," but "to be more stable and strengthened."[4] For a few months in 1789 he served as president of the new National Assembly, but as the Revolution steadily became more radical, with more tendencies toward violence, he resigned and soon went into many years of exile. He refused to return to France during Napoleon's rule, for he could not accept the emperor as the legitimate ruler of France. Finally returning in 1814, he was welcomed back to his see and was greatly honored by Louis XVIII, who persuaded Pius VII to make him a cardinal in 1817.

La Luzerne keenly pursued many intellectual interests all his life and devoted his writing talents especially to defending the Catholic faith in an age of turmoil and unbelief. The enforced leisure of exile enabled him to write extensively. Some of his major works include his *Dissertations sur la vérité de la religion, sur les prophéties, sur l'existence et attributes de Dieu, etc.* (6 vols., Langres, 1802–1810) and his *Explication des évangiles* (5 vols., Lyons, 1807). Recognized as an eloquent defender of the Church and of the primacy of spiritual values over political, Cardinal La Luzerne was also respected as an able proponent of the Gallican ecclesiology. Edgar Hocedez notes that as "a zealous prelate and orator of renown," he was "among the most illustrious defenders of this doctrine."[5] In particular, Henri Maret, one of the few defenders of Gallicanism left by the time of Vatican I, considered

---

3. Joseph Charonnot, *Mgr. de La Luzerne et les serments pendant la Révolution* (Paris: August Picard, 1918), esp. 2–7.

4. Charonnot quotes these ideas from La Luzerne but does not cite the specific source.

5. Edgar Hocedez, S.J., *Histoire de la théologie au XIXe siècle* (Paris: Desclée de Brouwer, 1948), 1:97.

La Luzerne second only to Bossuet in this respect and cited him frequently in his book on the general council. He was especially impressed by the cardinal's "merciless criticism" (critique impitoyable) of the notion of ex cathedra pronouncements.[6]

Joseph Charonnot is apologetic about the Gallicanism of La Luzerne and urges his readers to remember that the bishop was really always very devoted to the Holy See, especially against its revolutionary and schismatic enemies. "By word and example," he says in a summary sentence, "La Luzerne was an apologist for the rights and jurisdictional primacy of the Sovereign Pontiff."[7] He says that Pius VII recognized the piety and zeal of La Luzerne and quite willingly acquiesced in the king's request that he make him a cardinal.[8] Pius could not—fortunately, one surmises—have seen La Luzerne's book on the Gallican Declaration, which was published four years later in 1821. La Luzerne died later in that year, on June 27.

Papal Monarchy

At the beginning of *Sur la déclaration de l'Assemblée du Clergé de France en 1682*,[9] Cardinal La Luzerne states in a very brief "Avis de l'auteur" that he wrote this book "eight or ten years ago in emigration" with the intention of responding to Giuseppe-Agostino Orsi, who had undertaken a large-scale refutation of Bossuet's defense of the Gallican Articles (5). On returning to France in 1814, the year of the great military defeat and forced abdication of Napoleon, he thought that publishing it in such circumstances would be "unuseful." But now that Ultramontane ideas are being "defended and published by very estimable authors whose talents and virtues I honor, I believe that it is indispensable to publish this work to serve as a re-

---

6. Raymond Thysman, "Le gallicanisme de Mgr. Maret et l'influence de Bossuet," *Revue d'histoire ecclésiastique* 52 (1957): 410.
7. Charonnot, *Mgr. de La Luzerne*, 376.
8. Ibid., 377, not citing any source.
9. The original edition of this book was published in Paris by Méquignon-Junior in 1821. The edition used here is the 1843 new edition from the same publisher. We will cite this book by page number in parentheses in the text.

sponse to their maxims, and to maintain among us the precious and salutary doctrine of the Gallican Church" (ibid.). He does not name any Ultramontane authors here, but probably Joseph de Maistre, whose *Du pape* appeared in 1819, would have been the one foremost in his mind.

Proceeding into part I, entitled "Questions diverses," he reminds us of his large element of agreement with the Ultramontanes and then of the differences between their doctrines and the Gallican doctrines so mistakenly combated by "the learned Cardinal Orsi" (13). Gallican ecclesiology certainly recognizes that papal primacy is not simply a primacy of honor, but one of real jurisdiction. The preamble of the Declaration of 1682 reaffirms this essential Catholic dogma (14).[10] It is regarding "the *extent* of this pontifical jurisdiction that our doctrine differs from the Ultramontane system" (ibid.; emphasis added). We do not see that authority as being "as absolute as they believe it to be" (16).

Certainly, the most basic general concern of La Luzerne throughout this book is the rejection of the Ultramontane claim that the Church is an absolute monarchy, ruled by the Supreme Pontiff as an absolute monarch. This is the claim that the Gallican viewpoint sees as contrary to Scripture and the tradition of the Church. He says at the beginning of his principal chapter on this subject, "Orsi establishes as an incontestable principle that the government of the Church is monarchical, and as an immediate and necessary consequence that the pope, monarch of the Church, has a sovereign authority not only over all the members that make up the Church taken distributively but also over them taken collectively, and that he is not bound by the canons" (39).[11] Orsi does not, continues La Luzerne, take the trouble to prove this principle, which he regards as universally recognized (ibid.). For Orsi the Church is the kingdom of God on earth, and

---

10. He gives the whole text of the Declaration of the Gallican Clergy at the beginning of this book. Actually, the preamble affirms papal primacy but does not mention primacy of jurisdiction.

11. Unfortunately, La Luzerne usually does not cite Orsi's text either by book and chapter or by page number.

thus must have a king, the pope. Moreover, since "pure monarchy" is the most perfect form of government, this is certainly the form that Jesus Christ gave the Church (40). Thus in Orsi's ecclesiology of true and perfect monarchy, not only each member of the Church but the totality of the Church and all its members, both individually and collectively, depend on the monarch (ibid.). His inspiration, says La Luzerne, seems to be Roman laws and jurists, for he cites these in asserting his idea of the Church.

This reasoning, notes La Luzerne, is easily refuted. Human reasoning is not the source of ecclesiology. "It is not by likening it to human governments that one should infer what government Jesus Christ has given to the Christian society that is his Church; it is from Scripture and tradition that one must establish what constitution the Church has from its divine founder" (41). You certainly do not find anywhere that Jesus Christ has given the Church a government derived from civil constitutions. Thus Orsi's claim that the Church is a pure monarchy "is false" (ibid.). Gallicans hold that the constitution of the Church is "monarchy mixed with aristocracy," the aristocracy being of course the episcopate. The disagreement between Gallicans and the Ultramontanes has to do with the basic nature of the authority of the papacy, not just the manner of exercising it. "It is a matter of what tempers the authority; now, what tempers authority is not the use that one makes of it voluntarily and freely; it is the use that higher laws oblige it to make; it is the limit that is placed for it and that it cannot pass" (41–42). In the Gallican doctrine, the jurisdiction of the pope is tempered by canons that he does not have the right to infringe and by the episcopal body that has the power to resist him. But "in the Ultramontane system the power of the pope is tempered only by his [own] will, because he can do everything that he wants [*il peut tout ce qu'il veut*]" (42). A monarchical authority that is limited only by its own discretion is not monarchy tempered by aristocracy, but really just an arbitrary power.

La Luzerne dismisses Orsi's claim that Jesus chose pure monarchy for the Church because it is the most perfect form of government.

Besides being wrong in any case simply to borrow a form of government from the political realm, "one should not say that a certain kind of government is in itself the best and therefore Jesus chose it for the Church." Rather, "one should say that Jesus Christ gave a certain kind of government to the Church, and for this reason this is the best for it" (ibid.). The pure monarchy that Orsi wants is really "despotism," as is obvious from his references to the laws of the Roman Empire, which was certainly despotic.

La Luzerne makes short work of all of Orsi's monarchy exegesis. The "kingdom" often mentioned by Christ is the kingdom of God, not a kingdom of the pope (43). Together with the Ultramontanes, Gallicans certainly adore Jesus Christ as the supreme king. Also, "we recognize and revere with them the pope as his lieutenant, as his vicar, as the visible chief under the invisible chief of the Church on earth; but the lieutenant, the minister of the most absolute monarch is not himself an absolute monarch" (ibid.). No matter what titles he is decorated with, he has only the measure of power that has been conferred on him by his master. To understand this measure we need to go to the sources of Christian faith: Scripture and tradition.

Ultramontane writers often, unknowingly or more likely knowingly, caricature the Gallican ecclesiology in various ways. Thus Orsi claims that in the Gallican system the Church is neither properly monarchical nor aristocratic, but a kind of irregular republic, perhaps similar to the German Empire. "The absurdity of this statement leaps to the eyes. Never has any French Catholic imagined that each bishop in his diocese has an absolute authority and is not submitted to the Sovereign Pontiff, as the German princes in their states are independent of the emperor" (ibid.).

Orsi's three scriptural images—shepherd, householder, and head of the body—are all briskly dismissed by La Luzerne. One can at most draw some inferences from them about the way in which Christ wanted his ministers to guide his people. For example, the good shepherd story shows how concerned the pastor should be for every member of the flock (44–45). The head/body metaphor has very little significance for any moral body, such as the Church. The head of a physical body does rule the body as it wills. But in a moral body, like an assembly, "the rights accorded to the chief vary according to the laws that govern diverse assemblies" (47). The president of a judicial body, or a senate, does not have the absolute authority that Orsi attributes to the pope over all judges and senators.

Papal Power to Teach Doctrine

Among Gallicans' many significant areas of agreement with the Ultramontanes, continues La Luzerne, they agree that the pope's primatial power of jurisdiction includes the threefold powers of government, legislative, executive, and judicial, but do not believe that these powers are "as absolute as they claim" (20). It is with the pope's legislative power that La Luzerne places his principal discussion of papal teaching authority and the consensus of the Church. It will have been noted at a number of places in this study that the treatment of teaching authority in both Ultramontane and Gallican authors has a rather juridical quality. Both, in focusing on the question of what makes a doctrinal statement definitive or infallible, use the expression "irreformable," that is, not subject to a further authoritative or legislative act.

Concerning the pope's legislative power in the area of dogma, says La Luzerne, the Ultramontanes assert that Jesus Christ conferred on Peter and his successors the power to state infallibly what is of faith, and that the pope's statements made ex cathedra are irrefragable (ibid.). Gallicans basically agree with this, for Article 4 of the Declaration of 1682 says: "The Pope has the principal part in questions of faith, and his decrees apply to all the Churches and to each Church in particular." Considering that papalist authors consistently understate or ignore the general Gallican acceptance of the papal magisterium, it is useful to note things that La Luzerne states at this point. "We say, in consequence, that he decides with authority all questions of faith and morals, that he has the right to approve doctrines conformed to the Catholic faith, and to condemn those that are not, to apply various qualifications to propositions that he disapproves of, to give his approval or to stigmatize with his censures modes of expression that are conformed to or contrary to the doctrine of the Church" (ibid.).

La Luzerne then invokes the more controversial clause of Article 4. "But we maintain that the doctrinal decisions of the pope, though clothed with great authority, acquire the supreme degree of authority, the infallibility that renders them irreformable and irrefragable, only when the consensus of the teaching Church adheres to them" (ibid.). He comments only briefly on possible ways in which the consensus of the Church might be implemented. "We say that it is indifferent whether the consensus of the Church is antecedent, or concomitant, or subsequent to the pontifical decision; or whether it is given by the Church gathered or by the Church dispersed; whether it is express and formally enunciated by all the bishops, or given tacitly, that is, when no [sizable] part of them speak out against it" (20–21). We have noted that Ultramontane authors, and twentieth-century scholars, usually say that the Gallicans demand a *consensus subsequens,* whereby there would need to be some kind of process in which bishops of the world indicate their assent *after* the papal statement. La Luzerne's view is clearly much more flexible than this.

Thus, he continues, Gallicans do not consider the pope infallible in his decisions on the faith, but do believe, according to the word of Jesus Christ, that his faith is indefectible. The Ultramontanes confuse two things that Gallicans distinguish. "Infallibility, which we profess resides in a general council, and which the Ultramontanes say exists in the pope, consists in never falling at any time, even a short time, into any doctrinal error" (21). There is also indefectibility, which Gallicans say means that if the Roman Pontiff falls into an error in the faith, his fall is promptly repaired either by himself or at an early date by his successors. Thus the Holy See, the series of successors of St. Peter, cannot in matters of faith commit more than short-lived errors. La Luzerne considers this a unique prerogative of the See of Peter, one not shared by other bishops, and he also considers that such indefectibility is sufficient to ensure that the See of Peter continues to be the center of unity in the Church (ibid.). That is, to preserve the faith it is not necessary to claim infallibility for particular papal statements. La Luzerne does not mention the familiar terms *sedes* and *sedens* in this discussion, but he clearly has the ideas in mind.

Akin to papal legislative power in teaching the faith is his legislative power in disciplinary or administrative areas, "which according to the Ultramontanes is so universal and so absolute that he can not only make new canons of discipline, both particular and general, but can also annul, abrogate, and change according to his pleasure [*à son gré*] those that exist, even those that come from general councils, even those consecrated by the approbation of all the centuries, all the Churches, and by his own predecessors" (ibid.). Certainly, Gallicans do recognize that the pope's legislative power is very extensive, but they do not accept that it extends to absolutely all rules of discipline, or that he can purely by his own authority abrogate laws "consecrated by general respect" (22). The traditional canons of the Church, "since they have their stability from the union of common consent, cannot lose it except through the same concurrence of united wills" (ibid.). This consent of the community is as necessary for irreformability here as in teaching the faith. "When we say that the pope in the last resort is the judge of cases of faith, we do not exclude the necessity of the consent of the Church to imprint on his judgment the final character of irreformability" (23).

Papal Statements Ex Cathedra

For César-Guillaume La Luzerne, the expression *ex cathedra* was created by papalist theologians in modern times as a remedy to deal with the cases of popes who made mistakes in doctrinal pronouncements. "Theologians who sustain the infallibility of the pope, embarrassed by errors into which some Sovereign Pontiffs have fallen, have recourse to a distinction" (48). They distinguish three cases: (1) the pope writing in his own name but as a private doctor; (2) the pope teaching officially but not with the full solemnity of his authority;

and (3) the pope teaching with the full authority and solemnity of his see. It is the last that they term ex cathedra, and only it is to be regarded as infallible and irrefragable. This is the Ultramontane opinion.

Gallicans, who do not admit the infallibility of the Holy Father, but who recognize the indefectibility of the faith of the Holy See, do not recognize any decree of the pope as infallible by itself. "We believe that his dogmatic decrees, always respectable but not infallible, require exterior submission and do not impose the obligation of interior assent as long as they are not fortified [*munis*] by the consent of the universal Church, the only depositary, conjointly with him, of irrefragable authority" (49).

The Ultramontane doctrine that the pope is infallible when he speaks ex cathedra, errs ("pèche") in two basic ways: in its novelty ("nouveauté") and in its changeability ("versatilité") (ibid.). It is novel, for it is not found in the early centuries. Certainly, the question of how the community of faith can identify and preserve its most essential beliefs is of vital importance, and the early Church devoted much attention to it. But there is no mention in any ancient document of such an important kind of papal statement, and "never did antiquity attribute to the pope the prerogative of infallibility" (50). If there were such a thing as a papal ex cathedra pronouncement, which would definitively settle by itself any controversy, would we not find it mentioned in the early Christian sources? No, that kind of pronouncement was "unknown in ancient times, and has been imagined in modern times to get around an insoluble objection." It was invented by "the Ultramontanes of our days to palliate [*pallier*] the errors into which several popes have fallen" (ibid.).[12]

La Luzerne spells out over some seven pages his second major criticism, that of *versatilité*. This word in French is not favorable, for it means changeability or even fickleness. The main point of his criticism is the lack of clarity and what could be termed reliability in what papalists say about this papal teaching power. "The principle of

---

12. *Pallier* could also mean "obscure" or "conceal."

papal infallibility, but only when he speaks ex cathedra, should have been not only established by tradition, but even more clearly explained. The regulative principle of the faith should be as evidently defined as the articles of faith, since on this fundamental dogma depend the certitude and fixity of all the others" (51). If there are some infallible papal statements, the faithful need to be able to recognize them readily, so that they can be confident in assenting to them.

Some Ultramontanes say that you can recognize an ex cathedra statement because it is one that the pope issues "after a mature examination [*mur examen*]." "But how can you know the degree of attention that he devoted to the decree, and recognize there the character to which infallibility is attached?" (52) La Luzerne thinks that there is no persuasive answer to that question. He goes on to observe: "The most common opinion among modern Ultramontanes connects ex cathedra teaching to the counsels with which the pope surrounds himself." One these is Melchior Cano, O.P. (1509–1560), who seems to speak for a number of theologians when he says that "if ever a Roman Pontiff has erred in defining the faith it is because, before pronouncing his judgment, he did not give it all the attention that he should have, did not sufficiently examine the matter, or did not consult those whom he should have" (ibid.)[13] The pope should not rely simply on his own lights, Cano adds, but should consult many wise persons.

Echoing Cano, La Luzerne writes, Orsi says that popes have always observed certain wise practices before defining a doctrine. They do not define without consulting the Church of Rome, and if it is a very important matter, all the bishops of Italy, or at least those near Rome.[14] Orsi adds that the forms used by popes in this process have

---

13. He cites correctly but does not quote verbatim Cano's *De locis theologicis*, lib 5, cap 5, q 3, as in his *Opera* (Venice: Remondiniana, 1759), 133. Eighteenth-century papalist writers like Orsi and Ballerini avoid saying as Cano does "if a pope has erred in definitione fidei." If they think that a pope like Honorius I has made a mistake, they do not use the words "define" or "definition."

14. Giuseppe-Agostino Orsi, O.P., *De irreformabili romani pontificis in definiendis fidei controversiis judicio*, 3 vols. (Rome: Paulus Junchius, 1771), I, 1, 190; see also II, 264–267.

varied over time, but some have been considered necessary in each period. He then asserts that there is no record that Honorius I observed any such essential routines, and therefore his unfortunate statements on Monotheletism were not ex cathedra.[15]

Cano, Orsi, and other papalists seem to forget, says La Luzerne, that their claim is that Jesus Christ conferred infallibility on *St. Peter*, not on counselors gathered around Peter. Is it not strange that Christ would confer infallibility on Peter, on the condition that he consult high-quality counselors, but "not say a single word about this condition" (54). And how are the faithful to know how many advisers the pope has consulted, how well qualified they are, or how thorough, or mature, a study has been made? No, the Ultramontane "system is absolutely unsustainable; it is necessary that infallible authority be distinguished by characteristics such that those who are bound to submit cannot be mistaken." They say that there is no record of Honorius doing adequate consulting before speaking on the Monothelete controversy. Well, really there is no record that Celestine I did any consulting before writing to Cyril about Nestorianism, or that Leo I did so before writing to Flavian about Eutychianism. There is no record that either did any more than Honorius (55).

What about the "solemnity" with which they say an infallible definition must be issued? Orsi stipulates that for a papal statement to be ex cathedra it must be done after consulting the Roman Church and "with solemnity." But "he does not say in what this solemnity consists, nor what part of the Roman Church the pope is bound to consult in order to teach ex cathedra. He leaves this vague [*dans le vague*], even though this would be the thing that should be fixed with the greatest precision" (55–56). In practice, the popes have not adhered to any one procedure. They have sometimes consulted all the cardinals, sometimes only a few of them; sometimes they have formed congregations for the purpose, with varying memberships—perhaps bishops, perhaps theologians, perhaps jurists. But the "Ultramontanes give

---

15. Ibid., I, 1, 190–201.

us all the decisions rendered in one or other of these modes as irrefragable oracles to which we must submit just the same as to those of the Gospel" (56).

Gallicans say to the Ultramontanes: Kindly tell us who are these men established to give to the pope the privilege of infallibility. Tell us what qualities they have to possess, and cite for us the laws that confer on them this venerable power. Also tell us if the pope is infallible in his choice of consultors. If he is subject to error, then you are saying that despite error in choosing them, he is preserved from error in their decisions. Also, if he is infallible in this, then he has an infallibility independent of their counsel. Certainly, the pope is bound to take counsel in trying to decide important matters of doctrine. If every bishop is bound to consult competent people in running his diocese, it is all the more necessary for the pope to take good counsel in governing the whole Church. "But it is an obligation of conscience, not a means of [acquiring] infallibility. The caution prescribed for avoiding mistakes does not confer the great privilege of being unable to make a mistake" (57).

A very clear and succinct summary of the points that he has made in this chapter concludes: "I add that the Gallican maxim, which places infallibility in the union of the pope and the universal teaching Church, makes all these absurdities disappear, and presents a doctrine continually believed and always clearly known" (57–58).

The Roman Pontiff and General Councils

The Gallican ecclesiology, as La Luzerne presents it, also differs very markedly from the papalist regarding the relation of general councils to the Roman Pontiff. (He uses the term *ecumenical council* at times, but more frequently says *general council*.) He speaks of the differences briefly in chapter 1, where he says that Gallicans agree on some very important points with the Ultramontanes. For example, they agree that it belongs to the pope to convoke a council, that he has the right to preside over it either personally or through a legate, and that he has the principal role in directing its deliberations (18 and

76). But the Ultramontanes claim far more than this. They claim that the pope dominates and stands over all the bishops not only individually but also collectively, when they are gathered in council. They say that "not only is he superior to the council, but that all its authority comes to it from the pope, and that it is from his decision that a definition of the council has its irrefragable authority" (19). They also say that he is not bound to concur with the view of a large plurality of the bishops; rather, after listening to them, "he pronounces the decree as he pleases" [*ainsi qu'il lui plaît*]" (ibid.).[16] They say that they recognize the bishops as being not just advisers to the pope at a council but veritable judges. But they add that "in judging, the bishops are bound to follow the judgment of the pope as their principle and rule" (ibid.).

The Gallican view does not accept this. "We maintain, on the contrary, that it is not from the pope that an ecumenical council receives its authority, but from the promise of Jesus Christ and the assistance of the Holy Spirit; that a general council legitimately assembled is superior to the pope; and that the pope, in pronouncing the conciliar definition, is obliged to enunciate it conformably to the opinion of the greatest number of bishops" (ibid.). The Ultramontanes do acknowledge that there is one time when a pope can be judged by a council: when he falls into heresy. But it has to be a formal heresy already condemned at some time in the past. A present council cannot presumptuously undertake to judge a present pope. "We hold, on the contrary, that a pope obstinately refractory to the orders or decisions of a general council can be judged, condemned, and punished by the council" (ibid.).

Later, La Luzerne devotes a whole chapter to the relation of pope and council, and specifically to the question did Christ establish that a council has its authority from the pope? In view of the Ultramontane claim that it is the Roman Pontiff who is endowed by God with

---

16. He does not name any authors of these statements attributed to Ultramontanes, except Orsi, and he does not cite page numbers for him.

infallibility and he communicates some of it to the council, La Luzerne wonders why they recognize councils as having any useful role to play. He notes that "the Ultramontanes declare that conciliar deliberations and decrees add to the infallible decisions of the pope a greater solemnity and give them greater weight and render their authority more imposing." He comments, "I must say, I have trouble understanding what weight and what authority can be added to infallible authority" (76).

Orsi, responding to some historical argumentation of Bossuet, says that if some councils did examine and discuss statements of popes, that "proves nothing." "The things that were examined, he says, were already, before the examination, irreformable." If the council did examine a papal decree, that does not prove at all that the decree was reformable (77). Well then, is there any reason why the pope allowed the council to discuss it and reaffirm it? Orsi seems to mean, observes La Luzerne perceptively, that the pope "permits this through a sort of indulgence, to provide more gently for weak or ignorant persons. Thus the indulgent goodness of the popes has sometimes permitted a new judgment on questions of faith already sovereignly decided by themselves so that truths unshakeable in themselves, and already judged irreformably by [popes] are put in a new light" (ibid.).[17] Thus Leo I kindly permitted the Council of Chalcedon to discuss the case of Eutyches, which he had already settled definitively by himself.

La Luzerne is not indulgent toward this reasoning: "[I]t sins from one end to the other on many points" (79). A council does not simply rubber stamp a decision made by a pope. "This is not only a matter of questions already judged [at some time in the past], but of new judgments rendered by councils on questions [recently] decided by popes." It is a matter of judging the actual decree just made by a pope. Councils do not just judge the errors of Eutyches and Nestorius. "They also judge the decretal letters by which the popes condemned the errors and which the councils subject to their examina-

17. This wording is of course La Luzerne's.

tion, their deliberation, to their judgment" (ibid.). La Luzerne adds that when he discusses the Council of Chalcedon in depth in a later chapter, he will show that "it was not by the permission or indulgence of the holy pope that this great assembly condemned Eutyches anew; I will show that the council judged with deliberation and with jurisdiction the very letter of this great pontiff" (ibid.).[18] He adds that this is true of the councils generally. When they judge decisions made by popes, "they do this, as Orsi says, to render the truth more evident; but they make it such by rendering irreformable the judgment previously made that was not yet such" (79–80). When the pope and a council both pronounce on a doctrine, "they reciprocally communicate to each other a new degree of authority."

In a very good summation of his view, La Luzerne says, "It is the union of head and members that gives the Catholic Church, by the institution of Jesus Christ, the force of infallibility, and that elevates its decrees to the supreme degree of irreformability" (80). He says, correctly, that he is concurring with Bossuet on this, and he could add Tournely also. These three all agree in their critical assessment of the monarchical portrayal of the papacy given by the papalist authors and in their advocacy of a more collegial form of Catholic Church authority. La Luzerne is particularly clear, succinct, and pointed in his articulation of this ecclesiology.

18. The later chapter is part III, chapter 13.

CHAPTER 8

Alfonso Muzzarelli
1749–1813

A Writer in Exile

Born of an aristocratic family in Ferrara, Alfonso Muzzarelli attended a Jesuit school in Prato and entered the Society of Jesus in Bologna in 1768.[1] His professors there included several fine scholars, such as Giambattista Roberti in literature and Ferdinando Calini in Church history. When the Jesuit order was suppressed in 1773 by Pope Clement XIV, he continued studies for the priesthood and was ordained for the diocese of Ferrara in 1775. For many years he was occupied in education, both in his own further studies and in teaching, and soon began writing the books and articles for which he is mainly known. In 1803 he was invited to Rome by Pope Pius VII and appointed a theologian of the Sacred Penitentiary, which is the Church's tribunal for internal forum cases.

When Napoleon's military forces took over the Papal States and the city of Rome in 1808, Muzzarelli was one

---

1. Our best source for the life of Alfonso Muzzarelli are two articles by Giuseppe Mellinato, S.J.: "Muzzarelli," *Dictionnaire de spiritualité* 10: 1858–1860 (1980), and "Alfonso Muzzarelli, teologo tra fine Settecento e Restaurazione," *Ricerche di storia sociale e religiosa* 21 (1992): 25–35. Also still useful is J. Carreyre, "Muzzarelli," *DTC*, 10.2:2584–2585.

145

of those who refused to take oaths demanded by the French occupying power. For this he was arrested on August 31, 1809 and imprisoned. Pius VII had already been taken prisoner on July 6, and was held captive for three years at Savona in northern Italy and then from June of 1812 in France at Fontainebleau until the fall of Napoleon in 1814. (It may be recalled that Pius VI was also taken prisoner by the French, in February 1798, and died in captivity in August 1799.) Muzzarelli also was taken to France, and after a forced stay in Reims, was allowed to take up residence at a convent of the nuns of St. Michael in Paris. It was during his several years in exile in Paris that he wrote the essays in ecclesiology that proved to be significant in the Ultramontane Movement. He died on May 25, 1813, without ever being able to return to his homeland.

In his own lifetime Muzzarelli was most known for many writings on spiritual subjects and some apologetic works. His most popular book surely was one on Marian devotion focused on the month of May, *Il mese di Maria* (Ferrara, 1785). In saying that it was printed an infinite number of times ("stampato infinite volte"), the *Encyclopedia italiana* is only slightly exaggerating,[2] for it was printed some 150 times and was translated into a number of languages.[3] One of his interesting books was *L'Emilio disingannato* (Emile Disillusioned), a critical study of Rousseau (4 vols., Siena, 1782–1783). He also wrote a substantial book criticizing the *Histoire ecclésiastique* of Claude Fleury, a well-known Gallican history of the Church.[4] The work that his contemporaries tended to consider his most important was *Il buon uso di logica in materia di religione*. This was a collection of articles on very diverse subjects, totaling some thirty-seven pieces.[5] Some topics

---

2. *Encyclopedia italiana* (Rome, 1934), 24:174.
3. Mellinato, "Muzzarelli," 1859.
4. Concerning Claude Fleury and his history of the Church, see Richard F. Costigan, S.J., *Rohrbacher and the Ecclesiology of Ultramontanism* (Rome: Università Gregoriana Editrice, 1980), 88–95. Rohrbacher wrote his huge history of the Church in order to rectify Fleury's Gallican version of history.
5. The first edition of this work appeared in three volumes (Ferrara, 1787); others ranged up to ten volumes (Rome, 1807).

included the religion of the philosophers, the method to be observed in writing on religion, marriage as a sacrament, the Inquisition, and the temporal domain of the pope. In each of these essays he undertook to deal with the subject in what he considered a reasoned way.

One essay in *Il buon uso* concerned papal authority: "Primato e infallibilità del Papa," but most of Muzzarelli's works in ecclesiology were published only after his death. The one most often cited as influential in the Ultramontane Movement is *De auctoritate romani pontificis in conciliis generalibus* (2 vols., Ghent, 1815). Aubert says that this book was "destined to serve as an arsenal of arguments for later Ultramontanes."[6] Yves Congar states that it "exercised great influence," and together with works of Ballerini, Zaccaria, and Capellari "served the papal cause against Gallican and Febronian theses."[7] Hermann Pottmeyer notes that Muzzarelli, "though no independent thinker," was "an important mediator of the arguments of Italian apologists to French and German Ultramontanes."[8] He traces the influence of Muzzarelli on the German periodical *Der Katholik,* on Johannes Andries, on Matthias Scheeben, and on Klemens Schrader.[9] In the case of *Der Katholik,* he specifically mentions the German translation of *Il primato e infallibilità;* in the case of the others Muzzarelli is simply mentioned together with other Ultramontane authors such as Bellarmine, Ballerini, and Zaccaria. The book of Muzzarelli to which we shall devote most attention here is *L'infaillibilité du pape prouvée par la doctrine et la tradition de l'Eglise gallicane,* which Aubert thinks "shows a certain originality compared to the Italian production of the eighteenth century." He says that Muzzarelli "very ably invokes to defend

6. Roger Aubert, "La géographie ecclésiologique au XIXe siècle," in Maurice Nédoncelle et al., *L'ecclésiologie au XIXe siècle* (Paris: Cerf, 1960), 17.
7. Yves Congar, O.P., "L'ecclésiologie de la Révolution française au Concile du Vatican, sous la signe de l'affirmation de l'autorité," in the same volume by Nédoncelle, 93.
8. Hermann Josef Pottmeyer, *Unfehlbarkeit und Souveränität: Die päpstliche Unfehlbarkeit im System der ultramontanen Ekklesiologie des 19. Jahrhunderts* (Mainz: Matthias Grünewald, 1975), 46.
9. Ibid., 207 (*Der Katholik*), 254 (Andries), 277 (Scheeben), 329 (Schrader).

his positions the authority of Bossuet and Languet, the bishop of Soissons."[10]

In our review of the ecclesiology of Alfonso Muzzarelli we will study three of his writings: first a brief essay that he offers as a simple and convenient refutation of the Gallican doctrine, then a whole book *(L'infaillibilité du pape)* defending papal infallibility in more detail, and finally another brief essay featuring a great syllogism that is a convenient summary of his doctrine. It will be of interest to keep in mind in reading these that they were all written when Muzzarelli was living in exile in Paris and while Pius VII, the pope he admired very much, was a prisoner at Savona or a few miles away at Fontainebleau.

An Argument against the Gallicans

Worth reviewing first is his essay of only ten pages entitled *Argumentum contra gallorum opinionem de reformabilitate decretorum summi pontificis* (Argument against the Opinion of the French about the Reformability of Decrees of the Supreme Pontiff).[11] The argument is stated in a very succinct syllogism: "The thesis in which it is stated that papal decrees of faith are not irreformable, unless the consensus of the bishops is added to them, supposes that bishops can dissent from decrees of the Roman Pontiff. But this supposition or hypothesis is completely imaginary [*chimaerica*]. Therefore, this thesis is speculative, and metaphysical, and not practical" (19). In dismissing the thesis as speculative or metaphysical, Muzzarelli seems to mean that it could, if one wanted, be discussed as an academic exercise, even though it is really false.

In this essay, presented as an exercise in logical reasoning, several proofs for the minor premise follow immediately. The first of these is brief indeed: "This hypothesis is chimerical if there can never be dis-

---

10. Aubert, "La géographie ecclésiologique au XIXe siècle," 33n.
11. This essay was published in a volume with several others (Avignon: Seguin, 1826). *Argumentum* could also be translated as "proof." We will cite it simply by page numbers in the main text.

sent by bishops from a decree of faith of the Roman Pontiff. But this is so. Therefore the hypothesis is completely chimerical" (ibid.). This belief that there can never really be dissent from a papal decree of faith, which he does not bother to explain here, is spelled out at great length in his book on papal infallibility. Similarly brief, and also making points that are treated at length in the book, is a second proof for the minor premise. There can never be dissent by bishops from papal decrees (1) if Christ established a college of bishops immovably adhering in faith to Peter and his successors; (2) if Christ obtained from the Father this perpetual unity; and (3) if Christ promised his presence in preaching the faith to the college of apostles for absolutely all days. But all three of these truths are ineluctably demonstrated from the Gospel and tradition. Therefore, the hypothesis is chimerical, or imaginary (20).

Muzzarelli then offers several scriptural considerations that, incidentally, do not appear in the book. All four consist of citing familiar images of the Church found in the New Testament, and all four are presented as logically rigorous proofs. First is the image of building and foundation. Christ established the Church on the foundation of Peter. Now, a building cannot stand, or even exist, without its foundation for even a single day. If the Church were ever separated in doctrine from Peter for even a single day, then it would be separated from its foundation and could not exist. Thus its constitution, established by Christ to be indefectible, would have failed. Therefore, the hypothesis of the college of bishops dissenting in doctrine from the successor of Peter is completely chimerical (21–22).

Second is the image of unified community centered on and confirmed in faith by Peter. The unified community of faith cannot exist apart from Peter, for Christ said, "confirma fratres tuos" (strengthen your brothers) (Luke 22:32). Christ nowhere told the community to strengthen Peter. Muzzarelli also cites Christ's prayer for unity at the Last Supper. If the community were separated from its center of unity in faith with Peter, it would collapse; "the center would have disappeared, the nexus would be broken, the visible sign of unity would have vanished," and the promise of Jesus Christ would have failed. Therefore, the hypothesis is chimerical (24).

A third image is that of shepherd and flock. How could you ever suppose that the flock could make its way without the shepherd? And if it were possible for the shepherd to err in teaching the faith, then it would seem right for the flock to judge him, and perhaps even to dismiss him. But there is not the slightest mention in Scripture of Jesus giving any such right to the sheep. And if they were not given the right, then they were not given the grace to do such a thing. Thus it is unthinkable for the sheep to second-guess the shepherd. Rather, their salvation certainly lies in obeying the shepherd (25).

Finally, he invokes the image of the body consisting of head and members. Jesus Christ promised that through his daily presence he would provide infallibility to the "apostolic college" or "apostolic body," and this presupposes Peter as its head (16). Every body necessarily has a head and cannot subsist without it. If the apostolic body were ever separated from Peter, its head, it would no longer subsist, even for one day. Peter is "the principal dispenser of the mysteries of faith, the first deputy to announce the faith in the name of the brethren, the only one delegated to confirm his brother apostles in faith, and the foundation stone of the imperishable Church" (27). This ministry of Peter is "singular"; it cannot be disassociated from his person but remains perpetually present in his successor. Christ made the promise of infallibility not just to the members of the Church but to the whole body, which must always remain attached to its head. Thus it is impossible that a doctrine proposed by the members be contrary to that of the head. This means that the hypothesis of a possible contradiction between a definition of the Roman Pontiff and a definition of the episcopal college is arbitrary, absurd, and chimerical (28).

This is the end of this terse and blunt little treatise. Interestingly, it does contain several expressions that do not quite fit in the model of absolute papal monarchy. Muzzarelli uses the term *collegium apostolo-*

rum as the recipient of infallibility (26), but does not show any tendency to develop, here or in the book we shall now look at, the idea of collegiality. Also, he uses the word *ministerium* several times in speaking of the role of Peter (26, 27, 28), but does not seem to advert to its literal meaning of "service." Rather, for him it seems to mean only the "office" of the head of the Church. Actually, he seems to use these words because they occur in writings of Bossuet that he is drawing on.

Papal Infallibility and Article 4
Studying Gallican Writings

Muzzarelli's principal book-length critique of the fourth Gallican article was also written during his several years in France. He entitled it *L'infaillibilité du pape prouvée par la doctrine and la tradition de l'Eglise gallicane*.[12] He tells us in his preface that he had only ten books in his library at the convent in Paris where he lived, including five volumes of pastoral instructions, documents, and other writings of Jean-Joseph Languet, bishop of Soissons and archbishop of Sens.[13] Languet's ecclesial ideas are not Ultramontane, he says; rather, this prelate was completely devoted to the Gallican view and was a great admirer of Bossuet. But reading these writings day after day, he became convinced that you can actually find in them ample matter to defend *papal infallibility*. Thus in this book he will draw on the principles of the "contradictors" of papal authority to show that if they would advert to the inner implications of their own doctrines, they would come to adopt the true Catholic doctrine of papal infallibility (9, 11). The starting point is the professed belief of both Languet and Bossuet in Jesus Christ's promises of perpetual assistance to the Church. He will show that these promises really mean that the Gallican doctrine ex-

---

12. Avignon: Seguin, 1826. We will cite this book in the text by page numbers in parentheses.
13. Jean-Joseph Languet de Villeneuve de Gergy (1677–1753) was a doctor of the Sorbonne and a relative of Bossuet, bishop of Soissons from 1715, archbishop of Sens from 1731, a member of the French Academy (1721), and a tireless adversary of Jansenism in many writings and other efforts; see *DTC*, 8.2:2601–2606.

pressed in the fourth article is purely speculative or metaphysical. That is, the supposition of some occasional contrariety of papal teaching and episcopal teaching "can never happen." Explaining this belief that there really cannot be episcopal dissent from a papal definition of faith is the main substance of the book.

Muzzarelli grants that the Gallicans are Catholic, and says several times that the French have generally been in practice more devoted to the Holy See than one might expect from the regrettable doctrines contained in the Declaration of 1682. "Notwithstanding their great zeal for their opinion, they have always maintained the most sincere and edifying submission to the Holy See." For this reason, "I will not fail to show the respect due to a clergy regarded always by the Roman Church as, so to speak, the apple of its eye." He notes also that popes have declared the Gallican Declaration null and void, "but they have not qualified [as, for example, heretical] any of the four propositions" (12).

Jesus Christ promised the Church a remedy against the errors and uncertainties that from time to time in Church history might arise to disturb its peaceful unity of faith. It is a remedy sure, efficacious, universal, and perpetual: it is authority. The authority that Christ established is "the authority of the body of bishops united to that of the successors of St. Peter, in a word, the union of the consensus of the teaching of the head of the Church and that of the greater number of bishops who, with the head, form one body: perfect, complete, living, and speaking all days" (18). (*Consensus* here and throughout renders the French *consentement*.) The expression "the greater number of bishops" he believes is appropriate, because it is not necessary that there be absolute unanimity of bishops for Christ's promise of infallibility to be fulfilled (32). After citing some Scripture and some texts given by Languet, including statements of Bossuet, he says, "It is necessary and essential for the accomplishment of the promise [of Jesus] that to the judgment of the successors of St. Peter be united the judgment or the consensus of the successors of the other apostles" (30). If the bishops hold different beliefs from those of the Roman Pontiff, then the promise of Jesus has failed.

Muzzarelli says that he deduces this doctrine from "the recognized and avowed doctrine of the whole Gallican Church" (32), and this is correct. What he has said thus far is the same as the ecclesiology of Tournely and Bossuet. But after this starting point, the divergence between the papalist and the Gallican views is, to put it mildly, quite marked. Muzzarelli asserts that from this premise it follows that "the solemn judgment of the pope, pronounced from the chair of St. Peter, can never be subject to error, and in consequence . . . this judgment is always infallible; because if for one sole time, and on one sole day, this judgment were fallible and subject to error, it could happen that his judgment was erroneous, heretical, false, and contrary to the faith," and this would mean that Christ's promised remedy had failed (46–47). His defense of his reasoning on this, which is of course completely different from the Gallican viewpoint, occupies the remainder of the book.

His specific critique of Article 4 begins in chapter 11, the title of which states that when the pope issues a solemn decree on the faith, there is no need for the faithful to wait for the consensus of the greater number of bishops. They may and should regard it as infallible and submit to it at once (54). Reading his analysis here, one rapidly realizes that some of his expressions that looked like the basis for collegiality were really not such at all. The stress that he has placed on the whole college of the apostles led by Peter, and on the whole body of the bishops joined with its head the pope, is really intended to enforce the necessity of *their* adhering to and obeying the head. There is no mention of a need for the head to adhere to or share the faith of the body. All authority really belongs to the head, and the members must simply realize that and accept it.

Muzzarelli frequently addresses possible Gallican interlocutors: *you* say that, while *I* say this. You express Gallican ideas, while I respond with the true Catholic doctrine. Thus, referring to Article 4, you say that the papal pronouncement is reformable until it receives the consensus of the bishops (54). So you mean that the pronouncement could be reformed, and thus that the pope could utter a false doctrine. I say, first, that the greater number of bishops has not received the promise of infallibility; only the whole body of apostles together with Peter received the promise of Christ. The members apart from the head did not receive the promise, and they can err if they are separated from the head. They do err if they think they can reform what the Supreme Pontiff has said. Incidentally, Muzzarelli usually specifies that the papal statement is a definition, or solemn definition, or constitution of faith. Also, it will be noted that he always thinks in term of *consensus subsequens,* consensus of bishops given after the papal statement, and never mentions antecedent or concomitant consensus.

I say, second, that if you suppose that the statement is reformable, and that the pope may be mistaken, then you are supposing that at that time, on that day, the promise of Jesus Christ has failed. "Are you capable of uttering that impiety? Surely not. Then you must say that on that day, and on all other days, Jesus Christ has been with the successor of Peter, and that he has given him the assistance promised forever, and that the pope, with that supernatural assistance, has not made a mistake, that his constitution is infallibly Catholic, and consequently that it is irreformable" (55–56). If it is reformable, then we are "floating and uncertain in the faith" until the decision of the great number of bishops has been heard from, and "who knows when that will be?" If the great number of bishops decides that it needs to be reformed, then we are still floating and uncertain until a general council decides. Who knows how long that will be? It could be years, or even centuries, and we would be floating and uncertain until then! Muzzarelli exclaims, "My God, where is the remedy sure, universal, prompt, and efficacious that you have given to the faithful for all times, and for all days, against nascent heresies, against the ruses and snares of the errant?" (56)

No, it is essential for the infallibility of the promise of Christ that a "constitution of the pope be always and forever exempt from error" (57). And it must be accepted as such as soon as it is published. Muzzarelli concludes this chapter by asserting "this certain principle: that the number [of bishops] united to the head, whether large or small, will always form the body moral, complete, perfect, and visible in which the truth will always prevail and will be perfectly recognized."

He believes that it is true in fact that "the truth will be recognized by the consensus of the greater number of bishops united to the head of the Church." But their consensus is not necessary; when it is present it serves a useful purpose, for it "gives greater éclat to the knowledge of the truth" (62–63).

Muzzarelli pursues his rigorous scrutiny of Article 4 in the following chapter, in which he offers confirmation of the foregoing "by the testimony and principles of the Gallican Church" (63). By now it has probably been noticed that, like other papalist authors, he has an instinctive and fixed tendency to see any expressions of concurrence in faith as simply obedience of papal decrees. That is, when French bishops, or anyone else, indicate that they recognize a papal statement as Catholic doctrine, he assumes that they really do this (only) because they know they have to *obey* the supreme authority. The members of the Church are like the subjects of a king: they obey their ruler. He does not seem to realize at all clearly that the historic Roman Catholic faith community existing in France, as in many countries, *is* a community of inherited and shared Catholic faith, a faith of which popes and councils are recognized teachers. The community has through the centuries accepted papal and conciliar statements because they are recognized as expressions of Catholic faith. The authorities that issue them are revered because their role is understood to be important and necessary.

Muzzarelli considers what you find in French Church documents anomalous and surprising. You discover in the texts assembled by Jean-Joseph Languet that the same clergy who produced the Gallican Articles also still recognize the Roman Pontiff as the most important authority in the Church. He thinks that the Gallican Declaration should mean that the French Church separates itself from the rest of the Church, and no longer (at least sincerely) accepts papal authority. Clearly, he remains unable to see how people who claim to be Catholic can retain any ability, or right, to evaluate and criticize a papal statement. This is inexplicable to one for whom faith is simply obedience to a decreeing power.

Muzzarelli thinks that the first part of Article 4 understands faith in this sense. It says that the pope has the "principal part [*praecipuas partes*] in questions of faith," and "his decrees apply to each and every Church" (eiusque decreta ad omnes et singulas ecclesias pertinere). (*Church* here of course means the local or regional parts of the Roman Catholic Church.) *Pertinere* (which Muzzarelli renders in French as *regardent*) is a rather vague term, and by itself would tend to mean simply "extend to, reach to," or "belong to." This broad meaning is probably what Bossuet had in mind when he chose it for the declaration. He surely did not mean it to say that the authority merely *suggests* doctrine, but manifestly did not mean it to say that the authority strictly *imposes* doctrine on the Church. Muzzarelli assumes a maximal meaning of *pertinere*, and asks how you can say that a papal definition of faith is reformable unless or until it receives the consensus of the bishops (66). He thinks that the papal definition itself requires obedience, and it cannot be simply exterior obedience and respectful silence. It must be sincere obedience and "perfect submission of the spirit" that does not leave any room for doubt. And it must be obedience explicitly to the successor of Peter, and to him alone. "To obey the decrees of the pope after the judgment of all the bishops is to obey the Church universal and not the successor of Peter in particular; to submit to the body of pastors united to the pope is not to submit precisely to the authority of the successors of Peter" (67–68).

Muzzarelli believes that this must be the real meaning of the first part of Article 4 itself, if rightly and logically understood. Since this part is true, the second part must be false. If you say that the pope is *the* teacher of the faith, then you cannot say that a papal pronouncement is reformable. You cannot say it is uncertain until it receives the consensus of the bishops. If the pope could be mistaken, then we simple faithful are constantly exposed to the danger of error, which is something that Jesus Christ could not have wanted. The fact that we need not await the consensus of the bishops also "dispenses us from the laborious and impractical research, greater than our abilities, [of trying] to assure ourselves of the consensus of the greater number of bishops" (72).

Muzzarelli Criticizes Bossuet

Muzzarelli pursues his criticism of Gallican doctrine through more lengthy chapters, and it would be repetitious to report much more of it here. Just a few specifics are of interest, including some in a twenty-page chapter on the opinion on papal infallibility of "the celebrated M. Bossuet." He regards the bishop of Meaux as "the soul" of the meeting of March 1682 and identifies him (correctly) as the redactor of the declaration produced there (114). Like other papalist authors, Muzzarelli sees much to admire in Bossuet's famous "Sermon on Unity," given at the beginning of the Extraordinary Assembly of the French clergy on November 9, 1681. (Muzzarelli mistakenly places it at a session in March 1682.) In this sermon, which Muzzarelli seems to know only from excerpts given by Languet, Bossuet eloquently upholds papal primacy, extolling the papacy's role in the history of the Church, and saying that Peter lives on in the pontiff of Rome (112–113).[14] For Muzzarelli, it is inexplicable how Bossuet can glowingly extol the pope's supreme ministry and then strip it of its "essential prerogatives," like infallibility, without which the pope cannot fulfill Christ's mandate (115). He uses the word *ministry* several times in these pages, perhaps influenced by Bossuet's use of the word, though without dwelling on the service idea, which is significant to Bossuet.

Papalist writers generally avoid the term *personal infallibility* in order to clarify that they are not talking about the pope speaking as a private doctor, but rather speaking in his public capacity as the head of the Church. But Muzzarelli, perhaps naively, sometimes asserts the *personal* infallibility of the pope, as when he says here that Bossuet unfortunately "refuses the personal infallibility of the pope in solemn constitutions that regard points of faith" (120).[15] In doing this the

---

14. Bossuet devotes the whole of what he calls the "Premier Point" in the sermon to the all-important unifying role of the successors of Peter; see text in Bossuet, *Oeuvres complètes,* ed. Lachat (Paris: Louis Vives, 1863), 11:592–609.

15. He uses the expression again on 156 and also in another essay that will be studied below, *Argument démonstratif de l'infaillibilité du pape,* 3 and 5.

French prelate is not true to Catholic tradition. Rather, he has "brought forth a new system in order to adapt the authority of tradition and the councils to his own opinion" (ibid.). As though the whole Gallican ecclesiology were created by Bossuet, Muzzarelli exclaims, "Such is the system of M. Bossuet: a system all new, new in its entirety." His added comment, "which I do not flatter myself that I have well understood" (123), seems to be intended critically, for he says that Bossuet's distinction between indefectibility and infallibility is not really intelligible. This is "a system subtle and outside the understanding of the ancient centuries." "I do not understand it, and its obscurity alarms me against this system." On a matter so important for the faithful and for the Church, "obscurity is not the mark of a divine institution or of an assured doctrine" (124). Clarity in place of obscurity is ready to hand: "Therefore I adhere to the intelligible and reasoned system of the Ultramontanes, which maintains only that . . . the pope speaking solemnly ex cathedra can never err on the faith" (128). This is almost the only time that Muzzarelli uses the term *ex cathedra*.

Nevertheless, Bossuet still deserves respect for his many real merits. "Let no one think that we want to diminish at all the just esteem earned by the celebrated bishop of Meaux, for whom even Ultramontanes profess the greatest respect." Compared to some people, "the immortal Bossuet" shows the "moderation" that is "proper to great men," and "what does him the most honor, an inviolable attachment to the Apostolic See" (ibid.). Though he probably has them in mind, Muzzarelli does not mention some of the more antihierarchical writers such as Edmond Richer. The material that he has available to him does seem to be limited to the few volumes that he mentions at the beginning of this book. He seems, for example, not to have had a copy of Bossuet's *Defensio*, but only some excerpts given by Languet.

In a later chapter, Muzzarelli deals with a concern that some (not named) may have: has the Holy See really condemned the Gallican theses as fully and clearly as it should have? He responds in the affirmative. The Declaration of 1682 was declared in the constitution *Inter multiplices* of Alexander VIII (dated August 4, 1690 and published January 30, 1691) to be *nulla, irrita,* and *inanis* (null, void, and vain). Muzzarelli is aware, as we shall see a little later, that none of these terms mean that the Gallican Articles are heretical, but they do constitute a severely negative judgment (167). He adds that more recently Pius VI noted in *Auctorem Fidei* (August 28, 1794), among his many censures of the Synod of Pistoia, that the Gallican Declaration had been condemned ("improbata") earlier.[16] He reaffirms this judgment, stating, "[W]e [again] reprove and condemn [*reprobamus et damnamus*]" that injurious and scandalous doctrine, and want it to be regarded as "reprobata et damnata."[17] For Muzzarelli this is sufficient to answer people who might say that the Holy See has not clearly censured the Gallican doctrines (167). He surely noted, however, that Pius VI declines to use the term *heretica* for Gallican views, though he does use that word for a number of other ideas of the Synod of Pistoia, for example, for propositions 1, 2, 3, 4, and 15.

Moreover, it is incorrect, Muzzarelli thinks, to say that Bossuet's *Defensio* has not been condemned by the Holy See. He cites a document that does not really contain a condemnation, but that gives an interesting glimpse of papal discretion in handling this controversy. The document is a letter written by Benedict XIV to the Grand Inquisitor of Spain, saying that this book defending the Gallican Declaration certainly opposes the doctrine of papal infallibility, which is "received everywhere outside France." For this reason, Benedict recalls, during the pontificate of his predecessor Clement XII there was serious thought in Rome of proscribing it. "Finally it was decided to refrain from proscribing it, not so much for the memory of an author who had served religion well in so many other ways, as for the just fear of a new round of controversy."[18] Muzzarelli does not mention (and probably does not know) what action, if any, Benedict advised

16. DS 2699.   17. Ibid. 2700.
18. Muzzarelli quotes this statement of Benedict XIV on 168, giving as reference a collection of Benedict's works published in 1767.

the Inquisitor to take in Spain. He simply cites Benedict to remind his readers that the popes considered Bossuet very mistaken in his ecclesiology, even while showing "prudent dissimulation" (167) regarding this book. After all, since belief in papal infallibility is securely in place in every other country, it does not seem urgent to try to suppress every erroneous book produced in France.

No Reformability

Muzzarelli sometimes gets carried away in relentlessly pursuing his conviction that Article 4 simply cannot mean what it says. He does this at length and with growing vehemence in chapter 18, which is entitled: "In the Intention of the Gallican Clergy the Fourth Proposition of the Declaration of 1682 Cannot Entail a Meaning Contrary to the Infallibility of the Pope" (136). He exclaims, "If the pope is not infallible, his decisions, his definitions and condemnations, have the character of the most frightful usurpation, threaten the overturning of the whole Church, and destroy from top to bottom the order established by Jesus Christ" (138). If the pope's judgment is not infallible, then it is abusive and lacking in validity. You are bound to reject it, "if you do not want to participate in the crime of the Sovereign Pontiff, and make yourself responsible for the frightful consequences of his perpetual usurpation" (139).

More of this vehement language occurs in this thirty-three-page chapter when he reviews some incidents in French Church history, mainly relating to the Jansenist controversy. Each time the French concur with a papal doctrinal statement, Muzzarelli assumes it must be out of sheer obedience to the supreme authority. This makes it seem more and more unthinkable and outrageous that any papal pronouncement can be thought of as reformable. One example may suffice. In 1665 Pope Alexander VII issued a bull against Jansenism, *Regiminis Apostolici,* which imposed the signing of a formulary stating that five specified propositions were contained in the major work of Cornelius Jansen, *Augustinus.*[19] This bull was accepted and published by

---

19. Some standard brief treatments of this episode include Louis Cognet, "Ecclesi-

the French bishops. Muzzarelli says that if you claim that a papal pronouncement, when issued, is reformable—that is, possibly mistaken—then you must logically regard that bull as a wrongful overreaching of papal authority. His language is strong. "That bull of the pope should be regarded as a criminal attack [*attentat criminel*], and founded on error, by all those who maintain the reformability of constitutions of the pope before their acceptance by the bishops. How then [could they] accept and publish anew a bull that is so criminal, so deceitful, and so dangerous?" (163) Rather, there should have been a general outcry against it. Though he uses the words *accepter* and *recevoir* numerous times in this section, he is unwilling, and apparently unable, to see French acceptance of a papal doctrinal statement as simply their recognition of traditional mainstream Catholic theology. Rather, he sees it as their *obedience* to a decree of the supreme power. It is also not too clear in Muzzarelli's account that he understands that the Assembly of the Clergy of France and also King Louis XIV asked the pope for this statement against Jansenism. This bull of 1665, incidentally, largely reaffirms a similar bull from the same pope, *Ad Sacram* (1656), which was also requested by the French.[20]

In his conclusion to this book, it becomes evident that his indignation at the wrong ideas of the Gallicans does not extend to them as persons, for he always recognizes them as his fellow Catholics. The doctrine of papal infallibility he earnestly believes is a "very legitimate and almost necessary consequence of principles" that are commonly held by Catholics. But we should remember that "this truth has not yet been declared by the universal Church as a dogma of

---

astical Life in France," in *The Church in the Age of Absolutism and Enlightenment,* vol. 6 of Hubert Jedin and John Dolan, eds., *History of the Church* (New York: Crossroad, 1981), 45–49; and E. Préclin and E. Jarry, *Les luttes politiques et doctrinales aux XVIIe et XVIII siècles,* vol. 19 of Augustin Fliche and Victor Martin, eds., *Histoire de l'Eglise* (Paris: Bloud et Gay, 1955), 200–204.

20. See Pierre Blet, S.J., *Le clergé de France et la monarchie: Etude sur les Assemblées Générales du Clergé de 1615 à 1666* (Rome: Università Gregoriana Editrice, 1959), 2:175–220, 300–325; also Martimort, *Le gallicanisme de Bossuet* (Paris: Cerf, 1953), 202–277.

faith; the contrary opinion is tolerated in the Church." For this reason, "one cannot scorn those who are of a different sentiment, all the more because in practice they conform to the obedience and submission due to the judgments of the Sovereign Pontiff." He adds that he thinks that papal infallibility is "so well founded on arguments of authority and reason" that the Church could easily proceed to a formal declaration of it (180). By "reason" he presumably refers mainly to his rigorous deduction of the doctrine from Christ's promises to Peter in the Gospels, and also to traditional assumptions about monarchy as the most efficient form of government.

One Great Syllogism for Papal Infallibility

We looked earlier at a brief essay of Muzzarelli entitled *Argumentum contra gallorum opinionem*. Published together with it after his death is another brief essay that offers in one clear emphatic syllogism a proof for papal infallibility, *Propositio pro adstruenda infallibilitate summorum pontificum*.[21] It is long for a syllogism but seems worth giving in full, for it is a good summary of the thinking on papal infallibility that we have been studying in his writings. It is also a uniquely bold little tour de force of polemic. Putting it in sense lines should help to follow the train of thought.

> He wills and ought to be considered as personally infallible
>   who pronounces absolute dogmatic decisions,
>   and publishes and declares them to all the faithful and bishops,
>   not having sought the immediate or mediate, express or tacit
>   consensus of the bishops,
>   rather commanding their publication and execution of his decisions,
>   forbidding all to infringe on them, or to dare rashly to go against them,
>   under pain of excommunication ipso facto,
>   reproving bishops who may want to dispute his decisions,
>   testifying that he does not demand the advice of bishops, or ask for their
>   votes, or await their opinion, but enjoins their obedience,
>   as has been the usage of his predecessors through a long series of

---

21. Though available only in Latin, he also gave it a French title, *Argument démonstratif de l'infaillibilité du Pape* (Avignon: Seguin, 1826). Page references will be given parenthetically in the text.

centuries, without the Church remonstrating through so many centuries, but rather with the universal Church acquiescing and obeying,
and with those few bishops who did or said something contrary
becoming silent at his reproofs, or excusing themselves and repenting.
But [*Atqui*], thus the Supreme Pontiff in his dogmatic constitutions, and thus the Church in its praxis for many centuries [here are given a large number of references to documents, mostly papal, dated between 1653 and 1794].
Ergo, the Supreme Pontiff wills and ought to be considered personally infallible, because if he were not infallible, his dogmatic constitutions would amount to a tyrannical usurpation against the episcopate, a rash presumption
   against the Holy Spirit, and intolerable error causing the
   subversion and destruction of the faith of the universal Church,
   which God could not permit without defecting from his promise of
      perpetual assistance to the Church,
   and which the Church itself could not accept with silence, praise, and
      execution, because the Church does not do, approve, or tacitly
      condone what is against faith and good morals. (3–4)

Most of the remainder of this sixteen-page essay, explaining and defending the syllogism, is either of secondary significance or repetitive of what we have seen already. But there are two items of interest. First, he expressly dissociates himself from some of his fellow papalist theologians, whom he does not identify, on at least one significant point. Referring to Ultramontane or papalist theologians as "Romans," he says: "Although I am certainly Roman, I reject as improper" the idea that the Supreme Pontiff bestows infallibility on a general council. Rather, it is the Holy Spirit who grants infallibility to a council. A general council consists of head and members, and its decrees are decrees of the whole body, not just of the head, and not just of the members. In saying that only the Holy Spirit can bestow infallibility on the decrees (7), Muzzarelli differs from authors like Orsi and Ballerini, who say that the Roman Pontiff confers infallibility on a council. But this is to a great extent a verbal distinction, for Muzzarelli's papal authority remains very monarchical: the pope does not need a council to proclaim the faith to the community (10–11).

Second, he comments that it is understandable if the French are not familiar with differences among Roman theologians, for they do not have a "supply of [the books] of Ultramontane doctors," and have to try to learn their opinions from their Gallican opponents (15). As he informs us at the beginning, Muzzarelli himself had only a few books available to him at his residence in Paris, and those few were mostly Gallican texts that had been assembled by Bishop Languet. He seems not to have had complete texts of Bossuet's writings, such as the *Defensio,* or copies of standard treatises such as Tournely's *De ecclesia*. He also apparently had virtually no Ultramontane works, for he does not mention either Orsi or Ballerini, or even Bellarmine. Thus he may be unaware that he differs from these fellow Romans on another notable matter also. That is his comment, again in this syllogism, that the Church has not cried out against the pretension and usurpation that the papacy's claim of infallibility really would be if it were not willed by its founder, Jesus Christ. This could suggest an unstated but implicit idea of reception, or *consensus Ecclesiae,* that one does not find in Orsi or Ballerini, who simply take absolute papal monarchy as their starting point. But if he adverted to this possible implication of his words, Muzzarelli would probably rephrase his statements, for he would not want to encourage in any way the idea that the Church can ever judge the Roman Pontiff. The sheep can never judge the shepherd, and they can never teach him anything. It is the plan of God that the shepherd guides the sheep and does not need their advice or consent. People who talk about the chief pastor needing the consensus of the Church seem not to understand the plan of God for the Church.

CHAPTER 9

Giovanni Perrone, S.J.
1794–1876

A Very Roman Theologian

A native of Chieri, near Turin, Giovanni Perrone studied in the major seminary of Turin and earned his doctorate in theology there.[1] He joined the Society of Jesus soon after it was restored in 1814 by Pius VII, and when Leo XII returned the Collegio Romano (today the Gregorian University) to the society in 1824 he was assigned to its faculty. On November 2, 1824, he was given the chair of dogmatic theology, and spent the remainder of his life there, except for a term as rector of the Jesuit school in Ferrara (1830–1834) and three years of exile in distant Wales after revolutionary forces took over the city of Rome in 1848. He was briefly rector of the Collegio Romano and for many years prefect of studies (dean): from 1855 till he died in 1876.

Perrone's great influence in nineteenth-century ecclesiology is widely recognized. It was an influence exercised in two ways: first, through his teaching in Rome and his major textbook in dogmatic theology, and second, through

---

1. The one readily accessible account of the life of Giovanni Perrone remains the *DTC* article by C. Boyer: *DTC*, 12.1:1255–1256. Salvatore Casagrandi offers an account of Perrone's life and work in *De claris sodalibus provinciae Turonensis Societatis Jesu commentarii* (Turin: Jacobus Arneodus Eques, 1906), 315–329.

his extra-academic work in Rome, as consultor of several curial congregations, and as participant in the preparation of both the definition of the Immaculate Conception[2] and Vatican I's dogmatic constitution on the Church. Perrone's principal statement of his ecclesiology appears in his *Praelectiones theologicae*, which he first published beginning in 1835. This nine-volume work went through some thirty-four editions, and its two-volume compendium went through forty-seven editions. Most of these "editions" were really reprintings rather than new editions in the present-day sense, but he also did a considerable amount of revising in them over the years. In the faculty of the revived Roman College, Roger Aubert observes, "one name dominates all the others, Giovanni Perrone."[3] In addition to the growing number of students whom he taught personally, his teaching spread across the Catholic world through the adoption in many seminaries of the *Praelectiones*. Gustave Thils calls him "the oracle of dogmatic theology" who "formed several generations of theologians,"[4] and also notes Perrone's influence at Vatican I.[5] Both Roland Minnerath and Klaus Schatz, in his major recent history of Vatican I, mention Perrone's significant role as a *peritus* for the Deputatio de Fide, the drafting committee of the council's documents.[6] (The drafting committee at Vatican I was called the Deputation on Faith, while its counterpart at Vatican II was called the Theological Commission.)

2. Perrone's role in the definition of the Immaculate Conception is briefly mentioned in Roger Aubert, *Le pontificat de Pie IX*, vol. 21 of Augustin Fliche and Victor Martin, eds., *Histoire de l'Eglise* (Paris: Bloud et Gay, 1963), 278–279.

3. Roger Aubert, "La géographie ecclésiologique au XIXe siècle," in Maurice Nédoncelle et al., *L'ecclésiologie au XIXe siècle* (Paris: Cerf, 1960), 33. Pages 33–35 deal with Perrone.

4. Gustave Thils, *La primauté pontificale: La doctrine de Vatican I, les voies d'une révision* (Gembloux: Duculot, 1972), 22.

5. Gustave Thils, *L'infaillibilité pontifical: Source, conditions, limites* (Gembloux: Duculot, 1969), 34.

6. Klaus Schatz, S.J., *Vatikanum I, 1869–1870* (Paderborn: Ferdinand Schöningh, 1992–1994), 1:17, 149, 152–153, and 3:15, 17, 167. Roland Minnerath, in *Le pape: Evêque universel ou premier des évêques?* (Paris: Beauchesne, 1978), has an interesting chapter on "L'intention des consulteurs de Vatican I," 13–37, which gives information on Perrone's role in particular, 16–22.

Besides the *Praelectiones theologicae,* which in its nine volumes covers the principal areas of theology, Perrone wrote several other significant works. One was a book on matrimony, another was a book on the divinity of Christ, and one dealt with the Immaculate Conception of Mary.[7] He also wrote one criticizing the theology of Georg Hermes,[8] and two books on Protestantism. John Henry Newman in 1847, not long after his conversion to Catholicism, asked Perrone's comments on an essay that he entitled, "On the Development of Catholic Dogma" (written in Latin). He was very pleased with the detailed notes with which Perrone replied. James Gaffney says, "Perrone read the work sympathetically and perceptively and criticized it with amiable candor."[9] He developed a "warm esteem for Newman" from this time and defended him in Rome.[10] Perrone himself was highly esteemed by Pius IX, who is said to have wanted to make him a cardinal. Contemporaries maintain that he was generally admired not only for his learning but also for his humility and good nature, and unlike most theologians he was well known to the people of Rome. Salvatore Casagrandi reports: "When he walked through the streets of Rome, passers-by pointed him out as the prince of theologians of the time."[11]

Papal Supremacy

Giovanni Perrone's *Praelectiones theologicae* is a work of scholastic rigor and clarity. It is also a work of great erudition, showing very wide reading not only of traditional treatises of Catholic theology but also of many modern authors, including non-Catholic ones. He had knowledge, rare in Rome at that time, notes Aubert, of books

---

7. *De matrimonio christiano,* 3 vols. (Rome, 1858); *De D.N.J. Christi divinitate,* 3 vols. (Turin, 1870) (D.N.J. is Our Lord Jesus); *De immaculata B.V.M conceptione* (Rome, 1855).
8. *L'ermesianismo* (Rome, 1838–1839).
9. John Henry Newman, *Roman Catholic Writings on Doctrinal Development,* ed. James Gaffney (Kansas City: Sheed and Ward, 1997). The comment is in Gaffney's introduction, 4.
10. Ibid.
11. Casagrandi, *De claris sodalibus provinciae Turonensis Societatis Jesu commentarii,* 318.

written in foreign languages.¹² He had read Johan Adam Möhler's *Symbolik*, and at the very beginning of his chapter on the constitution of the Church of Christ devotes two pages to a very positive appreciation of Möhler's idea of the Church as a continuing incarnation of Jesus Christ. He says that properly understood, this is a very good and useful—and scripturally based—way of conceiving the Church's nature.¹³ Numerous authors have noted Perrone's appreciation of Möhler's theology. "We are present here," says Aubert, "at the first penetration of the influence of German ecclesiology in the theology of the Roman College."¹⁴ Several recent authors, among them John Boyle and Richard Gaillardetz, briefly mention Perrone's respect for Möhler while noting that the Church in Perrone's ecclesiology really consists mainly of its centralized authority structure.¹⁵ Michael J. Himes makes the same perceptive comment in a major work on the theology of Möhler.¹⁶

That Möhler's idea of Church did not really penetrate deeply into Perrone's ecclesiology is clearly noted also in Hermann Pottmeyer's much longer (fifteen-page) treatment of Perrone, where he very correctly stresses that the Church in that ecclesiology is understood as an absolute authority system that centers around the sovereign power of

---

12. Aubert, "La géographie ecclésiologique au XIXe siècle," 33n.

13. Giovanni Perrone, S.J., *Praelectiones theologicae,* 31st ed. (Turin: Marietti, 1865), 2:23–25. It is this thirty-first "most-revised" edition that we are using throughout this study. The treatise "De ecclesia Christi" (7–193) and the immediately following "De romano pontifice" (194–343) are in volume 2. We shall hereafter cite this work simply by volume and page number in parentheses in the text.

14. Aubert, "La géographie ecclésiologique au XIXe siècle," 35. Perrone publicly praised Möhler's *Symbolik* in an address before the Academy of the Catholic Religion in 1837; see Gerald A. McCool, S.J., *Catholic Theology in the Nineteenth Century: The Quest for a Unitary Method* (New York: Seabury, 1977), 83.

15. John P. Boyle, *Church Teaching Authority: Historical and Theological Studies* (Notre Dame: University of Notre Dame Press, 1995), 79–80. Richard R. Gaillardetz, *Witnesses to the Faith: Community, Infallibility, and the Ordinary Magisterium of the Bishops* (New York: Paulist, 1992), 38–40.

16. Michael J. Himes, *Ongoing Incarnation: Johann Adam Möhler and the Beginnings of Modern Ecclesiology* (New York: Crossroad, 1997), 329. There is an unfortunate omission of a crucial "non" in his quotation of Perrone's idea of the Church. Perrone says, "Ecclesiae nomine hic *non* intelligimus coetum omnium fidelium" (By the word "church" here we do *not* mean the congregation of all the faithful) (329n).

the Roman Pontiff.[17] While our chapter here will show that this is certainly true, we should note that Perrone really does recognize at a number of points the basic spiritual nature of the Church. For example, he says that the institutional Church is a means to an end, which is the salvation of all the faithful (2, 8–14). He says that the soul of the Church is the sanctifying grace and other spiritual gifts possessed by its members (2, 25). He also notes that the prerogative of infallibility does not belong to Peter and the popes for their personal benefit, but for the good of the whole Church (2, 323).

Perrone is willing to use the word "ministry" (ministerium) quite a number of times in referring to papal authority. For example, speaking of the authority as witness ("testis"), judge ("iudex"), and teacher ("magistra"), he says that this teacher has the ministry of rightly informing people (2, 148). Using the same three terms in another place, he speaks of the Church authority as "an infallible teacher in daily ministry" (2, 168). Also, Jesus Christ conferred the deposit of faith on the apostles, and said that he would be with this ministry until the end of the world (2, 181). In defining doctrine, the Roman Pontiff, Perrone says, is exercising the "necessary ministry of unity committed to him by Christ" (2, 320). In none of these instances is it very clear that Perrone is adverting to the idea of "service," which is the literal meaning of ministry/ministerium, but he does think of the authority that he stresses so heavily as being intended for the good of the Church. Incidentally, he says in one place that the infallibility of the Church does not take away the need for the study of languages, history, and other subjects relevant to theology (2, 159).

In *Praelectiones theologicae* all of Perrone's ecclesiology is presented under the general heading of "De locis theologicis," in sections entitled "De ecclesia Christi," "De romano pontifice," and "De traditione." In what follows we are proceeding through his 150-page section, "De romano pontifice." Perrone asserts on every page a highly

17. Hermann Josef Pottmeyer, *Unfehlbarkeit und Souveränität: Die päpstliche Unfehlbarkeit im System der ultramontanen Ekklesiologie des 19. Jahrhunderts* (Mainz: Matthias Grünewald, 1975), 283–298.

pope-centered ecclesiology. Echoing a sentiment of Bellarmine, and using a rather untheological term, he states bluntly that papal primacy is the "supreme thing" that there is in Christianity. "When you talk about the head of the Church, you are talking about the supreme thing [*summa res*] on which the existence and salvation of the Church completely depend" (2, 193).[18] This must be asserted not only against non-Catholics, "but against not a few Catholics, who although they admit a primacy by divine right in the Church, still extenuate its power as much as they can, so that they almost reduce it to a mere name" (2, 194). Not naming any of these people here, he does name them at many points. The Gallicans are prime adversaries, particularly their viewpoint on the consensus of the Church. Against Richerians, Febronians, and Pistoians, he asserts the proposition: "Peter received primacy of jurisdiction immediately from Christ, not from the Church" (2, 227). Richer is especially targeted for claiming that the Church community receives the faith and authority from Christ and delegates it to bishops and the pope.

This is the opposite of true Catholic doctrine, for really all the Church's gifts and prerogatives were bestowed on it by Christ through the mediacy of Peter. "Through Peter the Church is one; through Peter the laws have their sanction and all authority is secured; through Peter it has its infallibility" (2, 229). Indeed, Christ founded the supreme office of the papacy before he founded the Church. He designated Peter the head and foundation before he established the Church, just as the wise architect lays the foundation before building the building. Thus the primacy of Peter must be considered the root of unity, and the root and principle from which authority and all the gifts of the Church flow. Peter did not receive the primacy from the Church, because the congregation of faithful never received power from Christ and thus could never confer it on Peter or on anyone (ibid.). In a footnote, Perrone admits that the other apostles did receive power from Christ also, but it was only "extraor-

---

18. Bellarmine uses this expression in *Tertia controversia generalis: De summo pontifice*, praefatio, 451.

dinary," granted to them only so that they could found churches in various places. This power ceased with their deaths (ibid.).

Perrone likes the architect/master builder image, which he sometimes links with other New Testament images like head/body and shepherd/flock. Like the master builder who lays the foundation first, Christ determined the head before he constituted the Church, he designated the rock for the foundation before he erected the building, he established the shepherd before there was a flock, and he gave this head-foundation-shepherd the fullness of power needed to govern the Church. Thus "the Church's constitution is purely monarchical, not at all democratic or aristocratic," as is alleged by the Richerians, Jansenists, and Pistoians, who really agree with the Protestants (2, 235). Surprisingly, he does not mention Gallicans in this section.

Christ did not intend that there be any limits on the primacy other than that the pontiff use his authority for the good and not for the destruction of the Church (2, 315). But even this is implicit and hypothetical. It is implicit because Jesus surely intended everything he did to be for the good of the Church, and he did not specify any limits on the primatial power. It is hypothetical because in reality the pontiff simply does not do anything that would tend to tear down the Church. "The pontiff cannot do anything that would tend to the destruction of the Church, and if anything of this sort were undertaken his acts would be deemed null" (2, 315–316). There is no indication here or elsewhere of what this enigmatic statement means, for there is no provision in Perrone's ecclesiology (any more than in that of Ballerini, Orsi, or Muzzarelli) for any judging or correcting of the Supreme Pontiff. In the meantime, the pope can do anything and everything for the building up of the Church. "Only by this and by no other limit did Christ want the authority of his vicar to be circumscribed" (2, 316). A few pages later, Perrone adds: "If the good of the Church demands it, the Roman Pontiff can use his power at times in a more restricted way, at times in a fuller way, and he alone can be the judge of things which, in the circumstances of times, places, and persons . . . tend to the building up of the Church. Any other rule [that some might suggest] is arbitrary and stems from a spirit of rebellion" (2, 318).

Thus it is idle and unuseful to imagine possible inconveniences that might come from the unlimited kind of supreme authority established by Christ, the divine and all-wise architect and founder of the Church (2, 315). No one should indulge in such pointless questions. In another place Perrone says that if it happened that the pontiff became a contumacious sinner, meaning evidently in his personal life, an inferior could discreetly and respectfully admonish him, but it is wrong ("nefas") to go beyond that. One should have recourse to prayer that in God's providence the sinner may repent and reform (2, 284).

Papal Infallibility and the Consensus of the Church

Perrone begins his discussion of the teaching authority of the Roman Pontiff by asserting that all the gifts or endowments of the Church as a whole are found in a more eminent way in its head, just as all the excellent qualities in the members of the human body are found in a more eminent way in the head (2, 318). This is true in particular of that very important gift of the Church, infallibility in teaching the faith. Those who affirm papal infallibility do not at all separate the Supreme Pontiff from the body of the Church, so that they consider the head apart from the body. Rather, they believe strongly in the unity of the head with the body, and that the head has its nature and its dignity as head only in union with the body. They consider that the pope, in defining doctrines, is performing the "necessary ministry of unity committed to him by Christ" (2, 320). When the Roman Pontiff issues his definitions of faith, he is not stating his own views but what is contained in the deposit of revelation and is transmitted to us in Scripture and tradition. Thus "it cannot happen" that the rest of the Church professes a faith different from that which is defined by the Roman Pontiff (ibid.).

If a different doctrine is expressed somewhere at some time, it is manifestly a novelty that needs to be branded as such and rejected.

"When some error or heresy arises somewhere, the leaders of the Church in the region in which the heresy begins are ordinarily the first to take up arms against the profane novelty; they inform the pontiff of the new error, and request his judgment and definition" (2, 320). Although he says later that there is no need to inquire how the pontiff arrives at his doctrinal decisions (2, 336), Perrone here sketches a loose sequence that involves many parties. The pope studies the question sent to him and launches a "lengthy inquiry" to ascertain the most prudent way to respond. In the meantime, "rumors are aroused, writings for this side and that appear, provincial and national councils are held to discuss the topic, several years pass before the Holy See issues its definition" (2, 320). Perrone notes in a footnote that such things happened during the long Jansenist controversy in the years before each papal statement, for example, the constitution *Cum occasione* of Innocent X in 1653, and more recently during the ten years after the "pseudo-synod" of Pistoia before Pius VI issued *Auctorem Fidei* in 1794 (2, 320n).

Thus when the Supreme Pontiff issues his final judgment the whole business ("negotium") has plainly matured. "For this reason it cannot happen either that the Church rise up against the dogmatic judgment of the pontiff or that it can reform [the judgment]; and certainly it never happens that the Roman Pontiff stands alone in dogmatic definitions" (2, 320). If bishops are divided, some concurring with the pontiff, others disagreeing, all good Catholics remember the ancient rule, "Ubi Petrus, ibi Ecclesia," and know that "those who arise against the pope are necessarily in error, for they constitute not the Church but a headless faction" (2, 320–321). Regarding such a period of controversy and debate Perrone seems to imply that the pope listens to what the parties say and takes it into consideration. He certainly does not say that the pope bases his decision on what any of these people say.

The comments that he has made thus far are asserted and defended systematically in a major proposition: "The Roman Pontiff defining ex cathedra in matters of faith and morals is infallible, and his dogmatic decrees, even before the consensus of the Church, are altogether irreformable, as sacred Scripture shows first of all" (2, 321). For Perrone, this doctrine is certainly and plainly taught in the New Testament in Christ's promises to Peter. "If Peter or the Roman Pontiff were not infallible, or if his faith could fail when he exercises his public magisterium in dogmatic decrees, it would be necessary to say either that Christ's prayer for Peter was inefficacious, or that Christ did not give the Church a sufficient remedy [for solving doctrinal disputes]" (2, 321–322). Since neither of these can be admitted without blasphemy and injury to Christ, it follows that this infallibility must be acknowledged in Peter and his successors. Moreover, if decrees of the pope could be reformed by the Church on the grounds that the Roman Pontiff could fail in faith, then two more problems arise against the promises of Christ. First, it would mean that the Church, as distinguished from its head, would be endowed with infallibility, but this does not belong to the Church community except insofar as together with its head it constitutes one body. Second, this would invert the order established by Christ, for it would mean that Peter would no longer confirm his brothers, but that they would confirm him (2, 322).

In Mt 16:17, Christ stated that he was building the Church on Peter the rock. If you say that the Church could ever somehow correct Peter you are saying that Christ was a "stupid architect" (stultum architectum), who to sustain an eternal building chose an unfit and unstable rock. If you do not want to say that Jesus was that stupid, then you must declare that Peter and his successors are infallible in matters of faith. In this same vein, Perrone adds that if a decree of Peter could ever be reformed by the Church, besides the absurdities just mentioned, it would follow that the Church building was not strengthened by its foundation, but that the foundation was strengthened by the building. This idea, which is the real purport of what the adversaries say, would mean again that Jesus was confused when he established the Church, and "even to think this would be both absurd and impious" (2, 322). A little later Perrone says that if the pope really made a mistake in teaching the faith, the gates of Hell would have prevailed against the rock foundation of the Church (2, 324). He does not elaborate on this.

In another New Testament text, Christ gives Peter the role of shepherd, saying "Feed my sheep" (Jn 21:16). Now, the function of the shepherd of the Church consists not only of administering the sacraments but certainly includes also "the ministry of true doctrine" (2, 322). The Supreme Pastor must always teach the true faith of the Church. "But if the Roman Pontiff in his public and solemn magisterium could possibly make a mistake in a matter of faith, would he not lead the whole flock into error?" (2, 322) Perrone does use the word "magisterium" here and in several other places. In the hypothesis of the adversaries the shepherd would no longer be leading the sheep along a safe path, but rather the sheep would be trying to recall a deviant shepherd back to the right path, which is contrary to the clear mind of Jesus. Gratuitously and wrongly the adversaries postulate a Church distinct from the head and, also endowed with infallibility, able to correct the head. There is nothing in Scripture about the body correcting the head (2, 323 and 2, 325).

The adversaries' stubborn failure to understand Christ's words "Feed my sheep" draws more comments from Perrone about the consensus of the Church allegedly needed when the Roman Pontiff defines the faith. "ABoutngly, the adversaries think that it is not reasonable obedience for the individual churches to obey the pontiff when he defines a dogma ex cathedra, unless they previously examine the specific reasons on which the pontiff relied when he issued the decree of faith" (2, 325). Could not all dissenters, and sectaries, and even the Protestants, make the same objection against the definitions of the Church? Really, the appeal to the consensus of the Church is a delaying tactic used by people who are trying to advance novel doctrines. "In practice, this doctrine [about the consensus of the Church] is supremely harmful, since all sectaries can elude decrees of the Roman Pontiffs proscribing their novelties, which need a present remedy, until an express or tacit consensus can be established; and in the meantime they can disseminate their errors far and wide with impunity" (2, 325–326). Perrone is not using the word "sectaries" in the present-day sense of fervent groups of evangelical or fundamentalist Christians, but in a looser sense of any group that is promoting ideas at variance with Catholic doctrine, such as rationalists, deists, freethinkers, Masons, or misguided Catholics. In a footnote here he mentions the Jansenists as sectaries.

In a long footnote, Perrone says that if you look attentively at those in France who are devising delays in the application of papal decrees, you will find that "it is not the Gallican Church and not the Gallican clergy who act this way, but rascals [*nebulones*] and agitators [*factiosos*]" (2, 326n). When these see that their novelties are about to be condemned by a papal decree, they evasively and craftily invoke the Gallican doctrine and claim that papal decrees are not infallible until the consensus of the Church has been ascertained. Then they use the delay to continue propagating their views. "Never," says Perrone, "do sincere Catholics and those who act in good faith resist papal definitions." He cites as an example the pious submission of Fénelon in 1699 to his condemnation for *Maximes des saints* (ibid.).[19] It may be noteworthy that he seems to consider, correctly, that the Gallican bishops and priests—and laity—really have been devoted to the Roman Catholic faith through history. But clearly his notion of Article 4 bears no resemblance to that of Bossuet and Tournely. It is not, as they believe, a legitimate appeal to a valid collegial or consensual tradition in Roman Catholic history. Rather, it is simply a ruse calculated to evade and impede the supreme shepherd's Christ-given authority. If Perrone has any respect for Bossuet, it is very limited, for he soon dismisses the distinction between *sedes* and *sedens* as another invalid attempt by Bossuet and others to evade the acceptance of the decrees of every pope (2, 330–331).

Can even a council examine a dogmatic definition of the Roman

---

19. Perrone does not cite sources regarding this famous example of docility toward the Holy See, but a very good account is given by Michael de la Bedoyere in *The Archbishop and the Lady: The Story of Fénelon and Madame Guyon* (New York: Pantheon, 1956), 212–234.

Pontiff? Perrone notes two kinds of examination, *examen confirmativum* and *examen dubitativum*. The former means to examine something simply in order to concur with it or confirm it. The latter means to examine with the liberty to assent to it or dissent from it. In the case of a papal definition of doctrine, no one, including a council, has the right or power to conduct a dubitative examination of it. Such a thing "is never permitted regarding dogmatic definitions of the Roman Pontiffs even before any consensus of the Church" (2, 333). He says that this is shown in the history of famous councils. Popes Celestine I, Leo the Great, and Agatho sent doctrinal missives to the councils of Ephesus, Chalcedon, and Constantinople I "as the norm that these councils were to follow, expressly warning in instructions that they gave their legates, that nothing in [the missives] relating to the faith could be changed" (2, 333).[20] Perrone simply uses the term "council" in this passage, not specifying ecumenical councils but obviously including them. Incidentally, the word *dubitativum* is probably intended to have a rather pejorative flavor, suggesting that people who want to do such an examination of a papal statement may have a dubious and not a strong and certain faith. The reason why a council may not presume to do any such examination is clear: "The dogmatic definitions of Roman Pontiffs have in themselves [*ex se*] total coercive force, so that no one truly Catholic can oppose or withstand them" (ibid.). "Total coercive force" renders literally his Latin "totam vim eamque coactivam." The phrase is of course reminiscent of Ballerini's key expression, "vis coactiva ad unitatem fidei." He does not cite Ballerini here, but does cite him in footnotes in this and in other sections.

While emphatically stressing the inferiority of councils to the papacy, Perrone does say that councils can at times have a useful role to play in the Church's life. Innovators are often quite troublesome; they manage to agitate multitudes and deceive the unwary. When this happens, there may be need for a council, at which "from the collec-

---

20. He does not cite any sources for this statement.

tive votes of many, and their solemn adhesion to a pontifical definition, the faith of the whole Catholic Church is made more evident" (ibid.). A number of popes have convoked councils as "a suitable means to discuss complex and difficult questions more securely" and effectively (2, 333–334). This may recall the stubborn innovators to unity, or if not then at least serve to show that their errors are solemnly condemned. But although the utility of councils is generally widely recognized, he comments, historical experience has unfortunately also shown that people who are unwilling to accept papal authority tend to be also unwilling to accept the decrees of ecumenical councils (2, 333).

Given that papal infallibility is not a defined dogma of faith, one could ask whether the papacy has the power to command internal assent to its teachings. Perrone answers in the affirmative, saying that the adversaries themselves and the constant practice of the Church maintain that "all the faithful are by the institution of Christ bound to obey the head of the Church when he solemnly decrees something of the faith" (2, 336).[21] Obedience, to be true obedience, should be from the heart: it should be interior and sincere. Thus "although it is not officially *de fide* that the Roman Pontiff possesses infallibility, still all are compelled to give interior assent to papal dogmatic definitions." Perrone thinks that from this fact of strict obligation to give interior assent to papal definitions "we can draw an argument to prove infallibility" (ibid.). He says that it would be difficult, if not impossible, to reconcile the strict obligation to adhere with mind and heart to papal dogmatic definitions with the opinion of those who say that the Roman Pontiff is subject to *error* even in ex cathedra statements. "How the adversaries can reconcile these things with each other I profess I just cannot comprehend" (2, 336n). His reasoning here is surprising, for he surely knows that the adversaries really do not say that the faithful are obliged to give definitive assent to an assertion made only by the pope alone. In addition, most people

---

21. He does not cite any adversaries here.

would tend to say that you should reason from authority to obligation rather than from obligation to authority. Perrone adds that in practice "the universal Church has always adhered, adheres, and always will adhere to the center of the unity of faith, the uniquely apostolic Church headed by the Roman Pontiff" (ibid.). Any persons who resist are "rebellious and refractory." But not heretical. Although Perrone uses strong language against those who fail to assent to papal statements, he consistently refrains from calling them heretics. "If this article were of faith, then whoever denied [papal] definitions would immediately be formal heretics and outside the Church" (2, 336).

Perrone adds that the pope's infallible teaching authority does not depend on the Church of Rome, that is, on the community of the faithful constituting the diocese of Rome, or any clergy, curial officials, or theologians in Rome. Christ endowed Peter and his successors with infallibility for the good of the Church when he conferred the primacy on them. "Since the primacy is personal it follows that the inerrancy of the pontiffs does not depend on the Roman Church, but rather all the privileges that the Roman See possesses flow to it from Peter and his successors" (ibid.). He adds a comment that is very significant for what it seems to say about his regard for the entire episcopate of the Church. "The true tradition of the Roman Church is made known to the faithful through them [Peter and his successors], and no necessity presses us to inquire into the means that the Roman Pontiff has used or should use in issuing his solemn dogmatic definitions" (ibid.). It is evidently not the concern of bishops or anyone else how the Supreme Pontiff arrives at his definitions of the faith, and people should not indulge in idle questions about this. He does not even mention, a point stressed by Giuseppe-Agostino Orsi, that the pope should consult learned men about the doctrinal matter at issue, though he would probably agree that it would be wise for the pope to do this.

Incidentally, Perrone does not mention in the sections that we have studied here the definition of the Immaculate Conception by Pius IX in 1854. That happened after the first edition of the *Praelec-*

tiones (1835–1842), but well before the thirty-first edition (1865) that we have been using. In any case, there is really no indication here that he would have advised Pius to consult the world episcopate about this definition. It would be quite consistent with what we do find him saying that he would have advised the pope simply to define it by himself.

The Consensus of the Church and Modern Errors

In 1874, shortly after the council, Perrone published a substantial book discussing various aspects of the dogmatic constitution on papal authority, *De romani pontificis infallibilitate, seu Vaticana definitio contra novos hereticos asserta et vindicata*.[22] Several chapters include some very significant comments about the *consensus Ecclesiae*. In one he responds to the objection made by some, not named, who said that papal authority has now absorbed into itself everything that belonged to the rest of the *Ecclesia docens,* that is, the whole body of bishops, whether dispersed around the world or assembled in council. Not so, says Perrone, though his explanation would not give much satisfaction to the objectors, whom he calls "detractors." The traditional role of the episcopate remains the same as always, though all must keep in mind that "the infallibility of the bishops even taken all together, depends on the infallibility of Peter, or the Roman Pontiff." This is because "unless the judgment [*suffragium*] of the Roman Pontiff is added as a complement and seal to the judgment of all the bishops, [their judgment] by itself can be subject to error" (121). The body of bishops is not infallible, and they "are not the *Ecclesia docens* except insofar as they are united to and subordinate to the visible head of the Church" (122). The efficient cause of the infallible teaching authority that belongs to the primacy is the assistance of the Holy Spirit. Thus infallibility is in no way derived from the express or tacit consensus of the bishops. "Rather, the Roman Pontiff communicates irreformability to the judgment of the bishops, and not vice versa" (124).

---

22. Turin: Marietti, 1874. This is a book of 224 pages.
This book also will be cited by page numbers inserted parenthetically in the text.

Yes, the Holy Spirit does assist the bishops also in their task of teaching, but the necessary condition of this, and the sign that he is helping them, is their concurrence with the head of the Church (ibid.). Thus Perrone reiterates here what he and our other papalist authors have consistently said. It is an idea reaffirmed by Cardinal Joseph Ratzinger in his statement on papal primacy in 1998. He says that the pope in the exercise of his teaching authority in every age is guided by the "necessitas Ecclesiae." "The Holy Spirit helps the Church to recognize this necessity, and the Roman Pontiff, by listening to the Spirit's voice in the Churches, looks for the answer and offers it when and how *he* considers it appropriate."[23] In the last sentence of this document, he states, "We are all invited to trust in the Holy Spirit, to trust in Christ, by trusting in Peter."[24]

Some critics of the council's declaration said that papal supremacy now absorbs, or usurps, into itself the role of ecumenical councils. Perrone rejects the criticism. One brief chapter explains why the new definition of papal power does not mean that councils are not still sometimes useful (125–131). Another says that the council's definition does mean that councils are certainly not necessary. *Pastor Aeternus* means that a council is never necessary, because the Roman Pontiff, possessing the fullness of power to rule and teach the Church, can settle controversies of faith and "nail" errors by papal power alone without the concurrence of the bishops (131).[25] "Now no one can resist a papal definition under the pretext that it lacks the consensus of the Church, either in a council or outside a council" (ibid.). An appeal to the consensus of the Church remains simply a hackneyed and discredited ruse of disloyal agitators.

The most opportune and providential aspect of the Vatican Coun-

---

23. Cardinal Joseph Ratzinger, "The Primacy of the Successor of Peter in the Mystery of the Church," *Osservatore romano,* November 18, 1998, 5–6. This statement is in paragraph 12; emphasis added. In this document "churches" refers to the various Christian churches, especially those interested in ecumenical dialogue with the Roman Catholic Church.

24. Ibid., paragraph 15.

25. "Nail" is a literal rendering of his word, *configere,* to pierce through.

cil's declaration, for Perrone, is that it comes just in time to serve the Church's greatest modern need: the condemnation of the many errors that plague both the Church and civil society. The Church has always had to contend with errors, but now the number and kind of errors are unprecedented, and the need for condemnations is greater than in any past time. A council of bishops simply cannot act fast enough to do this effectively. He devotes two pages to the factors that make a council slow in assembling and cumbersome in functioning (132–133). Errors simply must be condemned quickly and decisively, because otherwise they become more widely disseminated and consequently more and more difficult—perhaps impossible—to uproot. He cites the well-known, and huge, case of Protestantism, whose errors were not stopped promptly in the sixteenth century, so that after several generations it became a permanent, and finally seemingly "normal," part of Christendom (134, 135). He does not specifically fault Leo X, Adrian VI, Clement VII, or other popes for neglect in allowing Protestantism to take root, but rather blames the lack of full and clear recognition of papal infallibility at that time. "If infallible papal authority had been established by a dogmatic definition by that time, and if Protestantism were really solemnly proscribed by it, then either it could not have progressed at all, and invaded so many Catholic regions, or it would have done much less damage" (135).

Similarly, the Jansenists used Gallican opinions to defend their heresies, and despite several papal censures were able to prolong the controversy inordinately. But if a dogmatic definition of papal infallibility had existed then, they could not have engaged in so many evasions and crafty subterfuges, including vague references to a council. "Most opportunely therefore the papal magisterium has been defined as infallible 'ex sese, non autem ex consensu Ecclesiae,'" ruling out such evasive tactics for the future (136).[26]

Today, countless new errors are being spread, continues Perrone, and swift, decisive action is needed to stop them, both at the local level and at the level of the universal Church. In almost every region

---

26. He does not cite any historical works on the Jansenist controversy.

unbelievers, sectarians, pantheists, materialists, and atheists are spreading their false doctrines (136, 141). Rather than travel to a council, the bishops should stay in their own dioceses to guard their flocks, lest during a long absence "rapacious wolves" are able to come in and mislead the faithful (136). At the Church's center, the Roman Pontiff's supreme power to assert the faith and condemn errors must not be impeded by references to a supposed need for the assent of the bishops. "Who is unaware how difficult it is to collect the votes of so many prelates? And how easy it is to claim that not all the bishops concur with the judgment of the pontiff." Recently some so-called Liberal Catholics were doing this. Infected with Gallican ideas before the council, they tried to evade the encyclical *Quanta cura* and the *Syllabus of Errors,* claiming that they were being interpreted in different ways by different bishops, and that the consensus of the whole episcopate with the papal magisterium was not manifest. But "after the Vatican definition such evasions have been precluded, and this is the great utility of the definition" (137).

"Long experience has shown that if some novelty arises, and is not eliminated immediately, it spreads far and wide like a fire with immense harm to truth and to souls" (139). Once errors are diffused among the people, it becomes very difficult to extirpate them and to curb the rise of the dissensions, contending parties, and factions inevitably generated by errors (139–140). "But once the infallible authority of the Roman Pontiff has been established, the peoples are maintained in good order much more rapidly and easily, and not carried away by the wind of false doctrine" (140). This is true in the first place of Church order, but is true of civil society also, and this should be recognized by political leaders. History shows that the peace of society is disturbed by innovators preaching errors of various kinds. But if errors are condemned and repressed as soon as they arise, then innumerable evils are happily prevented. "Now with infallible papal authority established, so many evils can be much more easily blocked, and a remedy placed against errors before they infect the multitude" (141).

Perrone speaks of the errors being blocked and the problems remedied by swift and emphatic papal condemnations. He seems to think that since the older hindrances and mistakenly supposed limits on total papal supremacy have been cleared away by *Pastor Aeternus,* and specifically by its *ex sese* clause, papal power will ensure the peace and security of the Church. It could do the same for the world also, if modern people were not so enamored of errors and so obstinate in resisting truth. One might wonder just how he thinks that condemnations hurled from on high will, empirically speaking, really *bring about* the desired good results. Something of an answer can be found in his comments on the reaction to the *Syllabus of Errors* in 1864. There was an "incredible commotion" at that time, as "crazy people" vented their anger, and not only individuals but some governments, mostly controlled by "sectaries," attacked the Holy See for this salutary document (139).[27] But all the attacks of "impious men" were in vain, as the Catholic faithful everywhere accepted the document with due veneration. What can worldly men and governments do against truths taught by the apostolic authority? "They will perish, but the acts of the Supreme Pastor will endure until eternity." This can only be explained by the faith of the Catholic people "in the infallible authority of the magisterium with which Christ willed his vicar on earth to be endowed" (ibid.).

He seems to mean that you do not need to ask how the condemnations stop the errors or remedy the problems if you devoutly believe in the supreme, and divinely granted, *power* with which the pope issues them. The more you revere the gracious teaching power with which Jesus endowed his vicar on earth, the more confident you are that obeying the Holy Father is the one thing needful, and the more impatient you become with people who try to impede his power with idle and divisive talk about the consensus of the Church. Giovanni Perrone would like to be patient and charitable with these people but finds it very difficult, because they so stubbornly ignore

---

27. The strong expression "crazy people" renders literally *vesanos homines.*

the act of Almighty God Himself in founding the papacy. His view is that of Pius IX, as very perceptively noted by Klaus Schatz in speaking of the role of the pope during the latter months of the Vatican Council. "In all this Pius IX had little sense of the pastoral seriousness and important theological objections that underlay the reasoning of the minority."[28] For him, Schatz says, the minority bishops must be motivated by a timid yielding to the secular spirit of the age and to public opinion, and also a desire to please certain governments. "He regarded it as a question of proper supernatural attitude whether one would offer unconditional support to the Holy See at a moment when the 'gates of hell' were bringing all their forces against it."[29] For Pius it was self-evident that if you believe in Jesus Christ, and thus have a supernatural attitude, then you certainly and unequivocally believe in papal infallibility. If you do not believe in papal infallibility, but rather continue to talk about the consensus of the Church, then you have, regrettably, given in to materialism and the spirit of this world.

28. Klaus Schatz, S.J., *Papal Primacy from Its Origins to the Present* (Collegeville: Liturgical, 1996), 156–157.
29. Ibid., 157.

CHAPTER 10

Conclusion

It is clear that the Gallican and papalist ecclesiologies, as we find them expressed in the authors studied here, entail radically different views of the consensus of the Church, as what is naturally included in the former is naturally excluded from the latter. The basic difference can be stated briefly. In the papalist view the successor of Peter really is a benevolent and paternal absolute monarch in ruling and teaching, and there is no need for the involvement of the faithful of any rank in this task. In the Gallican view the primatial authority, recognized as genuine and essential, is exercised in conjunction with the rest of the episcopate in a way that today would be called collegial and consensual.

For the papalist authors studied here what is given from the beginning is the almighty primatial Power established by the divine founder of the Church and conferred on one man alone. This is the supreme, and really divine, Power to rule and teach the entire community, and specifically to effect and maintain its unity of faith. All revolves around this Power and all is deduced from this Power. Once understanding the nature and purpose of this tremendous Power, you can and necessarily must deduce from it in rigorous logical order all other aspects of the structure and functioning of the whole Church. Upholding and revering this majestic and benevolent Power is the prime and central concern of all the members of the Church, who should be grateful that God has wisely and magnanimously provided this Power to sustain and guide their faith community.

The papalist standpoint does not recognize as legitimate any questions about the participation of the members of the Church, including the entire episcopate, in the making of decisions about policy or doctrine. The instinctive tendency of this view is to perceive any suggestion about the involvement of the community as infringement on the Power, as some kind of attempt—overt or devious—to evade or depreciate the Power. For this reason the suggestion is rejected out of hand as being self-evidently wrong. There is no need even to discuss its possible merits because any discussion might imply some deficiency in the sovereign Power established by Jesus, and probably a lack of faith in the gentle Savior himself. Thus a proposal that a doctrinal definition of the Roman Pontiff needs the consensus of the community, and specifically of the world episcopate, is as obviously mistaken as any other failure to accept the plan of God. The great error of the Gallicans is to try to impose human conditions on the divine institution of the primacy.

For the Gallican authors whose work we have reviewed here what is given from the beginning of Christianity is the whole community, which needs and has a number of ministers. The congregation of the faithful is not an unstructured one, and it is not at all a democracy. It is a fully structured, hierarchical, and indeed monarchical institution. This ecclesiology genuinely accepts papal primacy, a specifically Roman primacy, not merely of honor but of jurisdiction over the whole Church, and at no time intends to minimize or depreciate papal authority. This view and the papalist view differ only regarding the prerogatives entailed in the primacy. Bossuet, Tournely, and the other Gallican authors say that only the Church, meaning the hierarchy as a whole, can infallibly decide an important question of faith, not the Roman Pontiff by himself. For them the consensus of the Church has been an essential part, from the beginning, of a community of faith endowed by its founder with bishops as well as a pope, and is not a mere "human condition" concocted later by persons who are not sincere when they say that they accept papal primacy.

Yves Congar summed it up with admirable succinctness when he said of the ecclesiology of mainstream Gallican theologians: "One can, I believe, characterize it in the history of ecclesiological doctrines as the will not to let the pole *Ecclesia* be absorbed by the pole *papacy*."[1] The Gallicans believed, he continued, that the divinely established authority of the Church is shared between the power of the episcopate and the power of the pope in such a way that "neither can be validly exercised without the other."[2] Both are essential and neither should be reduced to a merely nominal role. Bossuet, Tournely, and the others, committed Roman Catholic theologians, can be seen as depreciating the papacy only from a standpoint that thinks that the only genuine "primacy" is one totally vested in one person and not limited by any "human condition," that is, not shared with any other ministers of the Church, all of whom are simply subjects and agents of the Roman Pontiff.

The fact that the papalist authors describe papal primacy as absolute monarchy could be taken by present-day readers as simply showing a concern for power in and for itself, a kind of determination to assert Roman power to dominate all. Attributing this motivation to them is really not just, for these authors really think of themselves as devoted to the words of Jesus. The piety that pervades their treatises is a genuine piety. For them the devout Catholic does not seek or need "proofs" for the supremacy and infallibility of the Holy Father beyond the Petrine texts of the Gospels. Surely Christ's words are clear: Peter is the firm rock on which the Church is built, the shepherd who lovingly feeds all the sheep, and the ever-reliable sustainer of the faith of the brethren. Surely Christ, the divine Son of the divine Father, is supremely wise and supremely dependable. Pa-

---

1. Yves Congar, O.P. "Gallicanisme," in G. Jacquemet, ed., *Catholicisme* (Paris: Letouzey, 1956), 4:1736.
2. Ibid.

palist authors speak reproachfully to any who do not seem to realize this. Bellarmine says that Christ obviously chose absolute monarchy for the Church because it is the best form of government. After all Jesus has done for you, how could you even suggest that he would choose an inferior form of government for his Church? Ballerini says that if you say that the Roman Pontiff's power to enforce unity of faith is not absolute, that is, "not subject to any conditions," then you are saying that Jesus provided badly for unity and does not keep his promises. How could you ever say that about Jesus? Muzzarelli says that if the pope ever made a mistake in teaching doctrine, then Christ's promise has failed. Moreover, if the pope is not infallible, then he is guilty of dreadful usurpation. How could you ever utter such impieties about Jesus and St. Peter? Perrone says that if you say that the Roman Pontiff is not infallible, then you are saying that Jesus was a "stupid architect," who was so clueless that he did not create a solid rock foundation for his Church. After all Jesus has done for you, how could you ever say such a thing about him?[3] The earnest piety in these readings of Scripture speaks from a very powerful certainty that not only obviates the need for any other study, but also throws a shadow of *impiety* on anyone that asks questions about the matter.

Given this conviction about the scriptural basis of the papalist doctrine, these authors also tend to think that there is no real need for any "historical proofs" for papal supremacy. Specifically, there is no need for "proofs" of the exercise of a Petrine primacy from the first years of the Church community. That Peter certainly exercised total sovereign power from the beginning is assumed as a given. This means that any historical sources that could be cited, if looked at in a spirit of piety, show Peter (and then his successors) exercising the full monarchical power of ruling and teaching. This begins with the Acts of the Apostles, for the Council of Jerusalem (Acts 15) shows Peter determining the faith for the community. Orsi, for example, says that

3. In each of these instances, all of which were cited in their respective chapters, the reproachful question is implied. It will be noted that all the ideas of the authors cited in this conclusion were given in the chapters, with citation of their texts.

when Peter stated his view all discussion ceased, providing "the clearest proof that the judgment of Peter in matters of faith was regarded as irretractable and unchangeable." After Peter's statement, "no consensus of the sacred assembly was awaited so that it would have its force." Moreover, as noted in several chapters here, any mention of people in the early centuries seeking the judgment of the bishop of Rome on a question is assumed to mean recognition of his personal power to decide the question definitively. The papalist authors would agree with Alfredo Ottaviani when he says, speaking of the election of bishops by clergy and people in the early centuries, that this took place "by the tacit or express concession" of the Supreme Pontiff.[4] They would also presumably concur with his view of the very purpose of Church history: "The function of ecclesiastical history is to show how the Holy See applied its authority in various periods."[5] This viewpoint evidently does not perceive history as an empirical discipline in which one goes to the sources to learn what *they* say.

Congar has noted this as a deficiency of the historical scholarship of eighteenth-century papalist authors, mentioning by name Ballerini and Muzzarelli. He calls them "not researchers but apologists," saying that they do not actually seek the real history of Church institutional growth. Rather, to prove a position already determined, they use any possible historical bits and texts that they think can serve "their single idea," that the Church authority consists of a papal monarchy and that the supreme chief is endowed with infallibility.[6] He sees Gallican and Febronian authors as more scholarly in their historical analyses. Comparing these Ultramontane treatises with Gallican or Febronian treatises, "we are struck by this difference: the Gallican or episcopalian positions are elaborated *starting from* histori-

---

4. Alaphridus Ottaviani, *Institutiones iuris publici ecclesiastici,* 5th ed. (Vatican City: Typis Polyglottis Vaticanis, 1958; first published 1936), 1:377. "Authority" renders *influxus.*

5. Ibid., 1:376.

6. Yves Congar, O.P., "L'ecclésiologie de la Révolution française au Concile du Vatican, sous la signe de l'affirmation de l'autorité," in Maurice Nédoncelle et al., *L'ecclésiologie au XIXe siècle* (Paris: Cerf, 1960), 93.

cal facts and reflect their complexity. The Ultramontane authors use texts of the past to illustrate their affirmations; they follow their adversaries on the terrain of history to refute them, but their positions proceed really from an idea. They also have the simplicity and force [of the idea]."[7]

These comments, though they do largely apply to the authors studied here, do not quite do justice to the very industrious work of most of them. Giuseppe-Agostino Orsi, for example, does display great erudition and years of diligent study in his work. Even Pietro Ballerini, despite the obviously aprioristic nature of his relentlessly deductive treatise, does show considerable and creditable study of sources. This could be said also of some papalist writers not dealt with in this book: for example, two Spanish authors, Thyrso Gonzales de Santalla, S.J., and José Saenz de Aguirre, O.S.B., both of whom wrote huge responses to the Gallican Declaration of 1682. Thyrso Gonzales, professor of theology at Salamanca and later general of the Society of Jesus (1687–1705), produced a work of 916 large pages that especially targeted Article 4, and which shows very extensive study of many sources.[8] Aguirre, a professor in the same Spanish city, says that a wave of horror swept Salamanca when people heard what the French clergy had declared. He wrote, in about one year, a very large book (544 pages, plus an appendix of 160 pages) undertaking to refute in strong terms the ideas of Gallicanism.[9] Both these works are

---

7. Ibid.; emphasis his. Febronius was the nom de plume of Johann Nikolaus von Hontheim (1701–1790), who wrote a widely read treatise (1763) stating that Christ conferred authority on the whole community; as its ministers all the bishops and pope are equal and the pope has only a primacy of honor. Thus, Febronianism is sometimes called episcopalist or episcopalian. See Richard F. Costigan, S.J., "Hontheim, Johann Nickolaus von [Febronius]," in Patrick W. Carey and Joseph T. Lienhard, eds., *Biographical Dictionary of Christian Theologians* (Westport, Conn.: Greenwood, 2000), 252.

8. Thyrso Gonzales de Santalla, S.J., *De infallibilitate romani pontificis in definiendis fidei et morum controversiis extra concilium generale et non expectato ecclesiae consensu, contra recentes huius infallibilitatis impugnatores* (Rome: Felicis Caesaretti, 1689).

9. José Saenz de Aguirre, O.S.B., *Auctoritas infallibilis et summa cathedrae sancti Petri extra et supra concilia quaelibet atque in totam ecclesiam denuo stabilita.* (Salamanca: Lucas Perez, 1683).

written in a polemical style but show genuine industry in their authors. Moreover, it is proper and essential, for them or for anyone, to point out the numerous instances in which the pope did exercise a major role in the early centuries and thereafter.

Today it is generally recognized that in the early centuries the bishop of Rome did not rule the entire Church in the manner of an absolute monarch governing through a centralized bureaucracy. It is also understood that he did not determine the whole content of the faith simply by personal decree. Rather, the growth of the Roman primacy in both ruling and teaching took place gradually over many centuries.[10] Most would also tend to agree that the popes generally earned the great respect that cumulatively accrued to their office by their intelligent and responsible exercise of leadership through many controversies. Specifically, the popes earned recognition as the chief teachers of the faith by their consistent ability to articulate steadily and persuasively the beliefs of the Catholic Church as to the essential teachings of Jesus Christ. Gallican authors base their acceptance of the pope as the most important authoritative teacher of the faith on their understanding of this historical record. They see the record as showing how the papacy has fulfilled the role really given to Peter by Jesus Christ.

But this whole kind of thinking is quite foreign to the papalist standpoint. The idea of basing one's acceptance of papal authority on the pope's actual historical record of earning respect as an authoritative teacher does not fit in the papalist ecclesiology. In their Churchview, the pope does not *earn* respect or acceptance any more than God—Father, Son, or Holy Spirit—earns respect or acceptance.

---

10. Among numerous works on this, some that both summarize much scholarship and give many references, are: William Henn, O.F.M. Cap., *The Honor of My Brothers: A Brief History of the Relationship between the Pope and the Bishops* (New York: Crossroad, 2000), esp. 7–83; Klaus Schatz, S.J., *Papal Primacy from Its Origins to the Present* (Collegeville: Liturgical, 1996), esp. 1–77; Patrick Granfield, O.S.B., *The Papacy in Transition* (Garden City, N.Y.: Doubleday, 1980), esp. chap. 4, "The Pope as Monarch," 34–61; and Robert B. Eno, S.S., *The Rise of the Papacy* (Wilmington, Del.: Michael Glazier, 1990).

Rather, possession of divine power (that is, power directly bestowed by the divine founder of the Church) simply requires *obedience* in the subjects. It is assumed that the Holy Father certainly teaches the faith supremely well and better than any other, but it is not for the quality of his teaching that the devout subjects assent to his statements. Nor is it because they believe that his teaching expresses the consensus of the Church on the doctrine in question. It is because he has a supreme power to tell them what to believe and to compel them to believe it.

It has been noted in all the chapters on the papalist authors that in the Church as they understand it the Roman Pontiff has full power by virtue of his office to declare, and when appropriate to define solemnly, the faith of the Church. It is always understood by these authors that it is the faith of the Church that the pope teaches, and not just his own opinion. He cannot and does not create any new doctrines that have not been part of the Church's tradition. He cannot and does not claim any new "revelation," for like everyone in the Church he knows that the deposit of faith was closed with the death of the last apostle. He cannot and does not create any new sacraments or discard any of the Church's traditional sacraments. The doctrines that he teaches are those that have been taught continuously by councils and previous popes. The papalist authors are aware that the community's agreement on these doctrines can legitimately be called "consensus," and that the pope is bound to teach the doctrines of that consensus. Nonetheless, they maintain consistently and adamantly that the Supreme Pontiff alone is competent to decide what the doctrines of the consensus are, for this was the manifest intention of Jesus in establishing the primacy.

Thus all the papalist authors reject any suggestion that the faith community, and specifically the episcopate, in whole or in part, has any role in formulating that consensus. As noted above, the instinctive tendency of this viewpoint is to view any such suggestions as some kind of infringement on the divine power that Jesus bestowed on the primacy. Surely it is self-evident that divine power is unlimited power, and all true Catholics realize this. Dissenters like the Gallicans, who call themselves Catholics, must know it also, but act as though they do not. When they maintain that the Church needs some way to see that a papal pronouncement expresses the consensus of the Church (episcopate), they show that they do not really respect the divine character of Christ's mandate to Peter. They may be doing this in good faith and "innocently," or they may be doing it out of some kind of willfulness (this interpretation is preferred), but in either case they are certainly failing to accept the divine will of Jesus. Ballerini speaks most emphatically for this view when he says that the Gallicans err woefully in Article 4 when they try to "impose human conditions" on the divine power of the Roman Pontiff.

For these authors the Roman Pontiff does need to make sure that what he says, especially in a solemn definition, really articulates the belief (consensus) of the Church. He must not speak imprudently or hastily, before he is convinced that his statement is certainly Catholic doctrine. But there are no institutional requirements that he must observe in arriving at this certainty. Is it necessary for the pope to consult many bishops, or the cardinals, or learned men, or the clergy of Rome? No, it is not. Orsi, for example, says that the pope *should* use available human means, such as consulting learned cardinals, but it is not necessary. He can issue an irretractable definition even if he has done no consulting. Giovanni Perrone says that the pope, when a doctrinal controversy needs to be settled, studies the issue himself and consults others in a "lengthy inquiry." But how the pontiff arrives at his decision on the doctrine is purely his concern, and "no necessity presses on us to inquire into the means which the Roman Pontiff has used or should use in issuing his solemn dogmatic definitions." In other words, for Perrone, it is nobody's business how the pontiff handles this matter, and people should not indulge in idle speculation about it. Klaus Schatz's comment on these papalist authors of the seventeenth century and thereafter is very perceptive. For them, he says, the duty of the pope to ascertain the faith of the Church before defining "was seen more and more as purely an individual moral obligation of the pope, not an ecclesiological necessity; it was a subject belonging essentially to papal morals, not to ecclesiology."[11]

This view was expressed very explicitly and candidly at the council in 1870 by Bishop Vincent Gasser, bishop of Brixen, Austria, and a spokesman for the Deputation on Faith (the drafting committee of the documents of the council). His report to the council on July 11, 1870 is a major and authoritative statement of the ecclesiology of the deputation, of the council majority, and of the resulting dogmatic constitution *Pastor Aeternus*, solemnly voted through on July 18. Gasser says several times that the Roman Pontiff certainly is not separated from the consensus of the Church. "We do not separate the Pope, defining, from the cooperation and consensus of the Church, at least in the sense that we do not exclude this cooperation and consensus of the Church."[12] Again, he states: "It is true that the consensus of the present preaching of the whole magisterium of the Church, united with its head, is a rule of faith even for pontifical definitions."[13] But there are no rules that need to be observed by the pontiff when he decides what the faith is. Though he should be diligent in studying the issues, it is purely a matter of "the conscience of the Pontiff," for this pertains "to the moral order rather than the dogmatic order."[14] Thus there is no necessity that he seek any consensus from the rulers of the Churches or from the bishops. The reason for this is that the Holy Father has many ways to ascertain the faith of the Church. "I say this because this consensus is very frequently able to be deduced from the clear and manifest testimonies of Sacred Scripture, from the consent of antiquity, that is, of the Holy Fathers, from the opinion of theologians and from other private means, all of

---

11. Schatz, *Papal Primacy*, 133.
12. The Gasser text is given in *The Gift of Infallibility: The Official Relatio on Infallibility of Bishop Vincent Gasser at Vatican Council I*, trans. James T. O'Connor (Boston: St. Paul Editions, 1986), 43, 44.
13. Ibid., 50. His Latin for "consensus" is *consensio*. The translator in this English version actually renders it as "consent," but it seems legitimate for our purposes here to alter that to "consensus."
14. Ibid., 46.

which suffice for full information about the fact of the Church's consensus."¹⁵ Another means is "the Tradition of the Church of Rome, that is, of that Church to which faithlessness has no access."¹⁶ Given all these means conveniently available to the Holy Father at all times, it is surely vain and pointless to talk about any supposed need to seek the consensus of the episcopate. Gasser mentions the fact that Pius IX, before he proclaimed the Immaculate Conception of Mary in 1854, consulted the bishops of the world on the doctrine. Pius did this purely "for his own information."¹⁷

It will have been noted that what Gasser says in the first sentence quoted from him here, that "we do not exclude this cooperation and consensus of the Church," was explicitly contradicted in the final text of the document. The phrase *non ex consensu Ecclesiae* was not in the text that he discussed on July 11, but was proposed by some of the majority after that day. It was added by the deputation on July 14 and was in a text presented to the council by Gasser on July 16. The council voted on it that same day, and again in the final vote on July 18.¹⁸

Is the word "absolute" properly applied to papal authority? The term is used explicitly by some papalist authors and implicitly by others. Ballerini definitely says that it is absolute: the power of the primacy must be "absoluta," for if it is to be efficacious to preserve unity of faith, then it "must not be tied to any condition of human judgment and will." Orsi says that the Gallicans, after seventeen centuries, rashly tried in 1682 to "prescribe limits on papal authority, which was circumscribed by no limits by Christ himself, the wisdom of almighty God." Perrone states that Christ did not intend any limits

15. Ibid., 50–51.
16. Ibid., 51.
17. Ibid. For an extended treatment of Pius IX's "poll" of the episcopate relative to the definition of the Immaculate Conception, see J. Robert Dionne, *The Papacy and the Church: A Study of Praxis and Reception in Ecumenical Perspective* (New York: Philosophical Library, 1987), 304–319.
18. See Cuthbert Butler, O.S.B., *The Vatican Council, 1869–1870* (London: Longmans Green, 1930; London: Collins and Harvill, 1962), 407.

on papal authority other than that it be employed for the good of the Church, and the pope alone can be the judge of what is good for the Church. "Any other rule is arbitrary and stems from a spirit of rebellion."

Bishop Gasser also comments on the word "absolute." He states that papal authority is *not* absolute. If some ask whether papal infallibility is absolute, "I reply and openly admit: in no sense is pontifical infallibility absolute, because absolute infallibility belongs to God alone." "All other infallibility, as communicated for a specific purpose, has its limits and its conditions under which it is considered to be present. The same is valid in reference to the Roman Pontiff. For this infallibility is bound by certain limits and conditions."[19] He adds that those limits are to be inferred from the will of Christ in his promises to Peter. Surely Vincent Gasser, and the members of the Deputation on Faith for whom he speaks, are sincere in all their statements about the doctrine in *Pastor Aeternus*. But when they add that the limits and conditions on papal infallibility are purely in the conscience of the Holy Father, and there are no rules that that he needs to observe in deciding on the faith, they nullify the assertion that papal authority is not absolute. It so happens that this is the meaning of the word "absolute": the ruler decides all things, and need not observe any rules known to the members of the community being ruled. This is the essence of absolute monarchy. The expression "absolute monarchy" should not be taken in a negative sense, for it is a respectable term in Western history, and quite compatible with traditional Catholic piety.

Gasser and all the papalist authors maintain that the Church community should not worry that the Supreme Pontiff will ever make a mistake in defining the faith. It simply will not happen, and all devout Catholics know that it will not happen. Devout Catholics, aware that Jesus Christ gave Peter complete authority to teach the faith unerringly, do not suffer any uncertainty or anxiety, and do not

19. Gasser, *Gift of Infallibility*, 45.

listen to people, like the Gallicans, who try to sow the seeds of doubt. Muzzarelli says most emphatically, and with great feeling, speaking of the "solemn judgment of the pope," that "if for one sole time, and on one sole day, this judgment were fallible and subject to error," then the faithful could be led into error. This would mean that Christ's promise had failed, and we know that Christ would not allow that to happen. This sentiment is certainly implied throughout the work of Orsi, Ballerini, and Perrone.

Some statements meant to be reassuring are interesting—and puzzling. Perrone, for example, says that the pontiff cannot do anything that would tend to the destruction of the Church, "and if anything of this sort were undertaken his acts would be deemed null." Perrone makes no attempt to explain what this means, and there is nothing in his ecclesiology that could explain it. Muzzarelli, in the last lines of his great syllogism, says that if the Supreme Pontiff is not infallible, then his claim to be so is an intolerable error tending to the destruction of the Church, which God could not permit, "and which the Church itself could not accept with silence, praise, and execution, because the Church does not do, approve, or tacitly condone what is against faith and good morals."[20] This is puzzling because, like the Perrone comment just quoted, it seems to suggest some rudimentary implicit notion of "reception" of papal decrees by the Church community, even though there is no provision for any such thing in his theory of the Church.

Gasser also offers reassuring comments. He says that in no way should it be feared that the universal Church could be led into an error about the faith through the bad faith or negligence of the pontiff. The divine assistance of Christ to the successor of Peter is a power "so efficacious that the judgment of the Supreme Pontiff would be impeded if it were to be erroneous and destructive of the Church."[21] If the unthinkable started to happen, God would somehow intervene

---

20. "Execution" (executione) seems to mean "obedience."
21. Gasser, *Gift of Infallibility*, 46–47.

and prevent the pontiff from making a mistake in defining. Thus the Church community need not worry. Gasser adds the most enigmatic statement to be found in any of the literature studied in this work. He says: "[O]r if in fact the Pontiff really arrives at a definition, it will truly stand infallibly." Trying to understand what this means would doubtless require lengthy study and discussion. It probably does not mean that if the pontiff asserts a doctrine that is not Catholic, God will intervene and somehow transform it into a Catholic doctrine. It might mean that the community will over time gradually see that the doctrine defined, even if at first it looks unfamiliar, can somehow be recognized as Catholic doctrine. In any case it is clear again that the Church, including the entire episcopate, is expected to acquiesce piously and passively, and not ask questions.

This brings us back to the starting point of this whole study: the ecclesial ideas of mainstream Gallican authors and their concerns about papal power, as actually expressed in their own writings in the years 1682–1870. We noted at the start that even the best modern historical scholars have not been accustomed to cite Gallican sources when they make statements about the "Gallican doctrine." For example, they typically say that the Gallican doctrine of *consensus Ecclesiae* means a consensus *subsequens,* one given by the bishops after the Roman Pontiff has issued a doctrinal pronouncement. We have seen that the views of the French authors on this point are much more nuanced than this, for they speak at least as often of a consensus that is *antecedens* or *concomitans*. Influenced by their knowledge of the first millennium of Church history, they think in terms of a faith that is the common possession of the whole Church community, and which is preserved and taught by the whole episcopate (which always includes the bishop of Rome). Thus they tend to think that decisions about the Church's basic beliefs should in principle be arrived at collegially and consensually, as was the case at the great councils.

It needs to be stressed again and very clearly that their ecclesiology is not democratic. *Church,* when they speak of the consensus of the Church, does not mean the whole membership of the community of faith, but only the hierarchy or episcopate, the bishops collectively. We have noted especially with Bossuet and Tournely that they reject in no uncertain terms, and emphatically, the Church-idea of Edmond Richer, according to which the Church is essentially a democracy. For Richer, Christ conferred authority on the whole community, which then delegates it to the pope and bishops, who exercise a ministerial role in governing and teaching. Thyrso Gonzales is absurdly mistaken when he says, twice, that the Gallicans entrust doctrine to "ignorant men, petty women, rustics, boys, shoemakers, the bleary-eyed, and barbers."[22]

For the Gallican authors, the Church is not only hierarchical but also certainly monarchical. They recognize that the pope is endowed with genuine monarchical authority, and exercises a primacy not only of honor but of jurisdiction. They consistently say that the Roman Pontiff is not just a primus inter pares, but the possessor of really supreme authority. It is difficult, indeed it may be impossible, for the papalist authors to grasp this. For them the only genuine primatial authority is absolute monarchy, that is, an authority that is not subject to any norms or limits. Anything less than this is not even real authority. Thus for them people cannot be really sincere when they say that they accept papal monarchy but as subject to some limits. For example, if you say that papal monarchy could possibly be embodied in some kind of constitutional structure, then you do not really believe in papal monarchy, or even in real primatial authority. Moreover, absolute monarchy is seen as somehow more spiritual than any other system. The other kinds are mere political systems, drawn from this world, while absolute monarchy is somehow not a political system, and not drawn from this world. Rather, it is God's own way. Thus any suggestion about possible ways to implement collegiality is seen as an attempt to import political and secular schemes into the sacred precincts of the Church. This surely shows a lack of faith in God's divine plan for the Church.

22. Gonzales, *De infallibilitate romani pontificis*, 13, 101. "Petty women," renders *mulierculae*.

The Gallican authors clearly do not agree that absolute monarchy is the only genuine kind of monarchy, and they do not believe that Jesus Christ intended that his Church be a monarchy of this kind. But none of them call for the creation of a "constitutional," or collegial, or conciliar regime in the Church. Indeed, they do not call for any changes in Church governance. Rather, they urge a reappreciation of the less centralized modes of authority already familiar in the Church's history. They consider that the early centuries of Church history already give the example of a broad but coherent faith community that makes the effort continually to preserve its unity, accepts without question the need of authority in doing this, and values the unique primatial role of the pontiff of Rome. But this history shows that the bishops of the world have been an essential part of the authority that the Church needs, and that they are not mere agents of a solitary supreme ruler. Tournely puts it with admirable succinctness: the Church is "truly monarchical," but it is not "purely monarchical," which latter would mean that the whole Church depends on the "arbitrium" (judgment) and "imperium" (power to command) of one man. "The regimen of the Church is not purely monarchical but tempered with aristocracy, and the exercise of apostolic power is to be moderated through the canons established by the Holy Spirit and consecrated by the reverence of the whole world." This way of referring to the first millennium is common in the Gallican authors. The Church, Tournely adds, is a spiritual communion consisting of free acts of faith and piety and "cannot be ruled by force and external coercion through an absolute and monarchical power," but rather by "common and catholic consensus." Citing a number of popes from the early centuries who stated that they governed the Church in accordance with the canons, he concludes that the basic principle surely is that "the Church is governed *by law, not by absolute power.*"[23]

In the spirit of sincere piety and devotion to the will of Jesus Christ, the papalist authors maintain that the Savior conferred all

---

23. Emphasis his.

power of ruling and teaching on one man, Peter the fisherman. Thus the Church does depend on the *arbitrium* and *imperium* of one man, the successor of Peter. Gallican authors note that this portrayal of the pope as, seemingly, a kind of ecclesiastical emperor gives an opening to Protestant and secular writers to caricature the papacy and the whole Roman Catholic Church. We need to be aware that all the French authors studied here wrote not only to disagree with certain views on papal authority, but also to defend the whole Church and the papacy from Protestant and secular critics. The latter especially had long troubled Bergier and Bailly in particular. Writing in the late eighteenth century, they had both lived their whole lives in the French Enlightenment milieu, with all its scornful comments about Catholic beliefs. Both undertook earnestly to defend the Church. The hostile critics, Bergier says, claim that we make of the pope "a kind of god on earth, and attribute to him despotic, arbitrary, and tyrannical power." The pope can teach anything he wants, and Catholics are helpless to do anything about it. This is not true, Bergier says, for if the pontiff ever taught a wrong doctrine, the Church community, "far from being led into error by this judgment, would strongly bear witness through the speaking out of the body of pastors" to its authentic tradition. Bailly also says that an individual pope can make a mistake in teaching, but this does not cause the downfall of the Apostolic See or of the Church, which survive papal mistakes.

Bossuet very clearly maintains that if the Church can survive corruption and wrongdoing in the papacy (which has happened many times), then it can surely survive a papal mistake in teaching the faith. History, he says, shows "that they are refuted who think the Catholic Church would at once perish if any Roman Pontiff defined something false: as if this were the one thing that the authority of the Catholic Church could not supply." (It will be recalled that he is speaking here of how the Church of the primatial see of Rome has at times been saved by the universal Catholic Church.) Is this, saving the faith itself, the one case where the Holy Spirit sent by Christ fails the Church? For Bossuet a prime example of the universal Church surviving a serious papal mistake is the theocratic claim made by medieval popes like Gregory VII and Boniface VIII to have power to depose kings and emperors. These excessive claims, he says, did great harm by confusing the faithful and leading many astray, but the harm was limited and not irreparable because the universal Catholic Church did not approve and accept the mistaken claims.

Bossuet would have been quite pleased with the comments of Pius XII on the claims of Gregory VII and Boniface VIII in his address to historians in 1955. Pius cites Leo XIII as saying (*Immortale Dei*, 1885) that church and state are each supreme in their own order, meaning that the Church (pope) is not superior to kings. Pius states, "It can be said that with the exception of a few centuries—for all the first thousand years as for the last four hundred—the statement of Leo XIII reflects more or less clearly the mind of the Church. Even during the intervening period, moreover, there were representatives of the doctrine of the Church—perhaps a majority—who shared the same opinion."[24] Bossuet would surely comment that those who, disagreeing with the theocratic claims, stood with "the mind of the Church" and were "representatives of the doctrine of the Church" were persons living not in Rome but in France and elsewhere. He would say that there was an ongoing and pervasive consensus in the universal Church regarding the legitimate scope of papal authority, and Gregory VII and Boniface VIII disregarded it. Their assertions of theocratic power over kings did not receive the *consensus subsequens* of the Church because they disregarded the *consensus antecedens* that was there.

Papalist and Gallican authors concur in their profound conviction that the Church, which has survived countless crises and tribulations for many centuries, will continue to survive no matter what its leaders, including the Supreme Pontiff, do. Both know that popes have

24. Pope Pius XII, "The Church and History," address to the Tenth International Congress of Historical Studies, Rome, September 7, 1955, in *Catholic Mind* 53 (December 1955): 746. He explicitly disowns Boniface VIII by name, though without mentioning the bull *Unam Sanctam* (November 18, 1302), 747.

committed many sins in their private lives and have made mistakes in governance, though papalists tend to admit this only if pressed. But the two sides differ on one major point: papal error in teaching the faith. Papalists say flatly that it does not and will not happen. Gallican authors state that popes can and have erred even in teaching the faith, but that this is not fatal to the Church. In general, Gallican authors tend to stress the numerous areas of agreement between the two sides, while papalist authors tend to stress the few areas of disagreement. In any case, the principal concern of this work has been to study very closely the ecclesiological ideas of the Gallican theologians as expressed in their own writings. We can all learn a great deal from a careful study of their books.

Bibliography

Primary Sources

Aguirre, José Saenz de, O.S.B. *Auctoritas infallibilis et summa cathedrae sancti Petri extra et supra concilia quaelibet atque in totam ecclesiam denuo stabilita.* Salamanca: Lucas Perez, 1683.

Bailly, Louis. *Theologia dogmatica et moralis.* 8 vols. Dijon: E. Bidault, 1826. Originally published in 1789.

———. *Tractatus de ecclesia Christi.* Dijon: E. Bidault, 1771.

———. *Tractatus de vera religione.* 2 vols. Dijon: E. Bidault, 1771.

Ballerini, Pietro. *De potestate ecclesiastica summorum pontificum et conciliorum generalium,* with *Appendix de infallibilitate.* Rome: Typis S. Congregationis de Propaganda Fide, 1850.

———. *De vi ac ratione primatus romanorum pontificum, et de ipsorum infallibilitate in definiendis controversiis fidei.* Edited E. W. Westhoff. Monasterii Westfalorum: J. H. Deiters, 1845.

Balmes, Jaime Luciano. *Protestantism and Catholicism Compared in Their Effects on the Civilization of Europe.* Baltimore: John Murphy, 1851.

Bellarmine, Robert, S.J. *Opera omnia.* 12 vols. Edited by Justin Fèvre. Paris: Louis Vives, 1870; Frankfurt: Minerva, 1965.

Bergier, Nicolas-Sylvestre. *Dictionnaire de théologie.* 8 vols. Liège: Société Typographique, 1789.

———. *Plan de la théologie par ordre de matières.* Besançon: Outhenin Chalandre, 1831.

Bossuet, Jacques-Bénigne. *Defensio declarationis cleri gallicani de ecclesiastica potestate.* Vols. 21–22 in *Oeuvres complètes.* Edited by F. Lachat. Paris: Louis Vives, 1862–1866.

———. *Discourse on Universal History.* Edited by Orest Ranum. Chicago: University of Chicago Press, 1976.

———. *Histoire des variations des Eglises protestantes.* 4 vols. Versailles: J. A. Lebel, 1817.

———. *Oeuvres complètes.* 31 vols. Edited by F. Lachat. Paris: Louis Vives, 1862–1866.

———. *Politics Drawn from the Very Words of Scripture.* Edited and translated by Patrick Riley. New York: Cambridge University Press, 1990.

Bibliography

Charlas, Antoine. *Tractatus de libertatibus ecclesiae gallicanae.* Liège: Matthias Hovium, 1684.

Durand de Maillane, Pierre-Toussaint, ed. *Les libertés de l'Eglise gallicane prouvées et commentées.* 5 vols. Lyon: Pierre Bruyset Ponthus, 1771.

Ehler, Sidney Z., and John B. Morrall, eds. *Church and State through the Centuries: A Collection of Historic Documents with Commentaries.* Westminster, Md.: Newman, 1954.

Federici, Luigi. *Elogi storici de' piu illustri ecclesiastici veronesi.* Verona: Ramanzini, 1819.

Gasser, Vincent. *The Gift of Infallibility: The Official Relatio on Infallibility of Bishop Vincent Gasser at Vatican Council I.* Translated by James T. O'Connor. Boston: St. Paul Editions, 1986.

Gonzales de Santalla, Thyrso, S.J. *De infallibitate romani pontificis in definiendis fidei et morum controversiis extra concilium generale non expectato ecclesiae consensu, contra recentes huius infallibilitatis oppugnatores.* Rome: Felicis Caesaretti, 1689.

La Luzerne, César-Guillaume. *Sur la déclaration de l'Assemblée du Clergé de France en 1682.* Rev. ed. Paris: Méquignon-Junior, 1843.

Lamennais, Félicité. *Oeuvres complètes de F. de Lamennais.* 12 vols. Paris: Daubrée et Cailleux, 1836–1837; Frankfurt: Minerva, 1967.

Maistre, Joseph de. *Du pape, suivi de l'Eglise gallicane dans son rapport avec le souverain pontife.* 2 vols. Brussels: H. Goemaere, 1852.

———. *Oeuvres complètes de J. de Maistre.* 14 vols. Paris: Emanuele Vitte, 1931.

Mansi, Giovanni Domenico, ed. *Sacrorum conciliorum nova et amplissima collectio.* 53 vols. Paris: Hubert Welter, 1903–1927.

Muzzarelli, Alfonso, S.J. *Argumentum contra gallorum opinionem de reformabilitate decretorum summi pontificis.* Avignon: Seguin, 1826.

———. *De auctoritate romani pontificis in conciliis generalibus.* 2 vols. Ghent, 1815.

———. *L'infaillibilité du pape prouvée par la doctrine et la tradition de l'Eglise gallicane.* Avignon: Seguin, 1826.

———. *Propositio pro adstruenda infallibilitate summorum pontificum.* Avignon: Seguin, 1826.

Newman, John Henry. *Roman Catholic Writings on Doctrinal Development.* Edited by James Gaffney. Kansas City: Sheed and Ward, 1997.

Orsi, Giuseppe Agostino, O.P. *De irreformabili romani pontificis in definiendis fidei controversiis judicio.* 3 vols. Rome: Paulus Junchius, 1771.

Perrone, Giovanni, S.J. *De romani pontificis infallibilitate, seu Vaticana definitio contra novos hereticos asserta et vindicata.* Augustae Taurinorum: Petri Marietti, 1874.

———. *Praelectiones theologicae.* 31st ed. Turin: Marietti, 1865.

Pius XII. "The Church and History." Address to the Tenth International Congress of Historical Studies, September 7, 1955. *Catholic Mind* 53 (December 1955): 742–750.

Ratzinger, Joseph. "The Primacy of the Successor of Peter in the Mystery of the Church." *Osservatore romano,* November 18, 1998.

Rocaberti, Juan Tomàs de, O.P., ed. *Biblioteca maxima pontificia.* 21 vols. Rome: Joannes Buagni, 1697–1699; Graz: Akademisch Druck, 1969.

———. *De romani pontificis auctoritate*. 3 vols. Valencia, 1691–1694.
Rohrbacher, René-François. *Histoire universelle de l'Eglise catholique*. 3rd ed. 29 vols. Paris: Gaume Frères, 1857–1859.
Tournely, Honoré. *Cursus theologicus scholastico-dogmaticus*. 11 vols. Paris, 1765.
Turrecremata, Joannes, O.P. *Summa de ecclesia*. In vol. 13 of Juan Tomàs de Rocaberti, O.P., ed., *Biblioteca maxima pontificia*. Graz: Akademisch Druck, 1969.

Secondary Sources

Alberigo, Giuseppe. *Lo sviluppo della dottrina sui poteri nella Chiesa universale: Momenti essenziali tra il XVI e il XIX secolo*. Rome: Herder, 1964.
Aston, Nigel. *Religion and Revolution in France, 1780–1804*. Washington, D.C.: Catholic University of America Press, 2000.
Aubert, Roger. "L'ecclésiologie au Concile du Vatican." 245–284 in Bernard Botte et al., *Le concile et les conciles: Contribution à l'histoire de la vie conciliaire de l'Eglise*. Paris: Cerf, 1960.
———. "La géographie ecclésiologique au XIXe siècle." 11–55 in Maurice Nédoncelle et al., *L'ecclésiologie au XIXe siècle*. Paris: Cerf, 1960.
———. *Le pontificat de Pie IX*. Vol. 21 of Augustin Fliche and Victor Martin, eds., *Histoire de l'Eglise*. Paris: Bloud et Gay, 1963.
———. *Vatican I*. Paris: L'Orante, 1964.
Audinet, J. "L'enseignement 'De ecclesia' à St. Sulpice sous le Premier Empire et les débuts du gallicanisme modéré." 115–140 in Maurice Nédoncelle et al., *L'ecclésiologie au XIXe siècle*. Paris: Cerf, 1960.
Balthasar, Hans Urs von. *The Office of Peter and the Structure of the Church*. San Francisco: Ignatius, 1986.
Barraclough, Geoffrey. *Papal Provisions*. London: Basil Blackwell, 1935.
Bedoyere, Michael de la. *The Archbishop and the Lady: The Story of Fénelon and Madame Guyon*. New York: Pantheon, 1956.
Blet, Pierre, S.J. *Les Assemblées du Clergé et Louis XIV de 1670 à 1693*. Rome: Università Gregoriana Editrice, 1972.
———. *Le clergé de France et la monarchie: Etude sur les Assemblées Générales du Clergé de 1615 à 1666*. 2 vols. Rome: Università Gregoriana Editrice, 1959.
———. "Fidèle au pape, fidèle au roi." 315–332 in Yves Durand, ed., *Hommages à Roland Mousnier: Clientèles et fidélités en Europe à l'époque moderne*. Paris: Presses Universitaires de France, 1981.
———. "Une légende ténace: Colbert et la Déclaration du Clergé en 1682." Académie des Sciences Morales et Politiques, Communications de la séance du 4 octobre, 1971, 25–45.
Bliss, Frederick M. *Understanding Reception: A Backdrop to Its Ecumenical Use*. Milwaukee: Marquette University Press, 1993.
Boyer, C. "Perrone, Jean." *DTC*, 12.1:1255–1256.
Boyle, John P. *Church Teaching Authority: Historical and Theological Studies*. Notre Dame: University of Notre Dame Press, 1995.

Butler, Cuthbert, O.S.B. *The Vatican Council, 1869–1870*. 2 vols. London: Longmans Green, 1930. One volume edition: London: Collins and Harvill, 1962.

Butterfield, Herbert. *The Origins of History*. New York: Basic Books, 1981.

Caillet, Louis. *La papauté d'Avignon et l'Eglise de France: La politique bénéficiale du Pape Jean XXII en France (1316–1334)*. Paris: Presses Universitaires de France, 1975.

Carreyre, J. "Muzzarelli," *DTC*, 10.2:2584–2585.

———. "Tournely." *DTC*, 15.1:1242–1244.

Casagrandi, Salvatore. *De claris sodalibus provinciae Turonensis Societatis Jesu commentarii*. Turin: Jacobus Arneodus Eques, 1906.

Chadwick, Owen. *From Bossuet to Newman: The Idea of Doctrinal Development*. Cambridge: Cambridge University Press, 1957.

Charonnot, Joseph. *Mgr de La Luzerne et les serments pendant la Révolution*. Paris: Augustin Picard, 1918.

Cognet, Louis. "Ecclesiastical Life in France." 45–49 in *The Church in the Age of Absolutism and Enlightenment*, vol. 6 of Hubert Jedin and John Dolan, eds., *History of the Church*. New York: Crossroad, 1981.

Congar, Yves, O.P. "Conclusion." 285–334 in Bernard Botte et al., *Le concile et les conciles: Contribution à l'histoire de la vie conciliaire de l'Eglise*. Paris: Cerf, 1960.

———. "De la communion des Eglises à une ecclésiologie de l'Eglise universelle." 227–260 in Yves Congar, O.P., and B. D. Dupuy, O.P., eds., *L'épiscopat et l'Eglise universelle*. Paris: Cerf, 1964.

———. "Ecclesia ab Abel." 79–108 in *Abhandlungen über Theologie und Kirche*. Düsseldorf: Patmos, 1952.

———. "L'ecclésiologie de la Révolution française au Concile du Vatican, sous la signe de l'affirmation de l'autorité." 77–114 in Maurice Nédoncelle et al., *L'ecclésiologie au XIXe siècle*. Paris: Cerf, 1960.

———. *L'Eglise de saint Augustin à l'époque moderne*. Paris: Cerf, 1970.

———. "Gallicanisme." 4:1731–1739 in G. Jacquemet, ed., *Catholicisme*. Paris: Letouzey, 1956.

———. "La 'réception' comme réalité ecclésiologique." *Revue des sciences philosophiques et théologiques* 56 (July 1972): 369–403.

Constantin, C. "Déclaration ou les Quatre Articles de 1682." *DTC*, 4.1:185–205.

Coriden, James. "The Canonical Doctrine of Reception." *Jurist* 50 (1990): 58–82.

Costigan, Richard F., S.J. "Bossuet and the Consensus of the Church." *Theological Studies* 56 (December 1995): 652–672.

———. "Bossuet, Jacques-Bénigne." 86–88 in Patrick W. Carey and Joseph T. Lienhard, S.J., eds. *Biographical Dictionary of Christian Theologians*. Westport, Conn.: Greenwood, 2000.

———. "The Consensus of the Church: Differing Classic Views." *Theological Studies* 51 (March 1990): 25–48.

———. "The Ecclesiological Dialectic." *Thought* 49 (June 1974): 134–144.

———."Hontheim, Johann Nickolaus von [Febronius]." In Patrick W. Carey and Joseph T. Lienhard, eds. *Biographical Dictionary of Christian Theologians*. Westport, Conn.: Greenwood, 2000.

———. "Lamennais and Rohrbacher and the Papacy." *Revue de l'Université d'Ottawa* 57 (July–September 1987): 53–66.

———. "Papal Supremacy: From Theory to Practice." *Vital Nexus* (Halifax, Nova Scotia) 2 (September 1996): 9–17.

———. *Rohrbacher and the Ecclesiology of Ultramontanism*. Rome: Università Gregoriana Editrice, 1980.

———. "Tradition and the Beginning of the Ultramontane Movement." *Irish Theological Quarterly* 48 (1981): 27–46.

Dansette, Adrien. *Religious History of Modern France*. 2 vols. New York: Herder, 1961.

Darricau, R. "Lumières nouvelles sur l'histoire du Clergé de France sous Louis XIV." *Revue d'histoire ecclésiastique* 69 (1974): 93–102.

Degert, Antoine. *Histoire des séminaires français jusqu'à la Révolution*. Paris: Beauchesne, 1912.

Dejaifve, Georges, S.J. "Ex sese, non autem ex consensu ecclesiae." *Eastern Churches Quarterly* 14 (Summer–Autumn 1962): 360–378.

Delaruelle, E., et al. *L'Eglise au temps du Grand Schisme et de la crise conciliaire (1378–1449)*. Vol. 14 of Augustin Fliche and Victor Martin, eds., *Histoire de l'Eglise*. Paris: Bloud et Gay, 1962.

de Meyer, A. "Ballerini, Girolamo et Pietro." *DHGE*, 6:400.

Derré, Jean-René. *Lamennais, ses amis, et le mouvement des idées à l'époque romantique, 1824–1834*. Paris: C. Klincksieck, 1961.

Dionne, J. Robert. *The Papacy and the Church: A Study of Praxis and Reception in Ecumenical Perspective*. New York: Philosophical Library, 1987.

Dublanchy, E. "Bergier, Nicolas-Sylvestre." *DTC*, 2.1:37.

Dubruel, M. "Gallicanisme." *DTC*, 6.1:1096–1137.

Duchon, Robert. "De Bossuet à Febronius." *Revue d'histoire ecclésiastique* 65 (1970): 375–422.

Ducros, Louis. *Les Encyclopédistes*. Paris, 1900; New York: Burt Franklin, 1967.

Eno, Robert B., S.S. *The Rise of the Papacy*. Wilmington, Del.: Michael Glazier, 1990.

Fabroni, Angelo. *Vitae italorum doctrina excellentiorum qui saeculis XVII et XVIII floruerunt*. Pisa, 1785.

Facchini, Tarcisio. *Il papato principio di unità e Pietro Ballerini di Verona: Dal concetto di unità ecclesiastica al concetto di monarchia infallibile*. Padua: Il Messagero di S. Antonio, 1950.

Fink, Karl August. "The Curia at Avignon." 333–344 in *From the High Middle Ages to the Eve of the Reformation*. Vol. 4 of Hubert Jedin and John Dolan, eds., *History of the Church*. Freiburg: Herder, 1970.

Fries, Heinrich. "Ex sese, non autem ex consensu ecclesiae." 480–500 in Remigius Bäumer and Heimo Dolch, eds., *Volk Gottes: Zum Kirchenverzeichnis der katholischen, evangelischen und anglikanischen Theologie*. Freiburg: Herder, 1967.

Gadille, Jacques. "L'épiscopat français au Premier Concile du Vatican." *Revue d'histoire de l'Eglise de France* 56 (July–December 1970): 327–346.

Gagnebet, M. R., O.P. "L'infaillibilité du pape et le consentemente de l'Eglise au Vatican I." *Angelicum* 47 (1970): 267–307, 428–455.

Gaillardetz, Richard R. *Witnesses to the Faith: Community, Infallibility, and the Ordinary Magisterium of the Bishops.* New York: Paulist, 1992.

Gérin, Charles. *Recherches historiques sur l'Assemblée du Clergé de France de 1682.* Paris: Lecoffre, 1869.

Gorce, M. M. "Orsi, Giuseppe-Agostino." *DTC*, 11.2:1612–1619.

Gough, Austin. *Paris and Rome: The Gallican Church and the Ultramontane Campaign, 1848–1853.* New York: Oxford University Press, 1986.

Granfield, Patrick, O.S.B. *The Limits of the Papacy.* New York: Crossroad, 1987.

———. *The Papacy in Transition.* Garden City, N.Y.: Doubleday, 1980.

Greenbaum, Louis S. *Talleyrand, Statesman Priest: The Agent-General of the Clergy and the Church of France at the End of the Old Regime.* Washington, D.C.: Catholic University of America Press, 1970.

Gres-Gayer, Jacques. *Le gallicanisme de Sorbonne: Chroniques de la Faculté de la Théologie de Paris (1657–1688).* Paris: Honoré Champion, 2002.

———. "Gallicans et Romains en Sorbonne d'après le nonce Bargellini (1670)." *Revue d'histoire ecclésiastique* 87 (July–December 1992): 682–744.

———. "The Magisterium of the Faculty of Theology of Paris in the Seventeenth Century." *Theological Studies* 53 (September 1992): 424–450.

———."The *Unigenitus* of Clement XI: A Fresh Look at the Issues." *Theological Studies* 49 (June 1988).

Heft, James, S.M. *John XXII and Papal Teaching Authority.* Lewiston, N.Y.: Edwin Mellen, 1986.

Henn, William, O.F.M. Cap. *The Honor of My Brothers: A Brief History of the Relationship between the Pope and the Bishops.* New York: Crossroad, 2000.

Himes, Michael J. *Ongoing Incarnation: Johann Adam Möhler and the Beginnings of Modern Ecclesiology.* New York: Crossroad, 1997.

Hocedez, Edgar, S.J. *Histoire de la théologie au XIXe siècle.* 2 vols. Paris: Desclée de Brouwer, 1948.

Horst, Ulrich, O.P. *Unfehlbarkeit und Geschichte: Studien zur Unfehlbarkeitsdiskussion von Melchior Cano bis zum I. Vatikanischen Konzil.* Mainz: Matthias Grünewald, 1982.

Hughes, Philip. *The Church in Crisis: A History of the Twenty Great Councils.* London: Burns and Oates, 1960.

Hurter, H., S.J. *Nomenclator literarius recentioris theologiae catholicae.* Oeniponte: Libraria Academica Wagneriana, 1893–1903.

Izbicki, Thomas M. *Protector of the Faith: Cardinal Ioannes de Turrecremata and the Defense of the Institutional Church.* Washington, D.C.: Catholic University of America Press, 1981.

Jedin, Hubert, and John Dolan, eds. *History of the Church.* 10 vols. New York: Crossroad, 1965–1981.

Jobert, Ambroise, ed. *Un théologien au siècle des lumières: Bergier, correspondance avec l'abbé Trouillet, 1770–1790.* Lyon: Centre André Latreille, 1987.

Kelley, Donald R. *Foundations of Modern Historical Scholarship: Language, Law, and History in the French Renaissance.* New York: Columbia University Press, 1970.

Kelly, J. N. D. *Oxford Dictionary of the Popes.* New York: Oxford University Press, 1986.

Köhler, Oskar. "The Established Church and the Enlightenment." 532–534 in *The Church in the Age of Absolutism and Enlightenment.* Vol. 6 of Hubert Jedin and John Dolan, eds., *History of the Church.* New York: Crossroads, 1981.

———. "Foundations and Forms of the Established Church in the Bourbon States of the Seventeenth and Eighteenth Centuries." 329–342 in *The Church in the Age of Absolutism and Enlightenment.* Vol. 6 of Hubert Jedin and John Dolan, eds., *History of the Church.* New York: Crossroad, 1981.

La Brosse, Olivier de. *Le pape et le concile: La comparaison de leurs pouvoirs à la Veille de la Réforme.* Paris: Cerf, 1965.

Lanson, Gustave. *Bossuet.* Paris: Lecène, Oudin, 1891.

Largent, A. "Bossuet." *DTC*, 2.2:1049–1089.

Latreille, André. "Innocent XI, pape 'janséniste,' directeur de conscience de Louis XIV." *Cahiers d'histoire* 1 (1956): 9–39.

Latreille, André, et al. *Histoire du catholicisme en France.* 2nd ed. 3 vols. Paris: Spes, 1962.

Lebrun, François, ed. *Histoire des catholiques en France de XVe siècle à nos jours.* Toulouse: Privat, 1980.

Lefebvre, Charles, et al. *Les sources du droit et la seconde centralisation romaine.* In *L'époque moderne (1563–1789),* tome 15, vol. 1 of Gabriel Le Bras and Jean Gaudemet, eds., *Histoire du droit et des institutions de l'Eglise en Occident.* Paris: Cujas, 1976.

LeGoff, Jacques, and René Rémond, eds. *Histoire de la France religieuse.* 4 vols. Paris: Seuil, 1988–1992.

LeGuillou, Louis. *L'évolution de la pensée religieuse de Félicité Lamennais.* Paris: Armand Colin, 1966.

Levesque, E. "Bossuet." *DHGE*, 9:1339–1391.

Lunt, William E. *Financial Relations of the Papacy with England, 1327–1534.* Cambridge, Mass.: Medieval Academy of America, 1962.

Marchal, L. "La Luzerne, César-Guillaume." *DTC,* 8.2:2465–2466.

Martimort, Aimé-Georges. *L'établissement du texte de la "Defensio declarationis" de Bossuet.* Paris: Cerf, 1956.

———. *Le gallicanisme.* Paris: Presses Universitaires de France, 1973.

———. *Le gallicanisme de Bossuet.* Paris: Cerf, 1953.

Martin, Victor. *Le gallicanisme politique et le clergé de France.* Paris: Picard, 1929.

———. *Les origines du gallicanisme.* 2 vols. Paris: Bloud et Gay, 1939.

Matt, Leonard von, and Hans Kühner. *The Popes: Papal History in Picture and Word.* New York: Universe Books, 1963.

Mayr, Johann. *Die Ekklesiologie Honoré Tournelys.* Essen: Ludgerus-Verlag Hubertus Wingen, 1964.

McCool, Gerald A., S.J. *Catholic Theology in the Nineteenth Century: The Quest for a Unitary Method.* New York: Seabury, 1977.

McManners, John. *Church and Society in Eighteenth-Century France.* 2 vols. New York: Oxford University Press, 1998.

Mellinato, Giuseppe, S.J. "Alfonso Muzzarelli, teologo tra fine Settecento e Restaurazione." *Ricerche di storia sociale e religioso* 21 (1992): 25–35.

———. "Muzzarelli." *Dictionnaire de spiritualité* 10:1858–1860 (1980).

Minnerath, Roland. *Le pape: Evêque universel ou premier des évêques?* Paris: Beauchesne, 1978.

Mollat, Guillaume. *The Popes at Avignon, 1305–1378.* London: Thomas Nelson, 1963.

Moroni, Gaetano. *Dizionario di erudizione storico-ecclesiastico.* Venice: Emiliana, 1840–1861.

Moulinet, Daniel. "Un réseau ultramontain en France au milieu du 19e siècle." *Revue d'histoire ecclésiastique* 92 (1997): 70–125.

Mousnier, Roland. *The Institutions of France under the Absolute Monarchy, 1598–1789.* 2 vols. Chicago: University of Chicago Press, 1979.

Nau, Paul, O.S.B. "Le magistère pontifical ordinaire au premier Concile du Vatican." *Revue Thomiste* 62 (1962): 341–397. Republished 161–220 in Roger Aubert et al., eds., *De doctrina Concilii Vaticani Primi.* Vatican City: Libreria Editrice Vaticana, 1969.

Neveu, Bruno. *L'erreur et son juge: Remarques sur les censures doctrinales à l'époque moderne.* Naples: Bibliopolis, 1993.

———. *Erudition et religion aux XVIIe et XVIII siècles.* Paris: Albin Michel, 1994.

———. "L'esprit de réforme à Rome sous Innocent XI (1676–1689)." *XVIIe siècle* 50 (1998): 203–218.

O'Gara, Margaret. *Triumph in Defeat: Infallibility, Vatican I, and the French Minority Bishops.* Washington, D.C.: Catholic University of America Press, 1988.

Ottaviani, Alaphridus. *Institutiones iuris publici ecclesiastici.* 5th ed. Vatican City: Typis Polyglottis Vaticanis, 1958.

Palanque, Jean-Rémy. *Catholiques libéraux et gallicans en France face au Concile du Vatican, 1867–1870.* Aix-en-Provence: Publications des Annales de la Faculté des Lettres d'Aix-en-Provence, 1962.

Palmer, R. R. *Catholics and Unbelievers in Eighteenth-Century France.* Princeton: Princeton University Press, 1939.

Pascoe, Louis B., S.J. *Jean Gerson: Principles of Church Reform.* Leiden: Brill, 1973.

Place, Michael. *The Response Due to Papal Solicitude in Matters of Faith and Morals: A Study of Selected Eighteenth-Century Theologians.* Ann Arbor: University Microfilms International, 1978.

Pottmeyer, Hermann Josef. "Reception and Submission." *Jurist* 51 (1991): 269–292.

———. *Towards a Papacy in Communion: Perspectives from Vatican Councils I and II.* New York: Crossroad, 1998.

———. *Unfehlbarkeit und Souveränität: Die päpstliche Unfehlbarkeit im System der ultramontanen Ekklesiologie des 19. Jahrhunderts.* Mainz: Matthias Grünewald, 1975.

Prandi, Alfonso. "La Istoria ecclesiastica di P. Giuseppe Orsi e la sua genesi." *Rivista di storia della Chiesa in Italia* 34 (July–December 1980): 430–450.

Préclin, E., and E. Jarry. *Les luttes politiques et doctrinales aux XVIIe et XVIIIe siècles.* Vol. 19 of Augustin Fliche and Victor Martin, eds., *Histoire de l'Eglise.* Paris: Bloud et Gay 1955.

Ranke, Leopold von. *History of the Popes.* New York: Frederick Ungar, 1966.

Rausch, Thomas, S.J. "Reception Past and Present." *Theological Studies* 47 (September 1986): 497–508.

Remanzacco, Candido da, O.F.M. Cap. "Vita e opere di Pietro Ballerini (1698–1769)." *Studia patavina* 9 (September–December 1962): 452–492.

Renouard,Yves. *The Avignon Papacy: The Popes in Exile, 1305–1403*. NewYork: Barnes and Noble, 1994.

Routhier, Gilles. *La réception d'un concile*. Paris: Cerf, 1993.

Salmon, George. *The Infallibility of the Church*. London: John Murray, 1923.

Schatz, Klaus, S.J. *Kirchenbild und päpstliche Unfehlbarkeit bei den deutschsprachigen Minoritätsbischöfen auf den I.Vatikanum*. Rome: Università Gregoriana Editrice, 1975.

———. *Papal Primacy from Its Origins to the Present*. Collegeville, Minn.: Liturgical, 1996.

———. *Vatikanum I, 1869–1870*. 3 vols. Paderborn: Ferdinand Schöningh, 1992–1994.

Schneider, Burkhart, S.J. "The Papacy under the Increasing Pressure of the Established Church." 563–566 in *The Church in the Age of Absolutism and Enlightenment*. Vol. 6 of Hubert Jedin and John Dolan, eds., *History of the Church*. NewYork: Crossroad, 1981.

Sonnino, Paul. *Louis XIV's View of the Papacy (1661–1667)*. Berkeley: University of California Press, 1966.

Stagaman, David, S.J. *Authority in the Church*. Collegeville, Minn.: Liturgical, 1999.

Sullivan, Francis A., S.J. *Magisterium: Teaching Authority in the Catholic Church*. New York: Paulist, 1983.

Thils, Gustave. *L'infaillibilité pontificale: Source, conditions, limites*. Gembloux: Duculot, 1969.

———. *La primauté pontificale: La doctrine de Vatican I, les voies d'une révision*. Gembloux: Duculot, 1972.

Thysman, Raymond. "Le gallicanisme de Mgr. Maret et l'influence de Bossuet." *Revue d'histoire ecclésiastique* 52 (1957): 401–465.

Tierney, Brian. *The Crisis of Church and State, 1050–1300*. Englewood Cliffs, N.J.: Prentice-Hall, 1964.

———. *Origins of Papal Infallibility: A Study on the Concepts of Infallibility, Sovereignty, and Tradition in the Middle Ages*. Leiden: Brill, 1972.

Vallin, Pierre, S.J. "Pour l'histoire du Vatican I: La démarche de la minorité auprès de Pie IX, le 15 juillet, 1870." *Revue d'histoire ecclésiastique* 60 (1965): 844–848.

Vanysacker, Dries. *Cardinal Giuseppe Garampi (1725–1792): An Enlightened Ultramontane*. Brussels: Institut Historique Belge de Rome, 1995.

Vidler, Alec. *Prophecy and Papacy: A Study of Lamennais, the Church, and the Revolution*. London: SCM Press, 1954.

von Pastor, Ludwig. *History of the Popes*. 40 vols. St. Louis: B. Herder, 1902–1953.

Vries,W. de. *Orient et Occident: Les structures ecclésiales vues dans l'histoire des sept premiers conciles oecuméniques*. Paris: Cerf, 1974.

Willaert, Léopold, S.J. *Après le concile de Trente: La restauration catholique, 1563–1648*. Vol. 18 of Augustin Fliche and Victor Martin, eds., *Histoire de l'Eglise*. Paris: Bloud et Gay, 1960.

Index

Adrian VI, 182
Agatho, 103,177
Aguirre, Jose Saenz de, O.S.B., 59, 191
Alberigo, Giuseppe, 33, 96, 107
Alexander VII, 160
Alexander VIII, 20, 107, 159
Andries, Johannes, 147
Arian controversy, 46
Aubert, Roger, 4, 147, 166, 167
Auctorem Fidei, 159, 173
Augustine of Hippo, 54, 94
Augustinus, 160
Avignon papacy, 7, 8, 10, 46–47
Azzolini, Cardinal Decio, 20

Bailly, Louis: life and work, 109–11; *De vera religione*, 110; *Theologia dogmatica et moralis*, 111–18; *Tractatus de ecclesia Christi*, 111–12; papal primacy, 112–15; papal infallibility, 115–18; mentioned, 34, 128, 202
Ballerini, Girolamo, 94
Ballerini, Pietro: life and work, 94–96; nature and force of the primacy, 97–103; papal infallibility as absolute, 103–8; on Bossuet, 99–100; on councils, 102–3; on doctrine of Irenaeus, 104–6; on Church as communion, 107–8; mentioned 39, 72, 83, 139, 147, 163, 164, 171, 177, 189, 190, 191, 194, 196,198
Balmes, Jaime Luciano, 37
Balthasar, Hans Urs von, 35–36
Baluze, Etienne, 84
Baronius, Cesare, 124

Bellarmine, Cardinal Robert, S.J., 22–29, 39, 53, 64–66, 72–73, 96, 115, 124, 147, 164, 170, 189
Benedict XIII, 10,11
Benedict XIV, 78, 95, 159
Bergier, Nicolas-Sylvestre: life and work, 119–21; *Dictionnaire de théologie*, 121–22; on papal infallibility, 115–18; mentioned, 34, 109, 110, 202
Blet, Pierre, S.J., 16, 61, 161
Boniface VIII, 48–50, 203
Bossuet, Jacques-Bénigne, Bishop of Meaux, life and work, 35–36; *Discourse on Universal History*, 36–37; defense of the Gallican Declaration, 38–43; criticized by de Maistre and Lamennais, 39–43; papal primacy and papal errors, 43–47; critique of Gregory VII and Boniface VIII, 48–50; on councils, 50–53; consensus of the Church, 53–57; Bossuet and history, 57–62; criticized by Muzzarelli, 157–60; mentioned, 4, 16, 17, 19, 20, 29, 30, 32, 34, 35, 78, 79, 82, 83, 88, 89, 97, 99, 100, 128, 131, 143, 144, 148, 151–53, 156–60, 164, 176, 187–88, 200, 202, 203
Bourbon Restoration, 41,60
Boyle, John, 168
Butterfield, Herbert, 36–37

Caillet, Louis, 9
Cajetan, Cardinal (Thomas de Vio, O.P.), 115
Calini, Ferdinando, 145
Calvin, John, 37, 67

215

Cano, Melchior, O.P., 65, 97, 115, 139–40
Casagrandi, Salvatore, 165, 167
Caulet, Etienne, Bishop of Pamier, 14, 30
Cavallerini, Giovanni, 21–22
Celestine I, 102, 140, 177
Chadwick, Owen, 38, 57–58
Chalcedon, Council of, 51, 111–12, 116, 143–44, 177
Charlas, Antoine, 29–30, 84
Charles VI, Emperor of Germany, 80
Charles VI, King of France, 11
Charonnot, Joseph, 130–31
Choiseul du Plessis-Praslin, Gilbert de, 17–18, 28–29
Clement VII, 182
Clement X, 14
Clement XI, 22, 63, 76, 80
Clement XII, 78–81, 159
Clement XIII, 78
Clement XIV, 145
Colbert, Jean, 16, 61
Colbert de Croissy, Charles, 21
Concordat of Bologna, 9
Congar, Yves, O.P., 4, 5, 6, 12, 32, 33, 58, 61, 65, 66, 96, 107, 147, 188
Constance, Council of, 18, 24, 42
Costantinople I, Council of, 91, 177
Cum Occasione, 57, 173
Cyprian, 54, 113
Cyril of Alexandria, 140

Declaration of the Gallican Clergy. *See* Gallican Articles
Diderot, Denis, 121
Dubois, Nicholas, 54
Dubruel, M., 12, 64
Duchon, Robert, 56
Ducros, Louis, 120
Durand de Maillane, Pierre-Toussaint, 31
Duval, André, 29, 84

Encyclopédie, 121–22
Ephesus, Council of, 177
d'Estrées, Cardinal César, 19
Eutyches, 101, 103, 116, 143, 144

Facchini, Tarcisio, 94–99
False Decretals, 123
Febronius, Justinus (Johann Nikolaus von Hontheim), 56, 191
Fénelon, François de Salignac, 176
Flavian, Patriarch of Constantinople, 140
Fleury, Claude, 84, 146
Florence, council of, 65, 126
Frederick II, Emperor, 116
Fries, Heinrich, 4

Gaffney, James, 167
Gaillardetz, Richard, 168
Gallican Articles (Declaration of the Gallican Clergy), 2; issuance of this document, 13–22
Gallicanism, 5–13; episcopal, 6, 32; parliamentary, 6, 12–13; origins, 7–12
Garampi, Giuseppe, 84, 96
Garibaldi, A., 111
Gasbert of Laval, 8
Gasser, Vincent, Bishop of Brixen, 195–99
Gerbet, Philippe-Olympe, 42n
Gérin, Charles, 15
Gerson, Jean, 24, 27–28
Gonzales de Santalla, Thyrso, S.J., 59, 191, 200
Gough, Austin, 3n, 110
Gousset, Thomas, 42n, 122
Gregory VII, 48, 80, 203

Harlay de Champvallon, François de, Archbishop of Paris, 17
Henn, William, O.F.M. Cap., 107, 192
Henry IV, Emperor of Germany, 80
Hermes, Georg, 167
Himes, Michael, 168
Hocedez, Edgar, S.J., 130
Holbach, Baron Paul Henri, 120
Honorius I, 81, 90, 139–40
Horst, Ulrich, 65, 97, 107
Hughes, Philip, 1
Hurter, H. S.J., 64, 129

Immaculate Conception, definition of, 166–67, 179, 196
Innocent I, 102, 116

Innocent IV, 116
Innocent X, 57, 173
Innocent XI, 14, 16, 19–20, 37
Innocent XII, 21–22
Inter Multiplices, 20–21, 107, 159
Irenaeus, 90, 104–6

Jansenism, 56–57, 63–64, 75, 151, 160–61, 173, 182
Jansenists, 171, 176
Jerusalem, Council of, 52, 87, 88, 124
John XXII, 8–9, 46–47
John Paul II, 62
Julius I, 71

Kühner, Hans, 80

Lainez, Diego, S.J., 71
La Luzerne, César-Guillaume, life and work, 129–31; papal monarchy not absolute, 131–35; papal teaching authority, 135–37; ex cathedra statements, 137–41; councils, 141–44; mentioned, 4
Lamennais, Félicité, 15, 79, 121
Languet, Jean-Joseph, Archbishop of Sens, 148, 151–52, 155, 157–58, 164
Lanson, Gustave, 38
Launay, Jean de, 84
Leo I, 51, 95, 103, 116, 140, 143, 177
Leo X, 182
Leo XII, 165
Leo XIII, 203
Le Roy, Pierre, 9–11
Letellier, Charles-Maurice, 17
Letellier, Michel, 17
Liberius, Pope, 56, 81
Louis XI, 31
Louis XIV, 13–17, 30, 36–37, 40, 61, 161
Louis XVIII, 130
Lumen Gentium, 3, 62
Lupus, Christian, 84
Luther, Martin, 37, 67
Lyon, Second Council of, 14, 116

Maistre, Joseph de, 15, 39–42, 60, 79, 132
Mansi, Giovanni Domenico, 84
Marca, Pierre de, 84

Maret, Henri, 58, 130
Martimort, Aimé-Georges, 4, 9, 16, 20, 22, 58, 61, 62
Martin, Victor, 7, 10, 11, 13, 15
Maximes des saints, 176
Melanchthon, Philip, 100
Migne, Jacques-Paul, 95
Möhler, Johan Adam, 168
Mollat, Guillaume, 8, 9
Monothelete controversy, 90–91, 140
Muratori, Ludovico, 84
Muzzarelli, Alfonso, life and work, 145–48; brief essay against Gallicans, 148–51; against consensus of Church, 151–56; critique of Bossuet, 157–60; great syllogism for papal infallibility, 162–64; mentioned, 115, 171, 189, 190, 198

Napoleon Bonaparte, 29, 41, 60, 130, 131, 145, 146
Nau, Paul, O.S.B., 4
Nestorianism, 140
Neveu, Bruno, 14n, 58
Newman, John Henry, 57, 167
Nicholas I, 71

Ordinances of 1407, 11
Orsi, Giuseppe Agostino, O.P., life and work, 78–82; determination to refute Bossuet, 82–85; scripture and papal primacy, 85–87; pope over councils, 87–89; against consensus of Church, 89–93; criticized by La Luzerne, 131–44; mentioned, 34, 46, 73, 96, 163, 164, 171, 179, 189, 191, 194, 196, 198
Ottaviani, Alfredo, 190

Pallavicino, Sforza, 71
Palmer, R. R., 120
Parlement of Paris, 30, 80
Passaglia, Carlo, S.J., 79
Pastor Aeternus, 1, 2, 3, 5, 34, 96, 114, 127, 181, 184, 195, 197
Pastor, Ludwig von, 80
Pavillon, Nicholas, Bishop of Alet, 14
Pelagianism, 102

Perrone, Giovanni, S.J., life and work, 165–67; papal supremacy, 167–72; papal teaching authority, 172–80; condemning modern errors, 180–85; mentioned, 203, 208, 210, 212
Petitdidier, Mathieu, 30
Philip IV, King of France, 48
Pistoia, Synod of, 159, 170–71, 173
Pius VI, 146, 159, 173
Pius VII, 130, 131, 145, 146, 148, 165
Pius IX, 1, 110, 118, 157, 179, 185, 196
Pottmeyer, Hermann Josef, 4, 79, 96, 125, 147, 168
Prandi, Alfonso, 84

Quanta Cura, 183

Ratzinger, Cardinal Joseph, 181
Reception, 19, 32–34, 47, 51, 57, 74–75, 103, 164, 198
Regiminis Apostolici, 160
Remanzacco, Candido da, O.F.M. Cap., 96, 98
Renouard, Yves, 8, 9
Richer, Edmond, 32, 55, 68–69, 113, 158, 170, 200
Riley, Patrick, 38
Roberti, Giambattista, 145
Rocaberti, Juan Tomàs, O.P., 30, 59–60
Rohrbacher, René-François, 15, 16, 42, 43, 75, 119, 121, 122, 146
Rousseau, Jean-Jacques, 120, 146

Salmon, George, 35
Schatz, Klaus, S.J., 185, 194

Scheeben, Matthias, 147
Schism, Great Western, 44
Schrader, Clemens, 79, 157
Scipio Africanus, 40
Spada, Cardinal Fabrizio, 22
Syllabus of Errors, 183–84

Thils, Gustave, 4, 166
Thomassin, Louis, 84
Thysman, Raymond, 58
Tourneley, Honoré, life and work, 63–67; Gallican ecclesiology, 64–67; papal primacy, 67–68; against Richer, 68–69; papal infallibility, 71–77; consensus of Church, 74–77; mentioned, 32, 84, 102, 128, 144, 153, 164, 176, 187, 188, 200, 201
Trent, Council of, 71, 124
Turrecremata, Ioannes de, O.P. (Juan de Torquemada), 28n

Ultramontane Movement, 3, 37, 43, 146, 147
Unam Sanctam, 48, 50, 203
Unigenitus, 63, 75–76

Vatican Council I, 1, 35, 96, 185
Vatican Council II, 3, 166
Vernant, Jacques de, 30
Vincent of Lérins, 55

Willaert, Léopold, S.J., 32

Zaccaria, Francesco Antonio, S.J., 147

 The Consensus of the Church and Papal Infallibility: A Study in the Background of Vatican I was designed and composed in Bembo by Kachergis Book Design of Pittsboro, North Carolina. It was printed on 60-pound Natures Natural and bound by Thomson-Shore, Inc., of Dexter, Michigan.

www.ingramcontent.com/pod-product-compliance
Lightning Source LLC
Chambersburg PA
CBHW031413290426
44110CB00011B/368